J. Bernard Keys
Robert M. Fulmer
Editors

DISCARD

Executive Development and Organizational Learning for Global Business

"Keys and Fulmer have produced an essential book for those concerned with management development. They have effectively compiled the ingredients that lead us to the future prospects for executive education and organizational learning."

Alan F. White
Senior Associate Dean,
MIT/Sloan School of Management,
Cambridge, MA

"This book provides an excellent overview of the challenge of developing leaders in a global environment. The sections on cross-cultural management issues and the use of simulation as a development tool provide an outstanding founda-

tion for addressing the challenge of transnational business development. The book is laced with detailed examples that help readers grasp the application of leading-edge learning methodologies to organizational development in a global context. The editors have compiled an impressive array of articles that help to define and delineate the challenge of developing leaders in a global business environment. It is a valuable reference tool that is sure to be well used by those who are seeking to develop globally minded leaders."

Albert A. Vicere, PhD
Professor of Business Administration,
Director of the Insitute for the Study
of Organizational Effectiveness,
The Pennsylvania State University,
University Park, State College, PA

Executive Development and Organizational Learning for Global Business

INTERNATIONAL BUSINESS PRESS
Erdener Kaynak, PhD
Executive Editor

New, Recent, and Forthcoming Titles:

How to Manage for International Competitiveness edited by Abbas J. Ali

*International Business Expansion into Less-Developed Countries:
The International Finance Corporation and Its Operations*
by James C. Baker

Product-Country Images: Impact and Role in International Marketing
edited by Nicolas Papadopoulos and Louise A. Heslop

The Global Business: Four Key Marketing Strategies edited by Erdener Kaynak

Multinational Strategic Alliances edited by Refik Culpan

Market Evolution in Developing Countries: The Unfolding of the Indian Market
by Subhash C. Jain

*A Guide to Successful Business Relations with the Chinese: Opening
the Great Wall's Gate* by Huang Quanyu, Richard Andrulis, and Chen Tong

Industrial Products: A Guide to the International Marketing Economics Model
by Hans Jansson

Euromarketing: Effective Strategies for International Trade and Export
edited by Salah S. Hassan and Erdener Kaynak

*How to Utilize New Information Technology in the Global Marketplace:
A Basic Guide* edited by Fahri Karakaya and Erdener Kaynak

International Negotiating: A Primer for American Business Professionals
by Michael Kublin

*The Eight Core Values of the Japanese Businessman: Toward an Understanding
of Japanese Management* by Yasutaka Sai

Implementation of Total Quality Management: A Comprehensive Training Program
by Rolf E. Rogers

An International Accounting Practice Set: The Karissa Jean's Simulation
by David R. Peterson and Nancy Schendel

*Privatization and Entrepreneurship: The Managerial Challenge in Central
and Eastern Europe* by Arieh Ullmann and Alfred Lewis

U.S. Trade, Foreign Direct Investments, and Global Competitiveness by Rolf Hackmann

Business Decision Making in China by Huang Quanyu, Joseph Leonard, and Chen Tong

International Management Leadership: The Primary Competitive Advantage
by Raimo W. Nurmi and John R. Darling

*The Trans-Oceanic Marketing Channel: A New Tool for Understanding Tropical Africa's
Export Agriculture* by H. Laurens van der Laan

Handbook of Cross-Cultural Marketing by Paul A. Herbig

Guide to Software Export: A Handbook for International Software Sales by Roger Philips

Executive Development and Organizational Learning for Global Business
edited by J. Bernard Keys and Robert M. Fulmer

Contextual Management: A Global Perspective by Raghbir (Raj) S. Basi

Japan and China: The Meeting of Asia's Economic Giants by Kazuo John Fukuda

Executive Development and Organizational Learning for Global Business

J. Bernard Keys
Robert M. Fulmer
Editors

International Business Press
An Imprint of The Haworth Press, Inc.
New York • London

Published by

International Business Press, an imprint of The Haworth Press, Inc., 10 Alice Street, Binghamton, NY 13904-1580

Cover design by Monica L. Seifert.

Library of Congress Cataloging-in-Publication Data

Executive development and organizational learning for global business / J. Bernard Keys, Robert M. Fulmer, editors.
    p.   cm.
   Includes bibliographical references and index.
   ISBN 0-7890-0479-8 (alk. paper).
   1. Executives—Training of. 2. International learning business enterprises—Employees—Training. 3. Organizational. I. Keys, Bernard. II. Fulmer, Robert M.
HD30.4.E94 1998
658.4′07124—dc21
                                                  97-37777
                                                 CIP

To Our Sons

CONTENTS

About the Editors   xiii

Contributors   xv

**Introduction: Seven Imperatives for Executive Education
and Organizational Learning in the Global World**   1

Think and Act Globally   1
Become an Equidistant Global Learning Organization   3
Focus on the Global System, Not Its Parts   3
Develop Global Leadership Skills   5
Empower Teams to Create a Global Future   6
Make Learning a Core Competence for Your Global
     Organization   7
Regularly Reinvent Yourself and the Global Organization   8

PART I: GLOBALIZATION AND LEARNING   11

**Chapter 1. Anticipatory Learning
for Global Organizations**   15
     Robert M. Fulmer
     Hildy Teegen

The Organizational Learning Imperative   15
All Learning Is Not Equal   16
The Organizational Learning Matrix   18
Forecasting versus Creating the Future   20
From the Forecasted Future to the Invented Future   20
Summary and Conclusion   21

**Chapter 2. Do Cultural Differences Make a Business
Difference? Contextual Factors Affecting
Cross-Cultural Relationship Success**   23
     Rosabeth Moss Kanter
     Richard Ian Corn

In Search of Cultural Differences   24
The Foreign Acquisitions Study   26
Culture versus Context as an Explanatory Factor   30

Contextual Factors as Key Determinants of Cross-Cultural
    Relationship Success   34
The Negative Side of Cross-Cultural Interaction:
    Threat and Prejudice   41
The Attribution of Organizational Problems
    to National Culture   42
Conclusion   45

Chapter 3. Managing Globally Competent People   **49**
    Nancy J. Adler
    Susan Bartholomew

Transnationally Competent Managers   50
The Globalization of Business: Strategy, Structure,
    and Managerial Skills   52
Transnational Human Resource Systems   56
Today's Firms: How Transnational?   58
Illusions and Recommendations   65

**Chapter 4. Creating a High-Performance
International Team**   **73**
    Sue Canney Davison

Establishing the Context of the Growing Number
    of International Teams   73
Creating and Managing an International Team   74
Managing the Geographical Distances   78
Working Within the Team   80

PART II: DEVELOPING THE GLOBAL EXECUTIVE   **87**

**Chapter 5. Selecting Training Methodology
for International Managers**   **91**
    J. Bernard Keys
    Linda M. Bleicken

A Model for Management Training for International
    Assignments   91
A Theoretical Base for Training Methodology   97
Management Development Methods   99
Developing Cognitive Competencies   100
Developing Behavioral Competencies with Experiential
    Methods   101

Developing Performance Competencies   105
Summary and Case Application of the Training Model   110
Recommendations for Future Research   111

Chapter 6. Creating Scenarios and Cases for Global
    Anticipatory Learning   **117**
        John A. Gutman

Review of Anticipatory Learning Program Issues   118
Scenario Planning   119
Cases   122
Conclusion   124

Chapter 7. A Culture-General Assimilator:
    Preparation for Various Types of Sojourns   **129**
        Richard W. Brislin

Introduction   129
Rationale for Materials Development   129
The Culture-Assimilator Format   132
Learning the Ropes   135
The Themes Around Which the One Hundred Incidents
   Were Developed   139
Uses for a Culture-General Assimilator   142
Conclusion   147

Chapter 8. Action Learning: Executive Development
    of Choice for the 1990s   **151**
        Louise Keys

What Is Action Learning?   152
Traditional Approaches to Action Learning   153
Unique Action Learning Adaptations   155
Summary   159

Chapter 9. Case Studies of International Management
    Development   **161**
        Charles Gancel
        Alison Perlo

Needs Analysis for International Training   162
Program Design and Development   162

Training for Trainers 163
Cultural Awareness 163
International Negotiation 164
Consulting in a Multicultural Environment 164
Communication in an International Context 165
Expatriate Preparation 165
Managing Internationally 165
An Application by ICM Management Training in Russia:
   Traps and Gaps 167

**PART III: DEVELOPING THE LEARNING
ORGANIZATION**   **179**

Chapter 10. Systems Dynamics and Anticipatory Learning **181**
   Peter M. Senge
   Robert M. Fulmer

Examples of Microworlds 184
Challenges of Using Microworlds 187
Conclusion 190

**Chapter 11. Microworlds and Simuworlds:
Practice Fields for the Learning Organization**   **193**
   J. Bernard Keys
   Robert M. Fulmer
   Stephen A. Stumpf

The Evolution of Practice Fields 194
Providing "Big Picture" Learning 195
Learning Leadership and Strategy in a Microworld 196
Reducing the High Risk of Organizational Learning 197
Overcoming Barriers to Learning 199
Promoting Focus on Competition and Collaboration 204
Encouraging Experimentation and Transfer of Learning 204
Initiating Organizational Learning with Simuworlds
   and Microworlds 205
Conclusion 210

Chapter 12. The Multinational Management Game:
A Simuworld   **215**
> *J. Bernard Keys*
> *Robert A. Wells*
> *Alfred G. Edge*

Playing the MMG Simuworld   216
The Case Study for the MMG Simuworld:
   Compaq Computer Corporation   218
Learning from MMG   221
Summary   227

Chapter 13. Leadership in a Global Village: Creating
Practice Fields to Develop Learning Organizations   **229**
> *Stephen A. Stumpf*
> *Mary Anne Watson*
> *Hermant Rustogi*

Global Village Practice Fields   230
Creating a Global Village Experience for Organizational
   Learning   232
Two Practice Field Applications   235
Leadership in a Global Village: The Results   238
Summary   240

Summary: What We Learned About
the Seven Imperatives   **243**

Think and Act Globally   243
Become a Global Learning Organization   244
Empower Teams to Create a Global Future   244
Focus on the Global System, Not Its Parts   245
Develop Global Leadership Skills   247
Make Anticipatory Learning a Core Competency
   in Your Organization   248
Use Practice Fields to Regularly Reinvent Yourself   249

Resources and Materials for the Global
Learning Organization   **253**

Index   **257**

ABOUT THE EDITORS

J. Bernard Keys is Fuller E. Callaway Professor of Business Administration at Georgia Southern University and directs the Center for Managerial Learning and Business Simulation in the College of Business Administration. He was previously Associate Dean and Director of Graduate Programs, The University of Memphis, where he taught the lead course in the Executive MBA Program and directed the Doctoral Program in Business. Dr. Keys recently served as a Visiting Scholar at the MIT Organizational Learning Center (now reorganized as The Society for Organizational Learning), as Visiting Erskine Scholar at The University of Canterbury, Christchurch, New Zealand, and Visiting Professor at The University of Hawaii.

Dr. Keys was Founder and first Fellow of the Association for Business Simulation and Experiential Learning and is an elected Fellow in the International Academy of Management, past editor and continuing North American editor for *The Journal of Management Development* and founding co-editor of *Executive Development*. He served as President of the Southern Management Association and The International Management Development Association and as Chair of The Management Education and Development Division of the Academy of Management. He is co-author of numerous management books, including three published business games. He has developed organizational learning, management development programs, and/or customized management gaming programs for well-known organizations throughout the world, such as Olivetta Consulting Company; ELEA, of Florence, Italy; Kimberly Clark; The Gulfstream Corporation; the Japan-American Institute of Management Science, Honolulu, Hawaii; and The Southeastern National Park Service. He presided over the World Congress on Management Development in Istanbul and as North American Coordinator of the World Congress on Management Development in London.

In his work for the Center for Managerial Learning and Business Simulation, Dr. Keys specializes in learning research based on simulations and in designing and delivering customized simulations for management development programs. He is the creator of the business game/case combination known as the Simuworld and co-author with Robert Wells, Georgia Southern University, of the *Multinational Management Game*, which has received high marks in programs such as the Eastman Chemical Company Business Dynamics Course and Arthur Little's MBA program.

Currently the W. Brooks George Professor of Management at the College of William and Mary, **Robert M. Fulmer** was previously a Visiting Scholar at the MIT Organizational Learning Center. Dr. Fulmer taught Organization and Management at Columbia University's Graduate Business School. As Director of Executive Education at Emory University, he directed the Executive MBA program as well as programs for general managers. He has also served as Director of Corporate Management Development for Allied Signal, Inc., and President of Executive Counsel, Inc., and he held an endowed chair at Trinity University.

As consultant, Dr. Fulmer has designed and delivered executive programs on six continents for top managers at Johnson & Johnson, Sterling, Inc., and Bertlesmann Music Group. He has received outstanding evaluations for his sessions on future trends, leadership issues, international team building, and implementation of strategy. Other clients include such groups as Barclays Bank PLC, Siemans-Bendix, Hoechst Celanese, Kodak, Union Camp, Coca-Cola, Nissan, The American Society of Association Executive, Citicorp, Kimberly Clark, BellSouth, NASA, and CDC.

Dr. Fulmer's writing has been widely read in both academic and professional circles. He is the author of four editions of *The New Management* (Macmillan), and co-author (with the late Harold Koontz of UCLA) of four editions of *A Practical Introduction in Business* (Richard D. Irwin, Inc.). Fulmer is the author of five other business books.

He is currently a Senior Research Associate with the international Consortium for Executive Development Research and a Fellow of the Academy of Management. He was chairperson of the Executive Education Exchange, is President of the Board of Editors for *Executive Development: An International Journal*, and a past president of the Southern Management Association.

CONTRIBUTORS

Nancy J. Adler is Professor of Management at McGill University in Montreal, Canada. Dr. Adler consults on strategic international human resources management, international negotiating, and developing culturally synergistic approaches to problem solving and organization development. She has authored numerous articles and edited the books *International Dimensions of Organizational Behavior* and *Women in Management Worldwide*. Dr. Adler has taught Chinese executives in the People's Republic of China, held the Citicorp Visiting Professorship at the University of Hong Kong, and taught executive seminars at INSEAD in France and Bocconi University in Italy.

Susan Bartholomew is a doctoral student in management at McGill University, Montreal, specializing in international organizational behavior. She has consulted at the national and international levels, including the United National Centre on Transnational Corporations.

Linda M. Bleicken is Associate Dean of the College of Business Administration and Associate Professor of Management, Georgia Southern University. She has been project director for a services marketing research firm, with major clients such as BellSouth, Trust Company Bank, and Georgia Ports Authority.

Richard W. Brislin served for a number of years as Senior Fellow and Director of Intercultural Programs at the East-West Center, FT, Honolulu, Hawaii. He has conducted seminars and consulting projects in intercultural management for major clients using the culture-general assimilator, which he assisted in designing. Presently Dr. Brislin serves as Director of the PhD Program in the College of Business Administration, University of Hawaii, Honolulu, Hawaii.

Richard Ian Corn at the time of this publication was a doctoral student at Harvard Business School, Boston, working with Rosabeth Moss Kanter.

Sue Canney Davison is Visiting Research Fellow at the London Business School, London. Dr. Davison's permanent affiliation is with Pipal International, Sharpthorne, East Sussex, U.K., where she frequently conducts research and consulting projects in international management development.

Alfred G. Edge is Chairperson of the Department of Management and Labor Relations and Professor of Management in the College of Business Administration, The University of Hawaii, Honolulu, Hawaii. He frequently consults and conducts seminars for organizations worldwide using the *Multinational Management Game,* which he co-authored. He is presently Visiting Professor at the University of Bangkok.

Charles Gancel is a consultant with Inter Cultural Management Associates, Paris, France. He consults with major organizations, primarily in the design of customized intercultural management programs.

John A. Gutman conducts research and consults in organizational learning and decision making in organizations. He has worked for Motorola, Cadbury Schweppes, Clorox, and Gemini Consulting in marketing, finance, operations, and strategic planning positions in the United States and Europe. He holds degrees from Princeton University, Columbia University, and the University of California, Berkeley.

Rosabeth Moss Kanter holds the Class of 1960 Chair as Professor of Business Administration at the Harvard Business School. Her newest book, *Rosabeth Kanter on the Frontiers of Management* (Harvard Business School Press), brings together many of the landmark articles she has published. She is also the author of *World Class: Thriving Locally in the Global Economy,* and many other best-selling business books. She has received eighteen honorary doctoral degrees and consults extensively with best-known companies of the world.

Louise Keys lectures in the area of Learning Support, Georgia Southern University, and is a principal in The MMG Group, a firm specializing in management game development, experiential learning, and action learning programs.

Alison Perlo, Inter Cultural Management Associates, Paris, France, consults with major organizations, primarily in the design of intercultural management programs.

Hermant Rustogi is an Associate in the Center for Leadership, University of Tampa, Tampa, Florida. He frequently assists with simulation projects with major clients.

Peter M. Senge is Chair of SoL, the newly formed Society of Organizational Learning, Inc., Cambridge, Massachusetts. He is a Senior Lecturer at Massachusetts Institute of Technology, where he has served for several years as part of the Organizational Learning and Change Group. He is author of the widely acclaimed best-selling book, *The Fifth Discipline: The Art and Practice of the Learning Organization,* and with his colleagues Charlotte Roberts, Rick Ross, Bryan Smith, and Art Kleiner, co-author of the *Fifth Discipline Fieldbook: Strategies and Tools for Building a Learning Organization.*

Stephen A. Stumpf is Dean of Internal Programs at Booz Allen Hamilton in New York City and served as Director of the Center of Leadership and Dean of the College of Business at The University of Tampa. Dr. Stumpf is the author of *Learning to Use What You Already Know,* co-authored with Joel DeLuca (Berrett-Koehler Publishers) and *Taking Charge: Strategic Leadership in the Middle Game,* co-authored with Tom Mullen (Prentice Hall).

Hildy Teegen is Assistant Professor of International Business at the George Washington University in Washington, DC. She teaches Foreign Market Entry and International Business Negotiations, both at George Washington and to executive audiences in the United States and Latin America. She consults with U.S. firms and acts as a facilitator in cross-border collaboration negotiations.

Mary Anne Watson is an Associate in the Center for Leadership, University of Tampa, Tampa, Florida. She frequently assists with simulation projects.

Robert A. Wells is an Associate in the Center for Managerial Learning and Business Simulation and Professor of Management in the College of Business Administration, Georgia Southern University, Statesboro, Georgia. He is the co-author of the *Mulitnational Management Game* (MMG) and two other simulations. He frequently conducts seminars and consults using MMG.

Introduction

Seven Imperatives for Executive Education and Organizational Learning in the Global World

The twenty-first century is dawning before us. The ideas that will shape competition in that century are emerging like the rays of morning's first light. This book explores the role of executive development and organizational learning processes in meeting the challenges of a new millennium. As learning becomes a major lever for achieving competitive advantage, we are confident that the following seven imperatives and appropriate responses will dominate executive and organizational learning programs around the world.

THINK AND ACT GLOBALLY

Challenges and organizations to meet these challenges are becoming more global or transnational. No one has captured this movement better than Kenichi Ohmae, head of McKinsey's Tokyo office.

In *Triad Power,* he was among the first to suggest that it is no longer enough for a company to be successful in its home region (Ohmae, 1985). A world-class competitor, he suggests, must have a presence and compete successfully in Europe, the United States, and the Pacific Rim. These three market areas require different skills, expertise, and experience, all of which must be managed successfully. In *The Border-less World*, Ohmae (1990) argues further that the global company must develop "the equidistant manager"—managers who see and think globally first. He clarifies as follows:

It may be unfamiliar and awkward, but the primary rule of equidistance is to see—and to think—global first. Honda, for example, has manufacturing divisions in Japan, North America and Europe—all three legs of the Triad—but its managers do not think or act as if the company were divided between Japanese and overseas operations. In fact, the very word overseas has no place in Honda's vocabulary, because the corporation sees itself as equidistant from all its key customers. (Ohmae, 1990, p. 18)

Bartlett and Ghoshal (1989) introduced the transnational concept as a successor to a multinational or global focus, two terms that we will refer to interchangeabley. Adler and Bartholomew (Chapter 3) suggest that "transnational managers must learn how to collaborate with partners worldwide, gaining as much knowledge as possible from each interaction and transmitting that knowledge quickly and effectively throughout the worldwide network of operations." Effective communications such as this requires managers who want to continuously learn from other cultures.

Yip (1995) of UCLA reports on research that distinguishes those firms with a truly global strategy from firms simply multinational in their operations. Managers who think globally must have access to development programs designed especially for intercultural management development such as the ones described by Gancel and Perlo (Chapter 9). These experienced consultants from Inter Cultural Management Associates in Paris, France, describe ongoing programs of their center and include a case study of an initiative focused on Russia.

Yet, we must not excessively emphasize cultural diversity. As the chapter by Kanter and Corn (Chapter 2) suggests, cultural differences do not necessarily increase the amount of tension between organizations or make partnerships among companies from different countries more difficult. Conflict often attributed to cultural differences may be attributable to the same sources that create tension among domestic departments or personnel. The equidistant manager must be able to discern when a cultural difference is the problem and when other issues are troubling the organization. To make such distinctions, diverse cultures must first be understood.

BECOME AN EQUIDISTANT
GLOBAL LEARNING ORGANIZATION

Too often organizations limit the cultures that will dominate learning—to the English speaking, the Japanese, the European, or some other dominant group. Frequently, learning is relegated to formal training programs, and often the style of teaching/learning is limited to a few cognitive approaches. In the global world of the equidistant manager (Ohmae, 1990) and the global human resource management program (Chapter 3), learning from any culture, anytime, in any manner possible must be facilitated (Slocum, McGill, and Lei, 1994).

Revans, venerable British creator of the action learning concept, asserts, "The pioneer of radical growth is the person able and ready to pose discriminating questions in conditions of ignorance, risk, confusion and to hold his ground in doing so" (Smith and Saint-Onge, 1996). Global organizational learning is more than an add-on or supplement to organizations. It permeates every aspect of organizational life or, as Marquardt suggests, includes five subsystems—learning, organization, people, knowledge, and technology (Marquardt, 1996).

It can be important to have an R&D presence in the local market of global customers and competitors, and to engage in joint ventures or alliances—all of these for the purpose of learning (Yip, 1995). For example, Boeing has formed an alliance with Fuji, Mitsubishi, and Kawasaki to help defray the $4 billion cost of building the 777 jetliner. Larry Clarkson, senior vice president, explains, "the day of an airplane being a sole Boeing product is past. . . . The big jet business . . . takes a lot of dollars and involves high risk, a long-term investment, and a limited customer base" (Phatak, 1997, p. 290). Competitive advantage in these relationships depends primarily on the ability to organize or position learning in such an equidistant way as to learn faster and more than others. Learning must not be inhibited by cultural dominance or limited perspective.

FOCUS ON THE GLOBAL SYSTEM,
NOT ITS PARTS

In addition to the obvious importance of being global on a geographical basis, it is also essential to recognize that strategic thinkers and the management development programs that help orient them must focus on the "big global picture" context. The history of industrial development in emerging economies has been based on achieving more and more specialization to achieve greater efficiencies of scale. With the advent of systems dynamics, managers are recognizing better how to treat global companies as total systems rather than as noninterrelated parts. This is reflected in such ideas as Jack Welch's demand for a "boundaryless" organization (Stewart, 1991) and Peter Senge's concept of the learning organization in *The Fifth Discipline* (1990, 1994).

In breaking down the silos of departments and sometimes even the boundaries that separate customers and suppliers, global thinking can create win-win situations across broad horizons. The Systems Dynamics Group at MIT has provided broad realization of the interconnectedness of the various components in the business system. Senge combines the rigor of systems thinking with the power of intuition, creativity, and leadership. Systems thinking can help break down the artificial barriers between the firm and its customers or suppliers. Systems thinking is a conceptual framework that helps make these patterns clearer and provides an understanding of how to change them or work within them. Nowhere is such a conceptualization more needed than within organizations engaged in global competition.

In Chapter 10, Senge and Fulmer elaborate on these ideas and provide a framework that integrates systems thinking and learning methodology. As one begins to push the concepts of systems thinking, a fundamental shift must take place between the kind of linear thinking most people have been taught and a more comprehensive systems worldview. The shift might cause change from seeing things as structure to seeing them as process. This is the thrust of Mike Hammer's recent work on reengineering (Hammer, 1993, 1995, 1996). For example, one might see a multinational corporation with offshore manufacturing sites and distribution networks throughout the world as a group of fragmented production and selling sites, or as a global system, in which each part is related by cause and effect to every other part. Diverse cultures, cross-cultural leaders, international organizations, and certainly international leadership development can be seen as ends within themselves or as parts of larger, more complex global systems.

DEVELOP GLOBAL LEADERSHIP SKILLS

Recently Cascio and Bailey (1995) surveyed 110 senior human resource managers from multinational companies in a variety of industries located in North America, South America, the Middle East, Asia, Europe, and Australia regarding compelling issues in international human resource management. They discovered that two critical issues within firms were "managing a multicultural workforce" and "developing management talent in a global business environment."

For the past two decades, John Kotter has promoted our understanding of the phenomenon of leadership in such books as *Corporate Culture and Performance* (Kotter and Heskitt, 1992), *The New Rules,* and *Leading Change* (Kotter, 1995). Kotter was among the first to articulate a most significant distinction between leaders and managers. Managers administer large bureaucracies and ensure stability. Leaders are vital forces in bringing about change. Going global requires leaders who can handle ambiguity, bring about change, and are even more flexible and resilient than their domestic counterparts. A new set of skills is required for managers to transcend the competencies historically required of expatriate managers. A globally competent and proficient human resource system is also essential. In Chapter 3, "Managing Globally Competent People," Adler and Bartholomew summarize eight ways in which these new skills exemplify themselves.

In Chapter 5, Keys and Bleicken suggest how the international management development process itself should be viewed as a system. Methodology for selecting international managers should be governed by level of cultural difference between the home and the host countries and the organization's international strategy—particularly the amount of interaction required between the home and host countries, as well as the existing competencies of expatriate managers. Suitable international management development techniques, based on these contingencies, are identified and reviewed.

For managers just starting down the road to cross-cultural encounters, and experienced expatriates, Chapter 7, "A Cultural-General Assimilator" by Richard Brislin will prove to be insightful. With considerable collaboration, Brislin has written 106 incidents that capture experiences, feelings, and thoughts that virtually all sojourners encounter. These were created to provide concrete examples of eighteen intercultural themes or commonalities central to an understanding of cross-cultural experiences.

In Chapter 6, John Gutman provides a rationale for a new emphasis on the use of cases in international management development. As Gutman suggests, "In business schools and executive education programs from INSEAD to Thunderbird, cases enhance the analytical skills of students and provide a framework for teachers to elicit participative class discussions." The new cases being developed in learning centers serve not only as a basis for class discussion but as scenarios to influence the evolution of organizational development. Furthermore, some scenarios are being supported by computer-based system dynamics models as discussed in Part III.

EMPOWER TEAMS TO CREATE A GLOBAL FUTURE

A former editor of the *Harvard Business Review* and author of one of our chapters, Rosabeth Moss Kanter (1989) exhorts in her best-selling book, *When Giants Learn to Dance*, "In the 1990s organization, the team is the competitive weapon." In an important American Management Association briefing, Marshall and Molly Sashkin (1994) described the evolution and key essentials for developing and using cross-functional teams. One of the ways in which teams offer tremendous potential for the new millennium is through their ability to reduce the time required to perform traditional tasks. This leads to strength in the important area of time-based competition. For example, Microsoft uses cross-functional teams extensively in their attempts to create a learning organization and to make large teams function as small teams do (Cusumano and Selby, 1995).

Teams can be a great stimulus for learning as well as for project success. One of the more effective team learning approaches is the action learning approach described and reviewed in our chapter, "Action Learning: Executive Development of Choice for the 1990s," by Louise Keys. Action learning is highly effective as a learning process in areas where no previous knowledge exists, which is often the case in global projects (Shenkar, 1995). General Electric, in their world-acclaimed executive programs, often begin with an action-learning process to promote team-building of culturally diverse teams from GE's far-flung operations. In our selection for Chapter 4, Sue Canney Davison illustrates the advantages of such diversity. Mixed nationalities in teams, she explains, can bring richer solutions and contribute significantly to company-wide networks. But she also finds they can bring increased communication difficulties, interpersonal conflicts, and higher costs. Davison provides suggestions for achieving the former while avoiding the negatives.

MAKE LEARNING A CORE COMPETENCE FOR YOUR GLOBAL ORGANIZATION

One of the most provocative phrases of the past decade comes from Arie de Geus, former head of strategic planning at Royal Dutch/Shell and author of a significant book on organizational learning, *The Living Company* (1997), who advises, "Over the long term, the only sustainable competitive advantage may be an organization's ability to learn faster than its competition" (de Geus, 1980, p. 71). Such thinking has led many companies in recent years to search for ideas and techniques that will assist them to become "learning organizations." A learning organization is one that develops a "strategic intent to learn, a commitment to experimentation, and an emphasis on learning from past successes and failures" (Slocum Jr., McGill, and Lei, 1994).

Other competitive advantages, whether capital resources, technical innovation, or even managerial talent, can be made obsolete by a competitor who reads the changing environment and learns in a more appropriate manner. Henry James once commented, "The mark of genius is simply the ability to see the world in unhabitual ways." A major challenge of international management development initiatives is to help participants learn to see the world in a new, richer global perspective.

A number of years ago the Club of Rome commissioned a significant study on learning titled *No Limits to Learning* (Botkin, 1979). Botkin and his associates concluded that while utilization or consumption of most raw materials leads to the depletion of the resource base, the utilization of "knowledge" with students or clients actually increases total knowledge resources.

The chapter titled "Microworlds and Simuworlds: Practice Fields for the Learning Organization" demonstrates how learning can be initiated and sustained in organizations. These management development labs are described in more detail by Keys, Fulmer, and colleagues in Part III of this book.

REGULARLY REINVENT YOURSELF AND THE GLOBAL ORGANIZATION

Individuals and organizations performing effectively today require "reinvention" in order to be equally successful in the twenty-first century. Reg Revans (1982, p. 1) crafts this thought well when he says "learning must be equal to or greater than environmental change or the organization will not survive." In order to seize control of an industry and create tomorrow's markets, Gary Hamel and C.K. Prahalad suggest that success depends on futuristic thinking (1994). Path-breaking organizations have always worked, not to justify past mistakes, but to "create tomorrow." The initial challenge is to start with a picture of an ideal future, then work backward to determine what must happen to make that future transpire. Developing the skills of change necessary for global competition will require practice by executives and their organizations—practice that must be generated by experience in the field or on practice fields such as the microworlds and simuworlds described in Part III.

The challenge of mastering the ever-changing and expanding needs of our constituencies may be overwhelming. Our job is to learn extensive amounts about our disciplines and prepare to learn it over again as circumstances change. We must blend the fields of strategy and behavior globally. We must balance the demands of strategy formulation and implementation in diverse environments. We must combine the challenges of global relevance and tactful rigor in our educational activities.

In Chapter 1, "Anticipatory Learning for Global Organizations," authors Fulmer and Teegen explain how futuristic planning and learning can be stimulated through the intriguing Merlin Exercise. The Merlin Exercise is a process ideally suited to the global future. It prompts top managers to suspend incremental, historically based restraints on planning and to project for their organizations an ideal future. Organizations such as Apple Computer and People's Express unconsciously crafted this type of strategy in their early days, but they failed to learn how to replicate the process. Fulmer and Teegen provide clarity and insight about the procedure with the Merlin analogy (Chapter 1).

Welcome to *Executive Development and Organizational Learning for Global Business* and to some of the most provocative writing on these subjects in recent years.

REFERENCES

Bartlett, C. and S. Ghoshal (1989). *Managing Across Borders: The Transnational Solution*. Boston: Harvard Business School.

Botkin, J. (1979). *No Limits to Learning*. Tarrytown, NY: Pergamon Press.

Cascio, W. and E. Bailey (1995). "International human resource management." In Oded Shenkar (Ed.), *Global Perspectives of Human Resource Management*. Englewood Cliffs, NJ: Prentice-Hall.

Cusumano, M. A. and R. W. Selby (1995). *Microsoft Secrets*. New York: The Free Press.

de Geus, A. (1980). Planning is Learning. *Harvard Business Review,* March-April: 71.

de Geus, A. (1997). *The Living Company.* Boston: Harvard Business School.

Hamel, G. and C. K. Prahalad (1994). *Competing for the Future*. Boston: Harvard Business School.

Hammer, M. (1993). *Reengineering the Corporation: A Manifesto for Business Revolution*. New York: Harper Business.

Hammer, M. (1995). *The Reengineering Revolution: A Handbook*. New York: Harper Business.

Hammer, M. (1996). *Beyond Reengineering: How Process-Centered Organization Is Changing Our Work and Our Lives*. New York: Harper Business.

Kanter, R. M. (1989). *When Giants Learn to Dance: Mastering the Challenge of Strategy Management and Careers in the 1990s*. New York: Simon and Schuster.

Kotter, J. (1995). *The New Rules*. New York: The Free Press.

Kotter, J. and J. Heskitt (1992). *Corporate Culture and Performance*. New York: The Free Press.

Marquardt, M. (1996). *Building the Learning Organization*. Alexandria, VA: McGraw-Hill.

Ohmae, K. (1985). *Triad Power: The Coming Shape of Global Competition*. New York: The Free Press.

Ohmae, K. (1990). *The Borderless World*. New York: Harper Collins.

Phatak, A. V. (1997). *International Management: Concepts and Cases.* Cincinnati: South-Western College Publishing.

Revans, R. (1982). "What is action learning." *The Journal of Management Development,* 1(1): 64-75.

Saskin, M. and M. Saskin (1994). *The New Team Work.* New York: AMA briefing.

Senge, P. (1990). *The Fifth Discipline: The Art and Practice of the Learning Organization.* New York: Doubleday.

Senge, P., A. Kleiner, C. Roberts, R. Ross, and B. Smith (1994). *The Fifth Discipline Fieldbook.* New York: Currency Doubleday Books.

Shenkar, O. (1995). *Global Perspectives of Human Resource Management.* Englewood Cliffs, NJ: Prentice-Hall.

Slocum, J. Jr., M. McGill, and D. T. Lei (1994). "The new learning strategy: Anytime, anything, anywhere." *Organizational Dynamics,* 23(2): 33-47.

Smith, P. A. C. and H. Saint-Onge (1996). "The evolutionary organization: Avoiding a Titanic fate." *The Learning Organization,* 3(4): 4-21.

Stewart, T. (1991). "GE keeps those ideas coming." *Fortune, 12,* (August): 41-9.

Yip, G. S. (1995). *Total Global Strategy.* Englewood Cliffs, NJ: Prentice-Hall.

PART I:
GLOBALIZATION AND LEARNING

The globalization process and the learning process are inextricably bound together. Globalization requires more flexibility in learning, more extensive learning, and more learning from sources previously overlooked by most organizations.

In our first chapter, Fulmer and Teegen review the Club of Rome's analysis of learning. Maintenance learning is focused on trying to discover better ways of doing what we already know how to do. The authors note that maintenance learning often misses important clues about a changing world environment or emerging challenges. A new global competitor arises, assets are nationalized, a war breaks out in an emerging market, and what they define as "shock" learning occurs. But learning that occurs under the stress of a crisis seldom includes creative solutions, relying instead on proven, familiar routines from the past. Chapter 1 recommends greater emphasis on innovative or "anticipatory learning." Anticipatory learning is participative since it cannot take place while there is an assumption that one country or business group has the answers which must be communicated to a less informed constituency. Anticipatory learning is also future oriented, focusing on what is likely or, more appropriately, possible for the future. Encouraging consideration of multiple futuristic plans enhances the firm's readiness for an uncertain tomorrow.

Building on concepts introduced by Fulmer and Teegen, Adler and Bartholomew, and others, we suggest four major ways that global organizations approach learning (see especially Table 1.1 of Fulmer and Teegen and Exhibit 3.1 of Adler and Bartholomew, Chapter 3). This matrix can guide firms in profiling their organization's approach to learning.

The first quadrant includes "Dominant Culture Learning." An authority figure in a particular country says that something is to be taught

TABLE I.1. Global Learning Matrix

1. Dominant Culture Learning
2. Decentralized Learning
3. Global Change Master Learning
4. Learning to Create a Synergistic Future Globally

or learned according to the practices and culture of a dominant head-quarters. Japan and the United States have both been notorious for following this approach with their overseas subsidiaries. This is the essence of maintenance learning. The second quadrant is defined as "Decentralized Learning." Left to their own devices, many international strategic business units or subgroups will find ways to learn effectively.

Fulmer and Teegen borrow from Rosabeth Moss Kanter to note that some strong global companies can be called Change Masters. They recognize the need for future-oriented change and insist that their companies learn to think or do business a new way. Thus, the third quadrant refers to "Global Change Master Learning." The fourth approach, modeled after Fulmer and Teegen and Ohmae's *The Borderless World*, is "Learning to Create a Synergistic Future Globally." The essence of anticipatory learning is for a group of motivated individuals to work together to create a future to which they feel committed, rather than simply forecasting a future. Like Kanter's Change Masters, they are anticipatory and committed to change, and as in the synergistic learning of Adler and Bartholomew (Chapter 3, Table 1), they are willing to work with and learn from people from many cultures simultaneously to create a culturally synergistic organization. Like Ohmae's equidistant manager, this organization sees and thinks globally first.

A model for preparing the global organization to use anticipatory learning would include the following requirements:

1. Stimulate Anticipatory Learning Within the Organization by Introducing the Merlin Exercise or a Similar Learning Process

In Chapter 1, Fulmer and Teegen explain how the Merlin Exercise can stimulate futuristic thinking and encourage participants to make quantum leaps in strategic planning.

2. Analyze Cultural Differences Between the Home and Host Countries Within the Global Organization

Chapter 2, by Rosabeth Moss Kanter and Richard Ian Corn, provides an in-depth look at difficulties of managerial and organizational learning within a critical change context, such as mergers of multicultural firms. The authors found that structural and technical differences in merged organizations may override differences of culture or national origin. Further, they learned that people of different national cultures who interact can be "remarkably adaptable." The ease of implementation of mergers across cultures depends on, among other things, mutual respect and efficient communication based on that respect, plus the willingness of the acquirer to invest in continued performance of the acquired firm.

3. Develop the Ability to Manage Globally Competent People by Developing a Global or Transnational Human Resource Management Function

Nancy Adler and Susan Bartholomew, in "Managing Globally Competent People" (Chapter 3), suggest that transnational firms need transnational human resource management systems. The mindsets or illusions that prevent this are outlined by the authors. Most can be recognized as symptoms of maintenance learning.

4. Extend and Maintain Global Organizational Learning Through Cross-Cultural Teams

Dealing with cross-cultural mergers and developing transnational human resource management can be improved by using effective team management. While chapters 3 and 4 emphasize the importance of cultural differences, it is clear that learning in such complex environments can be improved by well-organized international teams. Davison (Chapter 4) outlines an effective approach to international team building.

Chapter 1

Anticipatory Learning for Global Organizations

Robert M. Fulmer
Hildy Teegen

The 1990s have been described as the "decade of learning corporations." *Fortune* magazine has suggested "the most successful corporation of the 1990s will be something called 'learning organization,' a consummately adaptive enterprise." A host of articles and books has addressed the issue. Senior executives including Ray Stata, CEO of Analog Devices, and Arie de Geus of Royal Dutch/Shell have proposed that organizational learning may be the source of the "only sustainable competitive advantage" (Stata, 1988). A new "special interest group" at the Academy of Management focuses academic research on this increasingly important and popular theme and related new academic journals are titled *The Learning Organization* and *The Journal of Managerial Learning* (Senge and Fulmer, 1993).

THE ORGANIZATIONAL LEARNING IMPERATIVE

One group of authors refers to organizational learning as "sustained improvement by performance" (Hays, Wheelwright, and Clark, 1988, p. 21) Similarly, Stata (1988) cites reductions achieved in his firm in product defects, manufacturing cycle time, and late delivery percentage as indicators of learning.

___

Reprinted with permission of Robert M. Fulmer, Hildy Teegen, and the publisher. First published in *American Journal of Management Development* (MCB University Press), 1(3), 1995, pp. 18-25.

Organizational learning must extend beyond improvements in performance. These improvements may be the short-lived consequences of fortuitous circumstances rather than evidence of enduring changes in thinking and behavior.

Global organizations develop mental models of the "way things are" that are shared within and across countries." As Stata (1988, p. 21) puts it: "Organizations can learn only as fast as the slowest link. . . . Change is blocked unless all of the major decision makers learn together, come to share beliefs and goals, and are committed to take actions necessary for change."

Botkin and Matthews (1992) of the Club of Rome, a futuristic think tank, conducted several important studies focused on the significance of learning as a positive alternative to the excesses associated with unbridled economic and population growth (Botkin, 1979). Reflecting on the study, Barney (1991) concluded that much progress depletes finite resources, but applying or sharing knowledge consumes nothing; new resources are in fact created through the learning process.

ALL LEARNING IS NOT EQUAL

Learning has been greatly facilitated by the systems dynamics perspective pioneered at MIT (Senge, 1995). This perspective parallels the distinction between single-loop and double-loop learning described by Chris Argyris of Harvard and Donald Schon of MIT (Argyris and Schon, 1978). They emphasize the distinction between adjustments in behavior that occur *within a feedback structure,* which they call single-loop learning, and changes in *the structure itself,* which they refer to as double-loop learning. Single-loop learning is analogous to the continual adjustments made by a thermostat in regulating temperature. Learning *about* a structure, however, which leads to changes in the structure itself, is within the spirit of double-loop learning. Within the feedback structure created by existing information flows and operating policies, people are learning in the sense of modifying decisions and actions as new conditions develop. When global organizations merely adjust their inventories, personnel, or facilities across countries, they are engaging in single-loop learning. On the other hand, when they change the mental models that executives and key managers use as a basis for operating, or change their human resource and learning systems to become truly global, or what Adler and Bartholomew (Chapter 3) call "transnational"—they are engaging in double-loop learning.

In *No Limits to Learning*, Botkin (1979) and his associates described three types of organizational learning: maintenance learning, shock learning, and anticipatory learning. Maintenance learning, the most common, is focused on trying to discover more "correct" ways of doing what we already know. The United Parcel Service, for example, improved its competitive position by abandoning its former emphasis on maintenance learning, efficiency and reliability, in favor of promoting more anticipatory learning to improve its understanding of customers, and thus promote customer service.

Maintenance learning quite often misses important clues about a changing environment or emerging challenges. As a result, situations change, crises arise, and shock learning is introduced. Learning that occurs under the stress of a crisis can seldom anticipate fully the long-term consequences of managers' reactions. Research has shown that under conditions of high stress most individuals fail to exercise creativity, relying on proven routines from the past (Bartwick, 1991). A few years ago, when Michelin first attacked the market share of Goodyear auto tires in the United States, Goodyear tried matching the reduced prices of Michelin. Shock learning came with the realization they would have to reduce prices across a huge market share, while Michelin's initiative in the United States, required low margins on only a sliver of market. This caused Goodyear to search for better solutions. They quickly realized that a more effective retaliation was to enter Europe and reduce prices below the equivalent price/value of Michelin. After the Goodyear move, Michelin stopped their price-cutting in the United States.

As a result of the limitations associated with maintenance and shock learning, the Club of Rome recommends greater emphasis on innovative or anticipatory learning. Anticipatory learning would have led Goodyear, like IBM, to realize that the best defense for a home market attack is to be dominant in other countries early. This type of learning involves two challenges for organizations and managers. Anticipatory learning is *participative* and it is *future oriented*.

Peter Senge (1995) has noted the importance of informal network creation and maintenance for promoting participation in organizational learning. Organizational as well as national culture differences undoubtedly affect a firm's ability to encourage participation for organizational learning. Hofstede's study of over fifty IBM subsidiary offices worldwide highlights four defining dimensions of national culture: Uncertainty Avoidance, Individualism-Collectivism, Masculinity-Femininity, and Power Distance. Nations that are highly collectivist (e.g., Japan, Mexico) will embrace more readily a participative environment in their organizations (Hofstede, 1991). Even within highly individualistic countries (e.g., the United States), however, examples exist of firms with very consensual organization. Nations with low uncertainty avoidance (Singapore) tend to embrace the future and its potential; those with high uncertainty avoidance (Portugal) seek to protect against future outcomes.

THE ORGANIZATIONAL LEARNING MATRIX

Anticipatory learning involves two characteristics (future orientation and participation); a two-by-two matrix captures the essence of the different approaches. This matrix guides firms in profiling their organizational learning.

There are four major ways that organizations approach learning. The first can be referred to as "Because I say so." An authority figure says that something is to be done (or avoided) but concludes that the explanations of the reasons are too cumbersome for the learner to understand. This is the essence of maintenance learning. In many instances it is appropriate.

The second quadrant can be called "As you like it." Left to their own devices, many individuals and organizations will find ways to do things better. This is especially true in decentralized operations where performance is measured according to growth objectives, return on investment, or some other quantifiable measure.

To borrow from Rosabeth Moss Kanter, some strong CEOs can be called "Change masters" (Kanter, 1983). They recognize the need for future-oriented change and insist that their companies learn to think or do business a new way. Kotter and Heskitt (1992), in agreement with this viewpoint, conclude that significant, appropri-

FIGURE 1.1. How Organizations Learn

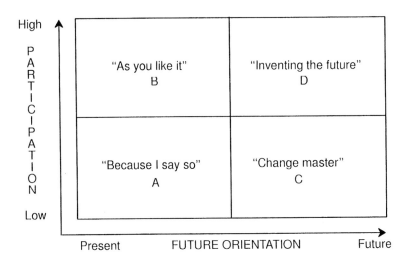

ate cultural change is unlikely to take place without strong leadership.

The fourth approach to learning is "Creating our future." The essence of anticipatory learning is for a group of motivated individuals to work together, not to forecast, but to create a future to which they feel committed. In 1992, when Ralph Larsen was planning an executive learning effort for the top 700 executives at Johnson & Johnson, the world's largest health care company, he resisted pressure to articulate the theme of the conference. Instead, he outlined the importance of thinking about change and the future along with the dangers of trading on past successes. He refused to give more specific directions for this strategic initiative. Supplemented with information from interviews involving almost 100 of their colleagues from eight countries, his key executives were required to devise a plan. The theme they ultimately chose was "Creating Our Future." The program that evolved from this mission included numerous computer group-ware applications (exercises that involved groups of people participating in debates affecting their future via computer hookups), discussion of a case titled "J&J 2002," and a comprehensive strategic exercise for "Creating Our

Future," which included Delphi forecasting. In this way, participation of many with a future focus was achieved—requisite characteristics for anticipatory learning.

Moving from Quadrant A to Quadrant B on the matrix (from "Because I say so" to "As you like it") moves the firm toward greater participation and invokes anticipatory learning. A shift from Quadrant A to Quadrant C (from "Because I say so" to "Change master") moves the firm toward heightened anticipatory learning in that the present is replaced by the future as the orientation focus. Quadrant D ("Inventing the future") is where techniques that are most consistent with anticipatory learning will fall. The following section will explore the importance of anticipatory learning and outline how organizational learning can (and should) move in this direction.

FORECASTING VERSUS CREATING THE FUTURE

Unless you believe in a deterministic world, the future is still in the process of evolving. Each person and organization has an almost infinite number of possible futures that could evolve from the current situation. Choice is the essence of creating the future.

The difficulty in choosing a future is that there is no right answer before the fact. Rather, we can anticipate only a few of the events and trends that will take place. Other possibilities are not yet noticed or mapped. Some that do not yet exist can be invented.

FROM THE FORECASTED FUTURE
TO THE INVENTED FUTURE

The *forecasted future* is a paradigm that managers already understand. In this model, managers analyze current trends, examine their global organization's strengths and weaknesses, explore core competencies and capabilities, and chart the projection of current trends. A whimsy by T. H. White provides an apt metaphor for the "future-first" perspective and, used effectively, can prepare managers to move toward the *invented future*. In White's *The Once and Future*

King, Merlin was a magician, mentor, and advisor to King Arthur who was described as having an uncanny ability to know the future. When asked about this insight, the magician explains:

> How did I know to set breakfast for two? . . . Now ordinary people are born forwards in Time, if you understand what I mean, and nearly everything in the world goes forward too. This makes it quite easy for ordinary people to live. . . . But unfortunately I was born at the wrong end of time, and have to live backwards from in front, while surrounded by a lot of people living forward from behind. (White, 1959, p. 34)

According to Charles E. Smith, "The Merlin Factor is the process whereby leaders transform themselves and the culture of their organization through a creative commitment to a radically different future" (Smith, 1992). In this model called alternatively "The Merlin Exercise" or "The Merlin Process," managers look first at what is desirable, unencumbered by current obstacles and past experiences. The "invention" conversation moves to a point where the desirability of the invented future is stronger than the burden of current circumstances. The challenge becomes one of "breaking through" and of inventing new ways of seeing and creating pathways to the desired future. A further discussion of the Merlin Exercise will be included in Chapter 11 of this text.

SUMMARY AND CONCLUSION

Good international managers are masters of maintenance learning and operate within existing paradigms. Excellent global leaders encourage anticipatory learning and help their colleagues move toward new paradigms to create a desirable future. Current thinking must be constantly challenged so that future prospects can be enhanced through anticipatory learning (Senge and Fulmer, 1993). Firms that succeed in jointly creating novel paradigms for guiding the organization will optimize their strategic outlook for the future.

A valuable model for enabling managers to focus on and steer toward the future for their organization would produce the following outcomes (Fulmer and Franklin, 1994):

- Give senior managers a global platform that will allow them to enthusiastically "play the game" they have chosen and rapidly begin the process of change.
- Produce an organization that can learn and respond rapidly across functions, countries, and global regions. Utilize the best knowledge currently available regardless of which country or region it originates within.
- Allow participants to leap from existing knowledge to design a challenging global future that can fully engage the organization and its people in providing significant competitive advantage.
- Engage the heads *and* hearts of global teams within the cross-cultural organization.

REFERENCES

Argyris, C. and D. Schon. (1978). *Organizational Theory of Action Perspective.* Reading, MA: Addison Wesley.

Barney, J. (1991). "Firm resources and sustained competitive advantage." *Journal of Management,* 17(1): 99-119.

Bartwick, J. M. (1991). *Danger in the Comfort Zone.* New York: Amacom, pp. 30-40.

Botkin, J. (1979). *No Limits to Learning.* Tarrytown, NY: Pergamon Press.

Botkin, J. and B. Matthews. (1992). *Winning Combinations.* New York: Wiley.

Fulmer, R. and S. Franklin, Sr. (1994). "The Merlin Exercise: Creating your future through strategic anticipatory learning." *Journal of Management Development,* 13(8): 38-43.

Hays, R. H., C. C.Wheelwright, and K. B. Clark. (1988). *Dynamic Manufacturing: Creating the Learning Organization.* New York: The Free Press.

Hofstede, G. (1991). *Cultures and Organizations.* New York: McGraw-Hill.

Kanter, R. M. (1983). *The Change Masters.* New York: Simon and Schuster.

Kotter, J. P. and J. L. Heskitt. (1992). *Corporate Culture and Performance.* New York: The Free Press.

Senge, P. (1995). "Learning infrastructures." *Executive Excellence,* 12(2): 7.

Senge, P. M. and R. M. Fulmer. (1993). "Simulations, systems thinking and anticipatory learning." *Journal of Management Development,* 12(6): 14-23.

Smith, C. E. (1992). *The Merlin Phenomena.* Unpublished working paper.

Stata, R. (1988). "Organizational learning—the key to management innovation." *Sloan Management Review,* Spring: 63-64.

White, T. H. (1959). *The Once and Future King.* New York: Putnam.

Chapter 2

Do Cultural Differences Make a Business Difference? Contextual Factors Affecting Cross-Cultural Relationship Success

Rosabeth Moss Kanter
Richard Ian Corn

I think Turks are Turks, and they are very different from Canadians, or North Americans or Brits or whatever. But when I went to Turkey, I was dealing with some Turks who had been dealing with Canadians for ten to fifteen years; they understood us and had adapted to our ways. Yes, they were still Turks, but they knew what Canadians expected. And they knew Canadians very well, so they forgave us when we made *faux pas,* they understood that we like Christmas Day off. They were patient and gave us a year to understand them.

> *Canadian executive, describing experiences in his company's joint venture in Turkey*

Of course, initially there were apprehensions about being bought by foreigners. Foreigners to us is anyone outside the local community.

> *American executive, describing his company's acquisition by a British company*

Reprinted with permission of the authors, Rosabeth Moss Kanter and Richard Ian Corn, Harvard Business School, Boston, Massachusetts, USA. *Journal of Management Development,* 13(2), 1994, pp. 5-23. Copyright 1993 by R. M. Kanter and R. I. Corn.

Portions of this article are based on research for the book *World Class: Thriving Locally in the Global Economy,* by Rosabeth Moss Kanter, New York: Simon and Schuster, 1995, which may be consulted for further information.

IN SEARCH OF CULTURAL DIFFERENCES

As economies globalize and organizations increasingly form cross-border relationships, there is a resurgence of interest in the management problems caused by national cultural differences—in values, ideologies, organizational assumptions, work practices, and behavioral styles—spawning research reminiscent of national character studies following World War II. Recent findings about the cultural propensities of major countries appear robust, replicated in surveys of the values of managers,[1-3] as well as used to explain institutional patterns within countries.[4]

Such findings are often consistent with stereotypes evoked by managers to explain others and themselves. Cultural generalizations roll easily off the tongues of people in our studies. For example, several Europeans predicted problems Volvo and Renault could have in combining Volvo's Swedish egalitarianism with Renault's French hierarchy. A German executive working in a French-American alliance commented that Germans and Americans had more values in common than either did with the French, invoking this as an explanation for why an American sent to London to lead the integration team was viewed as incompetent by the French partner for failing to make authoritative decisions.[5]

Furthermore, people often assume cultural heterogeneity creates tensions for organizations. Managers, even within a single country, often prefer homogeneity to heterogeneity, because shared experiences and culture are a basis for trust.[6]

Yet, while national cultural differences clearly exist at some level of generality, it is more difficult to specify how the presence of such differences affects organizational and managerial effectiveness. Evidence and observations in a range of situations raise questions about the usefulness of the "cultural differences" approach for managers. For example:

- When people of different national cultures interact, they can be remarkably adaptable, as in the Japanese history of borrowing practices from other countries.[7] And even though it is supposedly more difficult for managers to operate outside their home cultures, multinational companies have long succeeded even when expatriate managers make mistakes. Many industrial firms have operated successfully in foreign countries while showing insensitivity toward local values or treating host-country personnel less well than home-country personnel.[8]

- Technical orientation can override national orientation. There is evidence that similar educational experiences—e.g., for managers or technical professionals—can erase ideological differences; those within the same profession tend to espouse similar values regardless of nationality.[9,10] At Inmarsat, an international satellite consortium owned by companies from over sixty countries and staffed at its London headquarters by people of fifty-five nationalities, differences between functions were a greater source of conflict than differences between nationalities. Although stereotypes abounded ("Spaniards are often late"; "Indians like to talk"), engineers who shared a technical orientation quickly adjusted to each other's foibles—easily enough that a training program on cross-cultural management was poorly attended.[11]

- Tensions between organizations which seem to be caused by cultural differences often turn out, on closer examination, to have more significant structural causes. A Scottish construction company had difficulty in its first international partnership with a French company. The failure was widely explained by employees as caused by differences between a "beer culture" and a "wine culture." Its next partnership with a Dutch company was more effective, supposedly because of the greater compatibility with the Dutch. But in the first partnership, the companies set up many "dealbusters,"[12] from letting lawyers negotiate for executives, to ignoring assumptions about future business strategy. In the second case, they learned from their mistakes and changed the way they worked with their partner. National cultures had little to do with failure in the first instance and success in the second.

- Cultural value issues—and issues of "difference" in general—are more apparent at early stages of relationships than later, before people came to know each other more holistically. And outsiders of any kind, even from the next neighborhood, can seem different. But once people get to know each other beyond first impressions, relationship dynamics are often determined by power rather than culture. Resistance to the new American chief executive of a British retailer was resistance to change, not to culture differences. National culture issues were simply one more piece of learning as he moved from outsider to insider; they did not affect his ability to do his work of managing a fast and successful turnaround.[13]

- Central country value tendencies are often reported at a very high level of generality, as on average over large populations themselves far from homogeneous. Thus, they fail to apply to many groups and individuals within those countries. There are strong individual, regional, and ethnic differences within countries that are masked by the attempt to find country patterns. For example, an American who had served in Japan during the Second World War liked the docile women he saw there. He decided to marry a Japanese woman, only to discover after the marriage that she came from the one part of Japan that encouraged assertive, dominant women. And not only are there individual as well as ethnic differences within countries, but individuals themselves derive their behavior from many influences and can hold multiple identities. The chairman of Matra Hachette in Paris calls himself "a Gascon, a Frenchman, and a European."

- Finally, group cultural tendencies are always more apparent from outside than inside the group. Indeed, people often only become aware of their own values or culture in contrast to someone perceived as an outsider.[14] The British writer George Orwell observed that national identity and cultural similarity are salient only for those returning from abroad or when the country is threatened; otherwise, people hold firmly to their individuality and are more aware of differences among those within the same nation.

For these reasons, then, we wondered about the circumstances under which cross-cultural interaction would affect business performance.

THE FOREIGN ACQUISITIONS STUDY

To learn more about managerial issues provoked by cultural differences, we looked for situations in which cross-cultural interactions might produce organizational tensions. Kanter's studies of international strategic alliances and joint ventures, reported in a series of Harvard case studies and articles,[15] had uncovered a large number of strains between cross-border partners, but most of these involved strategic, organizational, political, or financial issues. But perhaps that was because the relationship between venture or alliance partners is assumed to be one of relative equality and independence; each partner retains its own cultural identity as well as control over its own operations, cooperating with the other for limited purposes while insulating core activities from the relationship.

We looked for another test in the realm of foreign acquisitions, in which cultural differences would perhaps play a greater role. Foreign acquisitions of U.S. companies increased over the last decade. In 1990, 446 such deals, valued at $46.2 billion, were completed, compared with only 126 deals, valued at $4.6 billion, in 1982. Foreign acquisitions of U.S. companies accounted for 28.1 percent of the total value of merger and acquisition activity involving at least one company in 1990, compared with only 7.6 percent in 1982.[16] This acquisition situation, we proposed, would heighten American managers' awareness of their own culture and its contrast to the acquirer's culture, as they merged operations or shifted control over decisions. Since American companies were more accustomed to acquiring foreign operations than being acquired, the reversal of roles experienced when being acquired would perhaps exaggerate tensions enough to bring cultural issues to the surface. Therefore, we developed a pilot project with eight companies.

The Companies

Approximately seventy-five interviews with senior and middle managers were conducted by Harvard Business School teams in 1992 and 1993 at eight midsized New England-based American companies which had been acquired by foreign companies in the period between mid-1987 and 1990 (with one exception acquired in 1984). All companies had enough experience with the foreign parent to provide time for cross-cultural contact to occur and any problems to surface; but the acquisition was also recent enough for managers to have fresh memories.

The circumstances surrounding the acquisitions differed in some respects. One was a strictly arms-length financial investment in which a well-known sporting goods manufacturer was acquired by a Venezuelan financial group as its only U.S. holding in a leveraged buyout from investors who had acquired it two years earlier; as long as profits were high, there was minimal contact with the parent. In two other cases, there was a history of relationships between the foreign parent and the acquired company prior to the acquisition. A family-owned retailer had developed a business partnership with a larger but also family-owned British chain four years before the acquisition as part of a succession plan. A metals manufacturer had formed a number of joint ventures with a Japanese conglomerate beginning seven years before the acquisition, turning to its Japanese partner as a defensive tactic against a hostile takeover threat. Other acquisitions also stemmed from financial distress: an armaments manufacturer was bought by a British conglomerate after the U.S. company faltered under a sequence of four different American owners; an abrasives manufacturer was bought by a French company as a "white knight" in a takeover battle with a British company; and a U.S. retailer was sold to a Japanese retailer when it no longer fit its U.S. manufacturing company parent's strategy. In many of the cases, then, foreign acquirers were sought by the U.S. companies to solve a problem.

Two of the companies, given the pseudonyms Metalfab and Hydrotech, were observed by the second author in particular depth. Both were engineering-oriented manufacturing companies with operations primarily in the United States and annual sales between $100 and $200 million. Both were previously owned by financially troubled U.S. parents whose core business was in a different industry, and both were bought by well-respected, internationally experienced companies in the same industry. Corn conducted thirty interviews at Metalfab, a manufacturer of fabricated metal products acquired about five years earlier by Fabritek, pseudonym for a Swedish manufacturer in the same business. He also conducted twenty-one interviews at Hydrotech, a designer and manufacturer of hydraulic systems acquired about three years earlier by Gruetzi, pseudonym for a German-Swiss manufacturer of industrial energy systems. But while Metalfab was acquired by a company of similar size and was operating at a pretax profit, Hydrotech's new parent was much larger and more diversified geographically and technologically, and Hydrotech was accumulating significant losses.

Overview of the Findings

The interviews at all eight companies focused on the history of the companies' relationships, their business situations and business strategies, the amount and kind of cross-cultural contact between managers, difficulties and how they had been resolved, and any organizational changes which had come about as a result of the merger. We expected cultural differences to play a prominent role in the dynamics of the integration, especially because so many questions probed these issues specifically—from asking for characterizations of "typical" American and parent country managers to comparing managerial styles in concrete situations. (The study was thus "biased" toward finding cultural differences and tensions because of them.) We expected many difficulties to arise, necessitating many organizational changes, and we expected American companies to resist learning from their foreign company parents. We also expected some combinations to be more volatile than others, such as the Japanese-American interactions, either because of prejudice or because of values and style differences.

We found, instead, that nationality-based culture was one of the less significant variables affecting the integration of the companies and their organizational effectiveness. We found that relatively few issues or problems arose which could be labeled "cultural," even though managers were able to identify style differences easily that fit common cultural patterns. We also found that very few measures were taken to facilitate cultural integration. Only a moderate number of difficulties were encountered or organizational changes necessitated, and U.S. companies learned from their foreign parents. Furthermore, there was no discernable pattern of cultural compatibility; all nationalities worked well with their American acquisitions.

In general, mergers and acquisitions create significant stress on organizational members, as separate organizational cultures and strategies are blended, even within one country.[17] Differences in national cultures are assumed to add another layer of complexity to the merger process. But our findings suggest that contextual factors play the dominant role in determining the smoothness of the integration, the success of the relationship, and whether or not cultural differences become problematic. These findings lead us to conclude that the significance of cultural differences between employees or managers of different nationalities has been overstated. Cultural values or national differences are used as a convenient explanation for other problems, both interpersonal and organizational, such as a failure to respect people, group power and politics, resentment at subordination, poor strategic fit, limited organizational communication, or the absence of problem-solving forums. Such differences are invoked as explanations for the uncomfortable behavior of others when people have limited contact or knowledge of the context behind the behavior.

CULTURE VERSUS CONTEXT AS AN EXPLANATORY FACTOR

Most interviewees were able to identify a number of ways in which they differed "culturally" from their foreign colleagues in values, interpersonal style, and organizational approach. Many of these "fit" the position of countries on dimensions Hofstede[18] identified, especially power distance and individualism/collectivism.

The first difference issue mentioned, however, was an objective one: language problems. A majority of Americans found the difficulty in overcoming language differences with all but the British acquirers to be the biggest "negative" surprise of their respective mergers. One American at Metalfab stated that "during initial meetings, we assumed that when we spoke English to the Swedes and they nodded their heads, they understood what we were saying. Now we realize the nods only meant that they heard the words." Employees at Metalfab and Hydrotech also recalled meetings in which their foreign colleagues would agree to adopt some new procedure, "only to go right back to doing things the same old way as soon as they left the meeting."

American employees noted cultural differences in decision-making styles. Many argued that their foreign parent's management team took a longer-term view. Americans at Hydrotech and Metalfab routinely expressed frustration with the unwillingness of German-Swiss and Swedish managers to make decisions without a great deal of analysis. Europeans noted the American reputation for fast, less thoughtful decisions. A British manager involved in the armaments company acquisition said, "Unlike American companies which manage by quarterly numbers, we at U.K. headquarters base our strategy and business policies on long-term positioning."

American interviewees also identified a number of differences in interpersonal style between themselves and their foreign colleagues which they attributed to national culture. The Swiss were described as "very orderly and efficient," the Swedes were universally described as being very serious. British managers were described as less emotional, less community-oriented, more deliberate, and much less likely to "shoot from the hip" than Americans. Europeans were described by nearly all American employees as being more formal, less open and outgoing, and slower to form friendships than are Americans. Japanese managers were described as very courteous and polite. Several Metal-fab employees stated that the Swedes were much more likely to argue with each other publicly than were Americans. One American official recalled that in the early days of the merger, he and an American colleague would stare at each other in board meetings while the Swedes argued among themselves. The American manager claimed that his American colleagues would have been much more likely to discuss such differences privately. The Swedes were also described as having less respect for authority and greater willingness to confront their superiors publicly than are Americans—signs of low power distance in Hofstede's terms. Other employees stated that Swedish managers are not as "results-oriented" as Americans when it comes to running meetings, ending meetings without a resolution or an understanding of the next steps. Swedes were described by several American employees as very critical, both of themselves and others. One American manager stated that "Americans are taught that it is more constructive to give pats on the back than to focus entirely on shortcomings as the Swedes are inclined to do."

In short, most of those interviewed found differences between themselves and their foreign colleagues to be clearly identifiable and immediately noticeable following their respective mergers. Employees attributed a majority of these differences to national culture. But a closer analysis of these responses reveals a tendency for employees to attribute to culture differences which are more situationally driven. For example, several employees stated the Swedes were unwilling or incapable of adjusting their planning and forecasting assumptions in light of changes in the environment, that the Swedes were more determined than are Americans to meet old budget targets. This may reflect the fact that as parent, the Swedes and German-Swiss have the ultimate responsibility for financial results. Similarly, slower decision making may reflect the fact that the Swedish parent involves more people in the decision-making process than does its American subsidiary. Of course, the use of greater participation may itself reflect differences in values between Americans and Swedes, but it may also reflect differences in the organizational culture of parent and subsidiary or in country-specific industry practices. Senior managers generally had more direct contact with the foreign parent and thus more contextual information. They were much more likely to identify differences in business context that explained apparent differences in "cultural values." Senior executives at the American retailer acquired by a British company attributed differences in management practices to differences in business environments in the United States and United Kingdom. For example, the British company appeared to be less interested in people and more interested in facilities. But this was because its operating expenses tended to be weighted more toward rent than to labor, because British supermarkets were typically located in expensive urban areas, whereas in the United States supermarkets were generally found outside the commercial core of the city, and U.S. chains had unions which drove up labor costs.

There was also a tendency for American employees to attribute interpersonal difficulties with foreign colleagues to cultural differences without recognizing that Americans act in much the same way. There are recent public examples of American board meetings interrupted by public bickering. The popularity of the view that committees rarely accomplish anything similarly attests to the fact that Europeans are not the only ones who have difficulty establishing clear agendas in their meetings. Finally, in the United States, American employees frequently complain about superiors who rarely hand out constructive criticism. In sum, Americans were routinely able to identify a number of differences between themselves and their foreign colleagues, but the attribution of these differences to nationality often seemed to be misdirected. Additionally, in many cases, these differences are more suggestive of perception than of reality.

Perhaps it was more convenient to attribute differences to culture than to context because of the popularity of national character stereotypes. The role of national stereotypes was made clear in contrasting what American managers said about their own foreign acquirers (whom they knew well) compared with other nationalities (which they knew less well). An American senior executive at the sporting goods manufacturer had highly positive things to say about his Venezuelan parent, calling Venezuelans "lovable, amiable, showing a high degree of concern for people." In contrast, he said, "The companies you do not want to have take you over are the Germans and the Japanese. They feel they know how to do it better and just come in and take over." But the companies in our study acquired by Japanese and German-Swiss parents reported just the opposite—that the Japanese, for example, were eager to learn from the American companies they acquired. In short, the greater the experience with managers from another country, the less reliance on negative stereotypes.

Furthermore, while many interviewees were able to identify behavioral style differences between American managers and their foreign parents, they also spoke of cultural compatibilities in values, business strategies, and organizational approach. Such similarities overrode style differences. Both retailers in the pilot study, for example, spoke of the common concerns and philosophies they shared with their foreign parents—one Japanese, one British.

Finally, just because people could point to differences, that did not mean that the differences had operational consequences. Interviewees were asked to assess the extent to which cross-cultural differences created difficulties in the relationship between parent and subsidiary. Interestingly, many employees felt that although differences exist between their cultures, such differences did not create significant problems for employees. This finding cuts to the heart of this study's central question: If cultural differences between a parent and subsidiary do not necessarily lead to significant interorganizational conflict, what factors moderate the relationship between cultural heterogeneity and organizational conflict? Why do American employees of foreign companies feel that cultural differences between their own firm and their foreign parent have not been particularly problematic? Here, our findings suggest that a number of contextual factors act as mediators in determining whether or not these differences will be problematic.

CONTEXTUAL FACTORS AS KEY DETERMINANTS OF CROSS-CULTURAL RELATIONSHIP SUCCESS

Six factors emerged in the pilot study that accounted for the ease with which the merger was implemented and the relatively few difficulties attributed to national cultural differences:

1. the desirability of the relationship, especially in contrast to recent experiences of the acquired companies;
2. business compatibility between the two companies, especially in terms of industry and organization;
3. the willingness of the acquirer to invest in the continued performance of the acquiree and to allow operational autonomy while performance improved;
4. mutual respect and communication based on that respect;
5. business success; and
6. the passage of time.

Relationship Desirability

The first issue sets the stage for whether the relationship begins with a positive orientation. When people are in distress, poorly-treated in previous relationships, have had positive experiences with their foreign rescuer, and play a role in initiating relationship discussions, they are much more likely to view the relationship as desirable and work hard to accommodate to any differences in cultural style so that the relationship succeeds.

First, almost all of the companies in the pilot study were acquired by foreigners after a period of financial distress. A Hydrotech employee said, "Everyone here was aware of the firm's financial problems at the time of the acquisition. News of the purchase was viewed favorably. Gruetzi kept our doors from being padlocked. Everyone recognized that without Gruetzi, Hydrotech might not have made it." While Metalfab did not have Hydrotech's financial problems at the time of its acquisition, its employees took comfort from Fabritek's strong financial condition at the time of the takeover. The abrasives company was rescued by its French acquirer as a "white knight in a takeover battle." In all these cases, people were thus more likely to view their acquirers as saviors than villains. Cultural problems were therefore not problematic.

When asked to describe their initial reaction to the acquisitions, interviewees in several companies began with a description of how difficult life had been under its former parent. Several foreign parents in our study therefore compared favorably with each subsidiary's former U.S. parents. Hydrotech and Metalfab's former parents had neither understood the business of its subsidiary nor shown any desire to invest in their subsidiary's long-term growth. The armaments company had four recent owners, several of whom stripped corporate assets and art collections, an experience one manager referred to as being "raped." Under new owners who cared about them, employees were therefore more inclined to tolerate and adapt to cultural differences.

In other cases, national differences were not a problem because the U.S. and non-U.S. companies had spent several years getting to know each other through joint ventures. The British retailer and the Japanese conglomerate had long worked closely with the American companies they eventually bought. Nearly every respondent at Metalfab and Hydrotech spoke with high regard for their parents' technical expertise, manufacturing skill, knowledge of the international marketplace, and reputation for quality. As one employee commented, "Our concerns about the takeover were quickly put to rest. After all, Gruetzi was not an unknown quantity. They were an industry leader and we had worked with them on several projects in the past." In contrast, respondents who were less familiar with the operations of their acquirer appear to have been the most concerned and apprehensive about the news of the merger when it was first announced. As one employee recalled, "At first I was sickened by the announcement, but when I saw Fabritek's product line and the obvious potential for synergy, I became extremely excited." Several respondents also mentioned that if the acquirer had a reputation for dismantling its acquisitions, they would have been far less sanguine about the takeover and the possibilities for success.

Reputation was based not only on past direct experience but also on assumptions about how "companies like that" behaved. One Metalfab employee claimed that compared with other countries, "the Swedes are just like us." The conventional wisdom at Metalfab was that Scandinavian firms had a history of keeping their acquisitions intact.

Finally, the ability to choose made a difference. In several cases, the companies themselves initiated the search for a foreign partner. The element of surprise that creates anxiety and uncertainty was missing. A Hydrotech employee stated, "We wanted to be sold; I viewed the announcement as a real positive—someone wanted to buy us!"

Business Compatibility

Organizational similarities were more important to most companies than national cultural differences. At the time of their respective mergers, employees of Metalfab, Hydrotech, and both retailers in the study took immediate comfort from the fact that their new acquirers were in the same industry as they, especially the retailer sold by an American manufacturer to a Japanese retailer. As one Hydrotech employee stated, "Our former parent showed no commitment to, or interest in, our business. Now, there is a much better fit." Another employee stated, "Everyone was initially apprehensive about the takeover but at least we were bought by a company which understands and cares about our business. This turned our initial apprehension into excitement." Along similar lines, Metalfab employees reacted very favorably to the news that "a metal company was purchasing a metal company."

Organizational similarity meant that employees could feel that they play important roles in carrying out their parent's strategy and believe that their parent values their contribution. As one Hydrotech employee stated, "Despite the fact that Gruetzi is a much larger company than our former parent was, it is easier to see how we fit into their plans." Thus, at both Hydrotech and Metalfab, the benefits of the merger were transparent to employees. As one manager stated, "This was an easy announcement to make; the merger spoke for itself."

Employees at Hydrotech and Metalfab felt that sharing a common technical orientation with their parent allowed both organizations to more easily overcome national differences. Several employees emphasized what a pleasure it was to work with a parent organization that understands the business they are in. As one engineer stated, "Our two firms are like twins that were separated at birth." Employees at both Hydrotech and Metalfab also feel that their parents' expertise and credibility in the industry has made it easier to accept them in the role of acquirer. One Metalfab employee's comment captured the attitude of the firm's employees toward foreign ownership when he claimed, "It doesn't bother me in the least that our parent is a foreign company because we speak the same language, *Metal!*" A majority of those interviewed concluded that they would now prefer being taken over by a foreign company in the same business than by an American firm in a different industry.

Investment Without Interference

Of all the actions taken by a foreign partner, none seems to have a more positive impact on morale and on attitudes toward foreigners than a foreign owner's decision to invest capital in its subsidiaries. Fabritek spent $11 to $12 million upgrading the production facilities of its U.S. subsidiary during each of the first two years following the acquisition and has invested an additional $6 to $8 million annually ever since. Gruetzi has similarly invested in new equipment for Hydrotech's Ohio production facility. To most American employees, such investment demonstrated that its new parent was committed to the company's long-term health.

When investment was accompanied by operational autonomy, the relationship was viewed very favorably and cross-cultural tensions minimized. In three cases—the sporting goods manufacturer acquired by a Venezuelan company and both the retailer and the manufacturer acquired by Japanese companies—feeling lack of cultural tensions was a function of the minimal interference of the foreign company in its new U.S. operations. "They let us do what we are good at," said an executive at the sporting goods firm, "which is make money."

Employees at Hydrotech and Metalfab were surprised by the extent to which their parents allowed them to manage their own operations. As one Hydrotech employee stated, "Things have turned out much better than I originally expected. Gruetzi has not overmanaged us, they kept our management team intact, and we have not been forced to spend a lot of our time defending ourselves." Metalfab employees were similarly pleased that their parent has allowed the firm to retain day-to-day control: "While our parent provides us with suggestions, they have allowed us to run the show here." We argue that American employees are less likely to view cultural heterogeneity as a problem when foreign management allows such autonomy along with adding resources.

It should be pointed out that complete autonomy was not welcomed by all employees; a minority of employees (those dissatisfied with their firm's policies) mentioned that they would be happier if the parent took a more active role in managing its subsidiary. At least one Hydrotech engineer wished that Gruetzi would force the company to standardize its designs and acquire better tools for its engineers to work with. At Metalfab, several employees expressed disappointment that its parent had not prevented the company from moving operations to Mexico. Furthermore, that high degrees of autonomy have possibly slowed down the speed with which the merged organizations develop a common culture. Several Metalfab employees reported that it has been difficult to "pull our two families together and get the message out to customers that we are *one* firm." Still, for the Americans autonomy generally meant that they did not feel foreigners were imposing "foreign ways" on them, which made them more tolerant of differences rather than resistant to them.

Open Communication and Mutual Respect

Nearly all interviewees agreed that open communication and showing mutual respect are critical to developing trust and ensuring a successful partnership. One retailer, for example, felt that its new Japanese parent wanted to learn from American practice, which made them feel valued and made rapport with the Japanese easy to develop. Tensions occurred, in contrast, when foreign colleagues did not show respect for American technology and expertise. At Fabritek, Swedish engineers and marketing personnel initially viewed Metalfab's traditional, composite products as inferior to their own, all-metal product, which required tighter engineering and manufacturing tolerances in order to ensure a perfect seal. As a result, Americans said that the Swedes saw themselves as "the real engineers" in the company. (But note here that the tensions were caused by *technical* differences, not cultural ones.) Similarly, Hydrotech engineers described their German-Swiss colleagues as very arrogant and protective about Gruetzi's products; there was a feeling that Hydrotech engineers should not "tamper" with their parent's designs.

Employee sensitivity to possible cultural differences played a significant role in reducing outbreaks of cross-cultural tension. One Hydrotech employee reasoned that cultural clashes had been avoided mainly because employees had been so concerned that such tensions could occur that they put more effort into trying to understand one another. Similar concerns led executives at Fabritek and Metalfab to schedule frequent meetings with each other soon after the merger; these meetings improved understanding and lessened tension between the two firms. Ironically, one senior American official recalled that he had rarely met with executives from the firm's former U.S. parent "even though they were located right down the road from the company." Though formal cross-cultural training programs were rare, open communication helped build relationships. Sensitivity to cultural differences and willingness to deal with problems directly minimized organizational tension.

Business Success

Nothing succeeds like success. People are willing to overlook cultural differences in relationships which bring clear benefits. But unsuccessful ventures produce squabbling even among people who are culturally similar.

Creating opportunities for joint success between parent and subsidiary promotes acceptance of cross-cultural differences and creates support for the relationship. Several months before Hydrotech's acquisition by Gruetzi, a company project had "gone sour" due to a technical malfunction. After the merger, Hydrotech used Gruetzi's technology to solve the problem. For the many employees who had suffered through the project's difficulties, this single act sold the virtue of the partnership. Another Hydrotech employee stated, "We had not realized how quickly Gruetzi's technology could be put to use. In only one year, our department was able to bid on two projects and win a $45 million contract." Nothing could possibly send a more positive message about the benefits of partnership than winning business because of it.

Ongoing financial performance affects the quality and nature of communications between parent and subsidiary, and thus plays a role in determining whether or not cultural differences are viewed as problematic. If success reduces tensions, deteriorating performance increases them. Employees noted that travel budgets came under increasing pressure during periods of poor performance, and thus, fewer meetings take place between American and foreign employees. In difficult times, communication between parent and subsidiary may deteriorate as employees in each organization focus on their own problems. Finally, poor performance leads to frustration, finger-pointing, and reduced trust. One Hydrotech manager noticed that as Gruetzi has encountered more financial difficulties, they became increasingly demanding of Hydrotech and focused more on the company's short-term operating results than in the past.

The Passage of Time

Does time heal all wounds? Time, at least, reduces anxieties and replaces stereotypes with a more varied view of other people. The levels of cross-cultural tension vary as a function of the stage in the relationship-building process. Anxieties at Hydrotech and Metalfab were highest during the days immediately following the announcement of each takeover. This initial anxiety declined as the merger entered a transition phase in which management showed reluctance to create conflict. Employees of both subsidiaries also reacted positively to foreign management's willingness to discuss issues and listen to their concerns at that time. According to one employee, "these meetings made us feel good about the changes and made us realize how alike our philosophies were." But during the transition phase, employees also underestimated the degree of cultural heterogeneity and the potential for conflict to erupt. As management began to focus on more substantive issues and the amount of communications between American and foreign employees grew, a new realization set in that the cultural differences between the two firms were greater than initially realized, which required more awareness and sensitivity to avoid conflict. It appears likely then, that employee perceptions of cross-cultural tension are affected by the passage of time and by the merger process itself. One might also expect that employee attitudes toward cultural heterogeneity will change as Americans and foreign employees work together and become more familiar with each others' customs and values.

Mistrust is always more likely at early stages of relationships. People at Hydrotech and Metalfab felt their new foreign parents were particularly guarded in discussing their technology during the first months together. As one employee mentioned, "It was like playing poker during the first year. You always got an answer to your question but the question was answered as narrowly as possible—even when, by withholding information, the answer was misleading." But another engineer recognized the significance of sharing technology, noting that, "when our parent provides us with technology, they are giving us their life's work."

THE NEGATIVE SIDE OF CROSS-CULTURAL INTERACTION: THREAT AND PREJUDICE

Positive views of the relationship between U.S. company and foreign parent predominated, but they were not universal in the companies studied. Top management and those with the greatest day-to-day contact were most likely to be favorable. Those at lower ranks anxious about the implications for their careers were more likely to express negative views, including prejudice and resentment, reacting the most nationalistically to the news of a foreign takeover. One American reported how "sick" he was over the fact that "this country is gradually being sold off to foreigners."

Some higher level managers commented that they would have been more comfortable if their acquirer had been American, but this preference did not seem to affect the relationship. A manager at the armaments company reported, "We would rather have been bought by a U.S. company. There is an element of national pride, especially in our industry. We are very patriotic. There is no one in the company that would say we are a British firm. We all wear and buy 'made in USA' products." Still, nationalist sentiments did not prevent this manager declaring the relationship a success and identifying very few cross-cultural problems.

The most significant factor in determining employee reactions to acquisition was self-interest: how the change would affect their own standing in the firm. Virtually all interviewees reacted to news of the acquisition with the same question: "How will this impact on my career in this organization?" Those employees who were most likely to suffer a loss of prestige or power, or who had reason to feel threatened by the mergers, were most likely to react unfavorably to it.

However, the fact that the vast majority of employees in both companies did not react in this way attests to just how apparent the benefits of these mergers were to most employees. Therefore threat could work both ways; if the foreign company improved performance, jobs would be saved. A manager at the U.S. armaments company observed, "The community and employees understand there are differences between us and the British. But for them, having good jobs is more valuable. When corporate survival is at stake, people cannot afford to have culture become an issue."

Attitudes were shaped by symbolic acts taken by the foreign parents as much as by more substantive actions. One Metalfab employee recalled the day that Fabritek's president arranged to have group photographs taken of all employees in the United States so that they could be shown to people back in Sweden. "Fabritek immediately impressed me as a very people-oriented company."

THE ATTRIBUTION OF ORGANIZATIONAL PROBLEMS TO NATIONAL CULTURE

Our findings suggest, then, that contextual factors act to either fan the flames of intergroup conflict and cross-cultural polarization or encourage organizational members to accept these differences. In the pilot study, organizational and technical compatibilities overwhelmed cultural differences. Cultural differences thus seem to be a residual category to which people attribute problems in the absence of a supportive context. Cultural differences do not automatically cause tensions. But when tensions do arise—often due to situational factors such as lack of communication or poor performance—people blame many of the organizational difficulties they encounter on cultural heterogeneity—on the presence of others who seem different—rather than to the context within which these problems took place. This view is consistent with Chris Argyris's perspective on defensive routines in organizations.[19]

Why do people blame culture for problems and ascribe differences between their own behavior and that of their foreign colleagues to dispositional factors (the kind of people they are) rather than to situational factors (the organizational context)?

First, cultural heterogeneity presents a conspicuous target for employees to point at when looking for an explanation for their problems. Such differences are readily apparent in early stages of contact between people who differ in a visible way, such as race, gender, or language, especially when there are only a few "tokens" such as expatriate managers among many "locals."[20] Preconceived notions and prejudices which employees bring into the evaluative process increase the likelihood that people will attribute behavior to nationality.

In-group favoritism is evoked in situations of cross-cultural contact. Research has shown that people want to favor members of their own group (the in-group) over others. Motivational theorists hold that self-esteem is enhanced if people value their own group and devalue other groups.[21,22] Such favoritism leads to a set of cognitive biases which reinforce the distinction between in-group and out-group members. People expect in-group members to display more desirable and fewer undesirable behaviors than out-group members.[23] As a result, people are more likely to infer negative dispositions from undesirable and out-group behaviors than from undesirable in-group behaviors, and are less likely to infer positive dispositions from desirable out-group behaviors than from desirable in-group behaviors.[24-27] Furthermore, people tend to remember behavior which is congruent with their expectations over behavior which is inconsistent with their views.[28,29] Thus, memories reinforce in-group favoritism as well. In-group biases are especially likely to form when individuals identify strongly with their group and when in-group members view other groups as a threat.[30]

During an acquisition process, employees who work for and identify with their company for many years suddenly find that another firm, with its own culture vision, values, and ways of doing things is responsible for their future. Cross-border mergers offer a particularly favorable environment for such biases to develop because group membership is clearly defined by national as well as organizational boundaries. At both Hydrotech and Metalfab, in-group favoritism and cognitive biases may have been the driving forces behind the tendency among Americans to attribute wrongfully "bad news" to their foreign parent (i.e., out-group members). In one case, Hydrotech management had frozen salaries and extended the required working week from forty to forty-four hours after the merger in an effort to "impress Gruetzi by showing a willingness to make a few difficult decisions." Many Hydrotech junior employees attributed this unpopular policy to Gruetzi's management. Ironically, according to one middle-level manager, when Gruetzi found out about these changes, they gave Hydrotech's president one month to reverse the policy.

In another example, soon after Metalfab announced plans to transfer some of its manufacturing operations to Mexico, rumors began circulating on the factory floor that the Swedes were behind the decision. When senior management in the United States found out about the rumors, the company's president called a meeting with all employees and took full responsibility for the decision. But many blue-collar workers continued to blame the Swedes for this unpopular move. They also attributed the decision to downsize the American workforce to the company's foreign parent.

A second explanation for why cultural differences are inappropriately invoked is called the "fundamental attribution error"[31]—a tendency to attribute one's own behavior to the situation but others' behavior to their "character." People attribute negative behavior of foreign colleagues to their nationality or culture (dispositional factors) rather than to situational or contextual factors which are operating behind the scenes.[32] For example, Metalfab interviewees initially viewed their Swedish colleagues as fractious (e.g., "Swedes are a stubborn people") before it occurred to them that language had caused many early misunderstandings. They attributed the fact that their Swedish colleagues were more engineering-oriented and less marketing oriented to national biases ("Swedes design bulldozers for the kind of work a garden shovel could do") rather than to differences in product features and to the requirements of the European market. For example, rigid engineering standards for Fabritek's all-metal products required engineers in Sweden to play a more central role in the parent's operations, whereas the competitiveness of the U.S. market demanded that marketing personnel play a more critical role in U.S. decision making. But those who had more direct contact with the foreign parent, such as senior managers, also had more contextual information and were less likely to make the "fundamental attribution error."

If in-group biases and the fundamental attribution error are behind the tendency to view cultural heterogeneity as problematic, what steps might management take to promote interorganizational cooperation in cross-border mergers? Our findings suggest that actions which make the relationship desirable, reduces uncertainty, show respect for the other group, create communication channels, and ensure business success will encourage employees to identify with their foreign colleagues and view the company as one organization. Creating an atmosphere of mutual respect, promoting open communication, investing in the future, maximizing opportunities to experience joint success, and taking steps to familiarize employees with their counterpart's products and markets reduces the likelihood that cultural differences will be viewed as a source of organizational tension.

CONCLUSION

These pilot study findings are only suggestive, of course. We have a small number of cases from one region. While none of them can yet be called a long-term success, they have survived a period of integration during which other companies which perhaps did experience debilitating cultural problems could have called off the marriage. We could be looking only at the "winners" that managed cultural differences well. Indeed, those companies experiencing problems were more likely to turn down our request to participate in the pilot study. But if tilted toward successes, then this research points to some of the circumstances that contribute to successful cross-cultural relationships. And since we "biased" the interviews toward identification of cultural differences and cultural tensions, the relative absence of tension gives additional weight to our argument that contextual and situational factors, such as technical fit, business performance, and abundant communication, are more significant determinants of relationship effectiveness.

Employees at each of the companies studied were able to identify a number of cultural differences between their own organization and that of their parent. Nevertheless, few employees viewed cultural heterogeneity as a significant source of tension in their firm. Such findings lend support to the notion that national cultural differences do not necessarily increase the amount of tension between organizations or make partnerships among companies from different countries untenable.

This article proposes that there are a number of factors which help to determine how employees react to foreign ownership. It calls into question the assumption that the larger the social distance or cultural gap between the national cultures of two merged organizations, the greater will be the potential for strain in the relationship between employees. The findings from our pilot study suggest contextual factors are extremely important mediators in cross-cultural relationships. These factors influence how cultural differences are interpreted and whether they are viewed by employees as problematic. Indeed, they may even determine whether "cultural differences" are identified at all.

REFERENCE NOTES

1. Hofstede, G., *Cultures and Organization,* McGraw-Hill, New York, 1991.

2. Kanter, R. M., "Transcending Business Boundaries: 12,000 World Managers View Change," *Harvard Business Review,* 69, May-June 1991.

3. Hampden-Turner, C., "The Boundaries of Business: Commentaries from the Experts," *Harvard Business Review,* 69, September-October 1991.

4. Lodge, G. C. and Vogel, E. F. (Eds.), *Ideology and National Competitveness: An Analysis of Nine Countries,* Harvard Business School Press, Boston, 1987.

5. Kanter, R. M., Applbaum, K., and Yatsko, P., *FCB and Publicis (A): Forming the Alliance,* Harvard Business School Case Records, Boston, 1993.

6. Kanter, R. M., *Men and Women of the Corporation,* Basic Books, New York, 1977.

7. Westney, E., *Imitation and Innovation: The Transfer of Western Organizational Patterns to Meiji, Japan,* Harvard University Press, Cambridge, MA, 1987.

8. Starbuck, W. H., "Learning by Knowledge-Intensive Firms," *Journal of Management Studies,* 29(6), 1992, pp. 713-740.

9. Haire, M., Ghiselli, E. E., and Porter, L. W., *Managerial Thinking,* Wiley, New York, 1966.

10. Wuthnow, R. and Shrum, W., "Knowledge Workers as a 'New Class': Structural and Ideological Convergence among Professional-Technical Workers and Managers," *Work and Occupations,* 10, 1983, pp. 471-487.

11. Myers, P. and Kanter, R. M., *Inmarsat 1991,* Harvard Business School Case Records, Boston, 1992.

12. Kanter, R. M., *When Giants Learn to Dance: Mastering the Challenges of Strategy, Management, and Careers in the 1990s,* Simon and Schuster, New York, 1989.

13. Kanter, R. M. and Gabriel, L., *BhS (A): Opening Boundaries,* Harvard Business School Case Records, Boston, 1992.

14. Kanter, *Men and Women of the Corporation.*

15. Kanter, R. M., "Competing on Relationships: How Companies Build Collaborative Advantage," *Harvard Business Review,* May-June 1994.

16. MckA *Almanac,* 26(6), 1992, p. 54.

17. Kanter, *When Giants Learn to Dance.*

18. Hofstede, *Cultures and Organization.*

19. Argyris, C., *Overcoming Organizational Defenses: Facilitating Organizational Learning,* Allyn & Bacon, Boston, 1990.

20. Kanter, *Men and Women of the Corporation.*

21. Taijfel, H. and Turner, J. C., "An Integrative Theory of Intergroup Conflict," in Austin, W. S. and Worchel, S. (Eds.), *The Social Psychology of Intergroup Relations,* Brooks/Cole, Monterey, CA, 1979, pp. 33-47.

22. Turner, J. C., *Rediscovering the Social Group: A Self-Categorization Theory,* Blackwell, Oxford, England, 1987.

23. Howard, J. W. and Rothbart, M., "Social Categorization and Memory for In-Group and Out-Group Behavior, *Journal of Personality and Social Psychology,* 38(2), 1980, pp. 301-310.

24. Taylor, D. M. and Jaggi, V., "Ethnocentrism and Causal Attribution in a South Indian Context," *Journal of Cross Cultural Psychology,* 5(2), 1974, pp. 162-171.

25. Allen, V. L. and Wilder, D. A., "Categorization, Belief Similarity, and Intergroup Discrimination," *Journal of Personality and Social Psychology,* 32(6), 1975, pp. 971-977.

26. Allen, V. L. and Wilder, D. A., "Group Categorization and Attribution of Belief Similarity," *Small Group Behavior,* 10(1), 1979, pp. 73-80.

27. Pettigrew, T. F., "The Ultimate Attribution Error: Extending Allport's Cognitive Analysis of Prejudice," *Personality and Social Psychology Bulletin,* 5(4), 1979, pp. 461-476.

28. Hastie, R. and Kumar, P. A., "Person Memory: Personality Traits as Organizing Principles in Memory for Behavior," *Journal of Personality and Social Psychology,* 37(1), 1979, pp. 25-38.

29. Srull, T. D., Lichtenstein, M., and Rothbart, M., "Associative Storage and Retrieval Processes in Person Memory," *Journal of Experimental Psychology: Learning, Memory and Cognition,* 11(2), 1985, pp. 316-345.

30. Taijfel and Turner, "An Integrative Theory of Intergroup Conflict."

31. Ross, J., "The Intuitive Psychologist and His Shortcomings: Distortions in the Attribution Process," in Berkowitz, L. (Ed.), *Advances in Experimental Social Psychology,* Vol. 10, Academic Press, New York, 1977, pp. 173-220.

32. Jones, E. E. and Nisbett, R. E., "The Actor and the Observer: Divergent Perceptions of the Causes of Behavior," in Jones, E. E., Kanouse, D. E., Kelley,

H. H., Nisbett, R. E., Valins, S., and Weiner, B. (Eds.), *Perceiving the Causes of Behavior,* General Learning Press, Morristown, NJ, 1971, pp. 79-94.

FURTHER READING

Locksley, A., Ortiz, V., and Hepburn, C., "Social Categorization and Discriminatory Behavior: Extinguishing the Minimal Intergroup Discrimination Effect," *Journal of Personality and Social Psychology,* 39(5), 1980, pp. 773-783.

Maass, A., Salvi, D., Arcuri, L., and Semin, G., "Language Use in Intergroup Contexts: The Linguistic Intergroup Bias," *Journal of Personality and Social Psychology,* 57(6), 1989, pp. 981-993.

Taijfel, H., "Social Psychology of Intergroup Relations," *Annual Review of Psychology,* Annual Reviews, Stanford, CA, 1982, pp. 1-39.

Chapter 3

Managing Globally Competent People

Nancy J. Adler
Susan Bartholomew

Top-level managers in many of today's leading corporations
are losing control of their companies. The problem is not that
they have misjudged the demands created by an increasingly
complex environment and an accelerating rate of environmental change, not even that they have failed to develop strategies
appropriate to the new challenges. The problem is that their
companies are incapable of carrying out the sophisticated
strategies they have developed. Over the past 20 years, strategic thinking has far outdistanced organizational capabilities.[1]

Today, people create national competitiveness, not, as suggested by
classical economic theory, mere access to advantageous factors of
production.[2] Yet, human systems are also one of the major constraints
in implementing global strategies. Not surprisingly therefore, human
resource management has become "an important fdocus of top management attention, particularly in multinational enterprises."[3]
The clear issue is that strategy (the *what*) is internationalizing
faster than implementation (the *how*) and much faster than individual
managers and executives themselves (the *who*). "The challenges
[therefore] are not the 'whats' of what-to-do, which are typically
well-known. They are the 'hows' of managing human resources in a
global firm."[4]

Reprinted with permission of Nancy J. Adler, Susan Bartholomew, and the publisher. First published in *Academy of Management Executive*, 1992, 6(2), pp. 52-65.

How prepared are executives to manage transnational companies? How capable are firms' human resource systems of recruiting, developing, retaining, and using globally competent managers and executives? A recent survey of major U.S. corporations found only 6 percent reporting foreign assignments to be essential for senior executive careers, with 49 percent believing foreign assignments to be completely immaterial.[5]

Which firms are leading in developing globally competent managers and executives, and which remain in the majority and lag behind? That majority, according to a recent survey of 1,500 CEOs, will result in a lack of sufficient senior American managers prepared to run transnational businesses, forcing U.S. firms to confront the highest executive turnover in history.[6]

By contrast, it describes the approaches of some of the world's leading firms that distinguish them from the majority. There is no question that world business is going global; the question raised in this article is how to create human systems capable of implementing transnational business strategies. Based on their research, the authors support the conclusion of the recent *21st Century Report* that "executives who perceive their international operations as shelves for second-rate managers are unsuited for the CEO job in the year 2000, or indeed any managerial job today."[7]

TRANSNATIONALLY COMPETENT MANAGERS

Not all business strategies are equally global, nor need they be. As will be described, a firm's business strategy can be primarily domestic, international, multinational, or transnational. However, to be effective, the firm's human resource strategy should be integrated with its business strategy. Transnational firms need a transnational business strategy. While superficially appearing to be a truism, transnational firms also need a transnational human resource system and transnationally competent managers.

As summarized in Table 3.1, transnationally competent managers require a broader range of skills than traditional international managers. First, transnational managers must understand the worldwide business environment from a global perspective. Unlike expatriates of the past, transnational managers are not focused on a single country nor

TABLE 3.1. Transnationally Competent Managers

Transnational Skills	Transnationally Competent Managers	Traditional International Managers
Global Perspective	Understand worldwide business environment from a global perspective	Focus on a single foreign country and on managing relationships between headquarters and that country
Local Responsiveness	Learn about many cultures	Become an expert on one culture
Synergistic Learning	Work with and learn from people of many cultures simultaneously	Work with and coach people in each foreign culture separately or sequentially
	Create a culturally synergistic organizational environment	Integrate foreigners into the headquarters' national organizational culture
Transition and Adaption	Adapt to living in many foreign cultures	Adapt to living in a foreign culture
Cross-Cultural Interaction	Use cross-cultural interaction skills on a daily basis throughout one's career	Use cross-cultural interaction skills primarily on foreign assignments
Collaboration	Interact with foreign colleagues as equals	Interact within clearly defined hierarchies of structural and cultural dominance
Foreign Experience	Transpatriation for career and organization development	Expatriation or inpatriation primarily to get the job done

limited to managing relationships between headquarters and a single foreign subsidiary. Second, transnational managers must learn about many foreign cultures' perspectives, tastes, trends, technologies, and approaches to conducting business. Unlike their predecessors, they do not focus on becoming an expert on one particular culture. Third, transnational managers must be skillful at working with people from many cultures simultaneously. They no longer have the luxury of dealing with each country's issues on a separate, and therefore sequential, basis. Fourth, similar to prior expatriates, transnational managers must be able to adapt to living in other cultures. Yet, unlike their predecessors, transnational managers need cross-cultural skills on a daily basis, throughout their career, not just during foreign assignments, but also on regular multicountry business trips and in daily interaction with foreign colleagues and clients worldwide. Fifth, transnational managers interact with foreign colleagues as equals, rather than from within clearly defined hierarchies of structural or cultural dominance and subordination. Thus, not only do the variety and frequency of cross-cultural interaction increase with globalization, but also the very nature of cross-cultural interaction changes.

The development of transnationally competent managers depends on firms' organizational capability to design and manage transnational human resource systems. Such systems, in turn, allow firms to implement transnational business strategies. Before investigating a firm's capability to implement transnational business strategies, let us briefly review a range of global business strategies along with each strategy's requisite managerial skills.

THE GLOBALIZATION OF BUSINESS: STRATEGY, STRUCTURE, AND MANAGERIAL SKILLS

Since World War II, industry after industry has progressed from dominantly domestic operations toward more global strategies. Historically, many firms progressed through four distinct phases: domestic, international, multinational, and transnational.[8] As firms progress toward global strategies, the portfolio of skills required of managers undergoes a parallel shift.

Domestic

Historically, most corporations began as domestic firms. They developed new products or services at home for the domestic market. During this initial domestic phase, foreign markets, and hence international managerial skills, were largely irrelevant.

International

As new firms entered, competition increased and each company was forced to search for new markets or resign itself to losing market share. A common response was to expand internationally, initially by exporting to foreign markets and later by developing foreign assembly and production facilities designed to serve the largest of those markets. To manage those foreign operations, firms often restructured to form a separate international division. Within the new international division, each country was managed separately, thus creating a multidomestic nature. Because the foreign operations were frequently seen as an extension—and therefore a replication—of domestic operations, they generally were not viewed as state-of-the-art.

During this international phase, a hierarchical structure exists between the firm's headquarters and its various foreign subsidiaries. Power and influence are concentrated at corporate headquarters, which is primarily staffed by members of the headquarters' national culture. It is during this phase that firms often send their first home-country managers abroad as expatriates. Cross-cultural interaction between expatriate managers and local subsidiary staff thus takes place within a clearly defined hierarchy in which headquarters has both structural and cultural dominance.

During this phase, international management is synonymous with expatriation. To be effective, expatriate managers must be competent at transferring technology to the local culture, managing local staff, and adapting business practices to suit local conditions. Specifically, international expatriate managers require cultural adaptation skills—as does their spouse and family—to adjust to living in a new environment and working with the local people. They must also acquire specific knowledge about the particular culture's perspectives, tastes, trends, technologies, and ways of doing business. Learning is thus single-country focused—and culturally specific—during the international phase.

Multinational

As competition continues to heighten, firms increasingly emphasize producing least-cost products and services. To benefit from potential economies of scale and geographic scope, firms produce more standardized products and services. Because the prior phase's multidomestic structure can no longer support success, firms restructure to integrate domestic and foreign operations into worldwide lines of business, with sourcing, producing, assembling, and marketing distributed across many countries, and major decisions—which continue to be made at headquarters—strongly influenced by least-cost outcomes.

During the multinational phase, the hierarchical relationship remains between headquarters and foreign subsidiaries. In addition, with the increased importance of foreign operations to the core business, headquarters more tightly controls major decisions worldwide. However, headquarters' decisions are now made by people from a wider range of cultures than previously, many of whom are local managers from foreign subsidiaries posted on temporary "inpatriate" assignments at corporate headquarters. These "inpatriates" are not encouraged to express the diversity of national perspectives and cultural experience they represent. Rather, they are asked to adapt as the firm implicitly and explicitly integrates them into the organizational culture, which is still dominated by the values of the headquarters' national culture. While multinational representation increases at headquarters, cultural dominance of the headquarters' national culture continues, remaining loosely coupled with structure.

For the first time, senior managers, those leading the worldwide lines of business, need to understand the world business environment. Similarly, for the first time, senior managers must work daily with clients and employees from around the world to be effective. International and cross-cultural skills become needed for managers throughout the firm, not just for those few imminently leaving for foreign postings. Expatriates and inpatriates still require cultural adaptation skills and specific local knowledge, but these are not the dominant international skills required by most managers in a multinational firm. For the majority, learning needs grow beyond context to encompass a need to understand the world business environment. In addition, multinational managers need to be skilled at working with clients and employees from many nations (rather than merely from a single foreign country), as well as at standardizing operations and integrating people from around the world into a common organizational culture.

Transnational

As competition continues to increase and product life cycles shorten dramatically, firms find it necessary to compete globally, based simultaneously on state-of-the-art, top-quality products and services, and least-cost production. Unlike the prior phase's emphasis on identical products that can be distributed worldwide, transnational products are increasingly mass-customized-tailored to each individual client's needs. Research and development demands increase as does the firm's need for worldwide marketing scope.

These dynamics lead to transnational networks of firms and divisions within firms, including an increasingly complex web of strategic alliances. Internationally, these firms distribute their multiple headquarters across a number of nations. As a result, transnational firms become less hierarchically structured than firms operating in the previous phases. As such, power is no longer centered in a single headquarters that is coincident with or dominated by any one national culture. As a consequence, both structural and cultural dominance are minimized, with cross-cultural interaction no longer following any predefined "passport hierarchy." It is for these firms that transnational human resource strategies are now being developed that emphasize organizational learning along with individual managerial skills.

Moreover, the integration required in transnational firms is based on cultural synergy—on combining the many cultures into a unique organizational culture—rather than on simply integrating foreigners into the dominant culture of the headquarters' nationality (as was the norm in prior phases). Transnational managers require additional new skills to be effective in their less hierarchical, networked firms: first, the ability to work with people of other cultures as equals;

second, the ability to learn in order to continually enhance organizational capability. Transnational managers must learn how to collaborate with partners worldwide, gaining as much knowledge as possible from each interaction and transmitting that knowledge quickly and effectively throughout the worldwide network of operations. This requires managers who both want to learn and love the skills to quickly and continuously learn from people of other cultures.[9]

TRANSNATIONAL HUMAN RESOURCE SYSTEMS

The development of such "transnationally competent managers," as discussed previously, depends upon firms' capability to design and manage transnational human resource systems. The function of human resource systems, in general, is to recruit, develop, and retain competent managers and executives. Beyond these core functions, we add utilization: human resource systems facilitate the effective "utilization" of those managers who have been recruited, developed, and retained. Therefore, a transnational human resource system is one that recruits, develops, retains, and utilizes managers and executives who are competent transnationally.[10]

Three Dimensions of a Transnational Human Resource System

For a transnational human resource system to be effective, it must exhibit three characteristics: transnational scope, transnational representation, and transnational process. We will describe each briefly, and then discuss their implications for recruiting, developing, retaining, and using human resources.

Transnational Scope

Transnational scope is the geographical context within which all major decisions are made. As Bartlett and Ghoshal have stated, global management is a "frame of mind," not a particular organizational structure.[11] Thus, to achieve global scope, executives and managers must frame major decisions and evaluate options relative to worldwide business dynamics. Moreover, they must benchmark their own and their firm's performance against world-class standards. They can neither discuss nor resolve major issues within a narrower national or regional context. An example is Unilever's "Best Proven Practices." This British-Dutch consumer products firm identifies superior practices and innovations in the subsidiaries worldwide and then diffuses the outstanding approaches throughout the worldwide organization.[12]

Transnational Representation

Transnational representation refers to the multinational composition of the firm's managers and executives. To achieve transnational representation, the firm's portfolio of key executives and managers should be as multinational as its worldwide distribution of production, finance, sales, and profits. Symbolically, firms achieve transnational representation through the well-balanced portfolio of passports held by senior management. Philips, for example, maintains transnational representation by having "the corporate pool." This pool consists of mobile individuals representing more than fifty nationalities, each having at least five years of experience and ranked in the top 20 percent on performance, and all financed on a corporate budget.[13]

Transnational Process

Transnational process reflects the firm's ability to effectively include representatives and ideas from many cultures in its planning and decision-making processes. Firms create transnational process when they consistently recognize, value, and effectively use cultural diversity within the organization; that is, when there is "no unintended leakage of culture specific systems and approaches."[14] Transnational process, however, is not the mere inclusion of people and ideas of many cultures; rather, it goes beyond inclusion to encompass cultural synergy—the combination of culturally diverse perspectives and approaches into a new transnational organizational culture. Cultural synergy requires "a genuine belief . . . that more creative and effective ways of managing people could be developed as a result of cross-cultural learning."[15] To create transnational process, executives and managers must be as skilled at working with and learning from people from outside their own cultures as with same-culture nationals.

TODAY'S FIRMS: HOW TRANSNATIONAL?

A survey was conducted of fifty firms headquartered in the United States and Canada from a wide variety of industries to determine the extent to which their overall business strategy matched their current human resource system, as well as identifying the extent of globalization of their human resource strategies. The results paint a picture of extensive global business involvement. Unfortunately, however, similar involvement in recruiting, developing, retaining, and using globally competent managers is lacking.

Global Strategic Integration

The fifty firms made almost half of their sales abroad, and earned nearly 40 percent of their revenues and profits outside of their headquarters country (the United States or Canada). Similarly, almost two fifths of the fifty firms' employees worked outside the headquarters country. Yet, when these firms reviewed their human resource systems as a whole, and their senior leadership in particular, they could not reveal nearly as global a portrait.

For example, in comparing themselves with their competitors, the fifty firms found themselves to be more global on overall business strategy, financial systems, production operations, and marketing. However, they found their human resource systems to be the least global functional area within their own organizations. Moreover, unlike their assessment in other functional areas, they did not evaluate their human resource systems as being more global than those of their competitors.

Similarly, the senior leadership of the surveyed firms was less global on all three global indicators—scope, representation, and process—than each firm's overall business performance. For example, an average of only eight countries were represented among the most senior 100 executives in each firm. Half of the companies reported fewer than four nationalities among the top 100 executives. Firms therefore have less than a quarter of the international representation in their senior leadership (8 percent) as they have in their global business performance (e.g., sales, revenues, and profits: 40 percent). Similarly, of the same top 100 executives in each firm, only 15 percent were from outside of North America. This represents less than half the internationalization of the senior executive cadre (15 percent) as of business performance (40 percent). Moreover, using experience rather than representation yields similar results. Of the same 100 leaders, almost three-quarters lacked expatriate experience, with only a third reporting any international experience at all. Not surprisingly, less than one in five spoke a foreign language. On no measure of international experience is the senior leadership of these North American firms as international as the business itself.

Transnational Human Resource Integration

Firms' organizational capability to implement transnational business strategies is supported by transnational human resource management systems. As discussed, such systems should exhibit all three dimensions—transnational scope, transnational representation, and transnational process. These three global dimensions are clearly important for each of the four primary components of human resource systems recruiting, developing, retaining, and utilizing globally competent people. Each will therefore be discussed separately. Unfortunately, the results of this study indicate that firms' human resource management systems have not become global either as rapidly or as extensively as have their business strategies and structures.

Recruiting

For recruiting decisions, transnational scope requires that firms consider their business needs and the availability of candidates worldwide. Similar to the firms' strategic business decisions, some recruiting decisions must enhance worldwide integration and coordination, others local responsiveness, and others the firm's ability to learn.[16] Local responsiveness requires that firms recruit people with a sophisticated understanding of each of the countries in which they operate; this includes recruiting host nationals. Worldwide integration requires that recruiting be guided by world-class standards in selecting the most competent people from anywhere in the world for senior management positions. Individual and organizational learning requires that people be selected who are capable of simultaneously working with and learning from colleagues from many nations: people who are capable of creating cultural synergy.

Transnational representation in recruiting requires that firms select managers from throughout the world for potential positions anywhere in the world. In a literal sense, it requires that talent flows to opportunity worldwide, without regard to national passport.

Transnational process in recruiting requires that firms use search and selection procedures that are equally attractive to candidates from each target nationality. Selection criteria, including the methods used to judge competence, must not be biased to favor any one culture.

Similarly, incentives to join the firm must appeal to a broad range of cultures. The antithesis of transnational process was exhibited by one U.S. firm when it offered new college recruits from the Netherlands one of the same incentives it offers its American recruits: free graduate education. The Dutch candidates found this "benefit" amusing given that graduate education in the Netherlands—unlike in the United States—is already paid for by the government and thus free to all students.

Rather than encouraging high-potential candidates, this particular incentive made Dutch students hesitate to join a firm that demonstrated such parochialism in its initial contact with them.

The fifty surveyed firms reported that their recruitment and selection activities were less than global in terms of scope, representation, and process. For a summary, see Exhibit 3.1, Transnational Recruiting.

Development

In managerial development, transnational scope means that managers' experiences both on the job and in formal training situations prepare them to work anywhere in the world with people from all parts of the world; that is, it prepares them to conduct the firm's

EXHIBIT 3.1. Transnational Recruiting

The 50 surveyed firms reported that their recruitment and selection activities were less than transnational in terms of scope, representation, and process. In selecting future senior managers, the 50 firms ranked an outstanding overall track record as the most important criterion, with foreign business experience, demonstrated cultural sensitivity and adaptability, and a track record for outstanding performance outside the home country ranked as somewhat, but not highly, important. Moreover, foreign language skills were not considered at all important. Similarly, while considering three out of four transnational scope and process skills to be somewhat important for promotion to senior management (understanding world issues and trends, working effectively with clients and colleagues from other countries, and demonstrating cultural sensitivity), none was considered highly important. Once again, foreign language skills were not considered important for promotion. Similarly, on transnational representation, only a third of the 50 firms stated that they "recruit managers from all parts of the world in which . . . [they] conduct business."

---

business in a global environment. Transnational firms search worldwide for the best training and development options and select specific approaches and programs based on world-class standards.

To achieve transnational representation, training and development programs must be planned and delivered by multinational teams as well as offered to multinational participants. To be transnational, programs cannot be planned by one culture (generally representatives of the headquarters nationality) and simply exported for local delivery abroad. By contrast, using a transnational approach, American Express created a multinational design team at headquarters to develop training approaches and programs which were subsequently localized for delivery around the world. At no time did American cultural values dominate either the process or the programs.

Transnational process in development requires that the approaches taken effectively include all participating cultures. Thus, the process cannot encourage greater participation by one nationality to the exclusion of other nationalities. Ericsson and Olivetti provide examples of a transnational development approach. Each company created a management development center in which both the staff and executive participants come from all regions of the world. To minimize the possibility of headquarters' cultural dominance, neither company located its management development center in the headquarters country—Sweden or Italy—but rather both chose another more culturally neutral country.[17]

For transnational firms, foreign assignments become a core component of the organizational and career development process. "Transpatriates" from all parts of the world are sent to all other parts of the world to develop their worldwide perspective and cross-cultural skills, as well as developing the organization's cadre of globally sophisticated managers. Foreign assignments in transnational firms are no longer used primarily to get a job done in a foreign country (expatriation) or to socialize foreign country nationals into the home country headquarters' culture (inpatriation), but rather to enhance individual and organizational learning in all parts of the system (transpatriation). Using a transpatriation approach, Royal Dutch/Shell, for example, uses multifunctional and multinational experience to provide corporate-wide, transnational skills. Shell's "aim is that every member of an operating company management team should have had international experience and that each such team should include one expatriate . . . [Similarly, at IBM], international experience is [considered] indispensable to senior positions."[18]

In the survey, the fifty firms reported that their training and development opportunities were less than global on all three dimensions of human resource strategy: transnational scope, transnational representation, and transnational process (for a summary of the research, see Exhibit 3.2, Transnational Development). Similar to recruitment, training and development approaches currently are not nearly as global as are overall business strategies. To reduce the gap between the relative globalization of firms' strategies and their less-than-global human resource systems, firms must learn how to recognize, value, and use globally competent managers. As one surveyed executive summarized, closing the gaps begins by having "the key organizational development activity . . . focused on allowing people of different nationalities to meet and to get to know each other, and, through these linkages, to meet the needs of the company."

Retaining

Transnational scope in retaining managers means that decisions about career paths must consider the firm's needs and operations worldwide.

EXHIBIT 3.2. Transnational Development

In the survey, the 50 firms reported that their training and development opportunities were less than transnational on all three dimensions of human resource strategy: scope, representation, and process. Fewer than one in four of the firms reported that the content of their training programs was global in focus, that they had representatives of many nations attending each program, or that their programs were designed or delivered by multinational training teams. Only 4 percent reported that cross-cultural training was offered to all managers. However, the firms did report offering a greater number of general development opportunities worldwide than specific international training programs. A third of the firms provide equivalent development opportunities for managers worldwide and 42 percent provide such opportunities for managers of all nationalities.

In reviewing foreign assignments, the 50 firms report using expatriates primarily to "get the job done abroad," not to develop the organization, nor to develop the individual manager's career. Given their emphasis on getting the immediate job done, it is not surprising that they did not report consistently selecting the "stars" (either high-potential junior managers or very senior, top-performing executives) for expatriate positions. To increase globalization in their development programs, the surveyed executives strongly recommended "transferring different nationalities to different countries several times in their career" and "making it clear to these employees that international assignments are important to career development." However, to date, the majority of the surveyed firms do not have such recommended programs in place.

Performance incentives, rewards, and career opportunities must meet world-class standards such that the firm does not lose its most competent people. Firms must benchmark excellence in their human resource systems against their most significant global competitors in the same ways that they assess the relative competitiveness of their research and development, production, marketing, and financial systems.

Transnational representation requires that organizational incentives and career path opportunities be equally accessible and appealing to managers from all nationalities. Firms with transnational human resource systems do not create a glass ceiling beyond which only members of the headquarters nationality can be promoted.

Transnational process requires that the performance review and promotion systems include approaches which are equally appropriate to a broad range of nationalities. The process by which promotion and career path decisions are made should not be innately biased toward any one culture, nor should it exclude particular cultures. The underlying dynamic in transnational process is not to institute identical systems worldwide, but rather to use approaches which are culturally equivalent. Shell, for example, ensures this transnational orientation by having managers' "career home" be in "a business function rather than a geographical place."[19] As one surveyed senior executive summarized, firms considered to be outstanding in transnational human resource management are "flexible enough in systems and practices to attract and retain the best people regardless of nationality."

Utilizing

Transnational scope in utilization means that managers' problem-solving skills are focused on the firm's worldwide operations and competitive environment, not just on the regional, national, or local situation. To assess the competitive environment in transnational human resource management, the fifty surveyed firms identified leading North American, European, and Asian companies. The top North American firm was perceived to be IBM, followed by General Electric and Citicorp. The surveyed firms identified Royal Dutch/Shell as the leading European firm, followed by Nestlé and Philips, along with British Petroleum and Unilever. Sony was selected as the leading Asian firm, followed by Honda, Toyota, and Mitsubishi. Yet, in reviewing the pattern of responses, a significant proportion of the surveyed firms do not appear to be benchmarking excellence in global human resource management at all, and an even greater number appear to be geographically limiting their perspective to a fairly narrow, parochial scope. For instance, almost a fifth of the surveyed firms (all of which are North American) could not name a single leading North American firm. Even more disconcerting, more than a third could not identify a single excellent European firm, and half could not name a single excellent Asian firm.[20]

Beyond scope, transnational representation in utilization means that managers and executives of many nationalities are included in the firm's critical operating and strategic planning teams. Managers from outside of headquarters are not "out of sight and out of mind"; rather, they are integrated into the worldwide network of knowledge exchange, continual learning, and action. For example, as Unilever's director of management development explains:

> In recent years, I have had several product group directors . . . [want] an expatriate on the board of the local company. Not just because they haven't got a national, not just because it would be good for the expatriate, but because it would be good for the company to have a bit of challenge to the one-best-way of doing things.[21]

Transnational process in human resource utilization means that the organization culture does not inherently bias contributions from or toward any particular cultural group. The human resource system recognizes the firm's cultural diversity and uses it either to build culturally synergistic processes that include all cultures involved or to select the particular process that is the most appropriate for the given situation.

ILLUSIONS AND RECOMMENDATIONS

From the prior discussion, it is clear that transnational human resource systems are both fundamentally important for future business success and qualitatively different from prior approaches to human resource management. Equally evident is the fact that North American firms' human resource systems are not nearly as global as their business operations on any of the three fundamental human resource dimensions: transnational scope, transnational representation, and transnational process. Competitive demands appear to have "outrun the slow pace of organizational change and adjustment . . . [with] top management beginning to feel that the organization itself is the biggest barrier to competitive and strategic development."[22] It is telling that in most cases the respondents found the survey itself to be important and yet very difficult to complete, primarily because their firms did not systematically collect or keep data on any aspect of global human resource management.

The remaining question is why. There appears to be a series of illusions—of mind traps—that are preventing firms from acting in a global manner, including recognizing the mental gap between their current human resource approaches and those necessary to succeed in a highly competitive transnational business environment. Many of the surveyed executives recognized that their firms simply "lack global thinking" and "lack global business strategies," largely due to the "massive U.S. imprint on human resource practices." According to many of the American executives, firms must "stop thinking that the world begins and ends at U.S. borders," "stop having a U.S. expatriate mentality," and begin to "realize that the world does not revolve around us." This pattern of responses suggests the following seven illusions.

Illusion One: If Business Has Gone Well, It Will Continue to Go Well

No, today is not like yesterday, nor will tomorrow be a projection of today. Business has fundamentally changed, and human resource systems must undergo similar transformational changes to stay relevant, let alone effective. As Kenichi Ohmae has pointed out, "Today and in the twenty-first century, management's ability to transform the organization and its people into a global company is a prerequisite for survival because both its customers and competitors have become cosmopolitan."[23]

Illusion Two: We Have Always Played on a Level Playing Field and Won

No. The North American economies (and therefore North American firms) have had an advantage: they were the only developed economies left intact following World War II and were thus "the only game in town." Today, Asia, Europe, and the Americas each have highly competitive firms and economies, none of which will continue to prosper without being excellent at including people and business worldwide. As Ohmae has observed, "The key to a nation's future is its human resources. It used to be its natural resources, but not any more. The quality and number of its educated people now determines a country's likely prosperity or decline"; so too with global firms.[24]

Illusion Three: If We Manage Expatriates Better, We Will Have an Effective Global Human Resource System

No. Doing better at what was necessary in the past (expatriate management) is not equivalent to creating systems capable of sustaining global competitiveness today. Whereas the temptation is to attempt to do better at that which is known (in this case, the simple expatriation of managers), the real challenge is to excel at that which is new. Transnational firms need transnational human resource systems to succeed. Better-managed expatriate transfers will only improve one small aspect of existing human resource management, not create an overall transnational system.

Illusion Four: If We're Doing Something, We Must Be Doing Enough

No. Focusing on only one of the three transnational dimensions—scope, representation, or process—is not enough to transform domestic, international, or multinational human resource approaches into truly transnational systems. Bringing a "foreigner" onto the board of directors, for example, gives the illusion of globalization, but is insufficient to underpin its substance.

Illusion Five: If "Foreigners" Are Fitting in at Headquarters, We Must Be Managing Our Cultural Diversity Well

No. This is a multinational paradigm trap. In multinationals, foreigners must adapt to the headquarters culture, including learning its native language. Multinationals typically see cultural differences "as a nuisance, a constraint, an obstacle to be surmounted."[25] In transnational firms, all managers make transitions, all managers adapt, and all managers help to create a synergistic organizational culture which transcends any one national culture.

Illusion Six: As National Wealth Increases, Everyone Will Become More Like Us

No. To the extent that the world is converging in its values, attitudes, and styles of doing business, it is not converging on a single country's national pattern, even that of the world's wealthiest nation. "The appealing 'one-best-way' assumption about management, the belief that different cultures are converging at different paces on the same concept of organization, is dying a slow death."[26] Moreover, transnational firms need to create transnational cultures that are inclusive of all their members, not wait for the world to converge on a reality that looks like any particular firm's national culture, even one that looks "just like us."

Illusion Seven: If We Provide Managers with Cross-Cultural Training, We Will Increase Organizational Capability

No. Increased cognitive understanding does not guarantee increased behavioral effectiveness, nor is enhanced individual learning sufficient for improved organizational effectiveness. Simply increasing the number of cross-cultural training programs offered to individual managers does not ensure that they will actually use the skills on a regular basis, nor that the firm as a whole will benefit from the potentially improved cross-cultural interaction. To benefit, the individual must want to learn that which is not-invented-here and the organization must want to learn from the individual. To enhance organizational capability, managers must continually work with and learn from people worldwide and disperse that knowledge throughout the firm's worldwide operations.

Despite the seemingly insurmountable challenges, firms are beginning to address and solve the dilemmas posed by going global. To date, no firm believes it has "the answer," the solution to creating a truly transnational human resource system. However, a number of firms are currently inventing pieces of the solution which may cohere into just such a system. For example, as John Reed, CEO of Citicorp, describes:

> There are few companies in the world that are truly global . . . Our most important advantage is our globality. Our global human capital may be as important a resource, if not more important, than our financial capital. Look at the Policy Committee, the top thirty or so officers in the bank. Almost seventy-five percent have worked outside the United States; more than twenty-five percent have worked in three or more countries.

Half speak two or more languages other than English. Seven were born outside the United States.[27]

Perhaps, then, a primary role of transnational human resource executives today is to remain open to fundamental change and to continue to encourage the openness and experimentation needed to create truly global systems.

REFERENCE NOTES

The authors would like to thank the Ontario Centre for International Business for generously funding this research. See "Globalization and Human Resource Management" (Nancy J. Adler and Susan Bartholomew) in *Research in Global Strategic Management: Corporate Responses to Global Change,* Alan M. Rugman and Alain Verbeke (eds.), Vol. 3, (Greenwich, CT: JAI Press, 1992) for further details of the research design and results of the study.

1. Christopher A. Bartlett and Sumantra Ghoshal, "Matrix Management: Not a Structure, a Frame of Mind," *Harvard Business Review,* July-August 1990, 138.

2. See Michael E. Porter, *The Competitive Advantage of Nations* (New York: The Free Press, 1990).

3. Paul A. Evans, Yves Doz, and Andre Laurent, *Human Resource Management in International Firms* (London: Macmillan Press, 1989), xi-1.

4. Ibid.; also see Gunnar Hedlund, "Who Manages the Global Corporation? Changes in the Nationality of Presidents of Foreign Subsidiaries of Swedish MNCs During the 1980s," Working Paper (Institute of International Business and the Stockholm School of Economics, May 1990).

5. See Donald C. Hambrick, Lester B. Korn, James W. Frederickson, and Richard M. Ferry, *21st Century Report: Reinventing the CEO* (New York: Korn/Ferry and Columbia University's Graduate School of Business, 1989), 1-94.

6. Ibid.

7. Ibid., 57.

8. See Nancy J. Adler and Fariborz Ghadar, "International Strategy from the Perspective of People and Culture: The North American Context," in Alan M. Rugman (ed.), *Research in Global Strategic Management: International Business Research for the Twenty-First Century; Canada's New Research Agenda,* Vol. 1 (Greenwich, CT: JAI Press, 1990) 179-205; and "Strategic Human Resource Management: A Global Perspective," in Rudiger Pieper (ed.), *Human Resource Management in International Comparison* (Berlin: de Gruyter, 1990), 235-260.

9. See Gary Hamel, Yves Doz, and C. K. Prahalad, "Collaborate With Your Competitors and Win," *Harvard Business Review,* 89(1), 1989, 133-139.

10. For a review of international human resource management, see Nancy J. Adler, *International Dimensions of Organizational Behaviour,* 2nd ed. (Boston: PWS Kent, 1991); Peter J. Dowling, "Hot Issues Overseas," *Personnel Adminis-*

trator, 34(1), 1989, 66-72; Peter J. Dowling and R. Schuler, *International Dimensions of Human Resource Management* (Boston: PWS Kent, 1990), Peter J. Dowling and Denise E. Welch, "International Human Resource Management: An Australian Perspective," *Asia Pacific Journal of Management,* 6(1), 1988, 39-65; Yves Doz and C. K. Prahalad, "Controlled Variety: A Challenge for Human Resource Management in the MNC," *Human Resource Management,* 25(1), 1986, 55-71; A. Edstrom and J .R. Galbraith, "Transfer of Managers as a Coordination and Control Strategy in Multinational Firms," *Administrative Science Quarterly,* 22, 1977, 248-263; Evans, Doz, and Laurent (1989) op. cit.; Andre Laurent, "The Cross-Cultural Puzzle of International Human Resource Management," *Human Resource Management,* 25(1), 1986, 91-101; E. L. Miller, S. Beechler, B. Bhatt, and R. Nath, "The Relationship Between the Global Strategic Planning Process and the Human Resource Management Function," *Human Resource Planning,* 9(1), 1986, 9-23; John Milliman, Mary Ann Von Glinow, and Maria Nathan, "Organizational Life Cycles and Strategic International Human Resource Management in Multinational Companies: Implications for Congruence Theory," *Academy of Management Review,* 16(2), 1991, 318-339; Dan A. Ondrack, "International Human Resources Management in European and North American Firms," *Human Resource Management,* 25(1), 1985, 121-132; Dan A. Ondrack, "International Transfers of Managers in North American and European MNEs," *Journal of International Business Studies,* 16(3), 1985, 1-19; Vladimir Pucik, "The International Management of Human Resources," in C. J. Fombrun, N. M. Tichy, and M. A. Devanna (eds.), *Strategic Human Resource Management* (New York: Wiley, 1984); Vladimir Pucik and Jan Hack Katz, "Information, Control and Human Resource Management in Multinational Firms," *Human Resource Management,* 25(1), 1986, 121-132; and Rosalie Tung, *The New Expatriates: Managing Human Resources Abroad* (New York: Harper and Row, 1988), and "Strategic Management of Human Resources in Multinational Enterprises," *Human Resource Management,* 23(2), 1984, 129-143; among others.

11. Bartlett and Ghoshal, op. cit., 1990.

12. Unilever's "Best Proven Practice" technique was cited by Philip M. Rosenzweig and Jitendra Singh, "Organizational Environments and the Multinational Enterprise," *Academy of Management Review,* 16(2), 1991, 354, based on an interview that Rosenzweig conducted with Unilever.

13. See Paul Evans, Elizabeth Lank, and Alison Farguhar, "Managing Human Resources in the International Firm: Lessons from Practice," in Paul Evans, Yves Doz, and Andre Laurent, 1989, op. cit., 138.

14. Kenichi Ohmae, *The Borderless World: Power and Strategy in the Interlinked Economy* (New York: Harper Business, 1990), 112.

15. Andre Laurent, op. cit., 1986, 100.

16. See C. K. Prahalad and Yves Doz, *The Multinational Mission: Balancing Local Demands and Global Vision* (New York: Free Press, 1987); also, for a discussion of global integration versus local responsiveness from a business strategy perspective, see Michael E. Porter, "Changing Patterns of International Competition," *California Management Review,* 28(2), 1986, 9-40; and Christopher A.

Bartlett, "Building and Managing the Transnational: The New Organizational Challenge," in M. E. Porter (ed.) *Competition in Global Industries* (Boston: Harvard Business School Press, 1986), 367-401, who explicitly developed the concepts, along with initial work and elaboration by: Christopher A. Bartlett and Sumantra Ghoshal, *Managing Across Borders: The Transnational Solution* (Boston: Harvard Business School Press, 1989); Yves Doz, "Strategic Management in Multinational Companies," *Sloan Management Review,* 21(2), 1980, 27-46; Yves Doz, Christopher A. Bartlett, and C. K. Prahalad, "Global Competitive Pressures and Host Country Demands: Managing Tensions in MNCs," *California Management Review,* 23(3), 1981, 63-73; and Yves Doz and C. K. Prahalad, "Patterns of Strategic Control Within Multinational Corporations," *Journal of International Business Studies,* 15(2), 1984, 55-72.

17. See Evans, Lank, and Farquhar, op. cit., 1989, 119.

18. Ibid., 130-131; 139.

19. Ibid., 141.

20. An even more disconcerting display of ignorance was that four surveyed firms listed 3M, Citicorp, Ford, and General Motors as European firms, and in another four responses, Dupont, Eastman Kodak, Coca-Cola, and Wang were identified as leading Asian firms.

21. Evans, Lank, and Farquhar, op. cit., 122.

22. Paul Evans and Yves Doz, "The Dualistic Organization," in Evans, Doz, and Laurent, op. cit., 1989, 223: based on the earlier work of Doz, "Managing Manufacturing Rationalization Within Multinational Companies," *Columbia Journal of World Business,* 13(3), 1978, 82-94; and Prahalad and Doz, op. cit., 1987.

23. Kenichi Ohmae, *Beyond National Borders* (Homewood, IL: Dow Jones-Irwin, 1987), 93.

24. Ibid., 1.

25. Evans, Lank and Farquhar, op. cit., 115.

26. Ibid., 115.

27. Noel Tichy and Ram Charan, "Citicorp Faces the World: An Interview with John Reed," *Harvard Business Review,* November-December, 1990, 137.

Chapter 4

Creating a High-Performance International Team

Sue Canney Davison

ESTABLISHING THE CONTEXT OF THE GROWING NUMBER OF INTERNATIONAL TEAMS

The number of international teams is growing rapidly as companies reorganize to compete in the global marketplace. The influence of different cultures makes interpersonal interaction in the team more complicated than within teams of one nationality. It affects the way the team works together, especially if the team is spread out across different countries. Each team is unique. High performance cannot be captured in a ready-made formula for creating synthesis among imaginary French, Japanese, Taiwanese, and Russian team members. High performance is created through channeling the forces at play.

In companies such as ABB, Unilever, the Hong Kong Shanghai Banking Corporation, GEC Alsthom, Alcatel, Royal Dutch/Shell group, and IBM, a matrix of international teams is already in place. In other companies such as Daimler Benz, Fiat, The Kone Corporation, Westpac, and The Broken Hill Proprietary Company, international teams are being used to shift the dominance of the headquarters national cultures.

Mixed nationalities in a team can bring richer and more appropriate solutions. They can broaden a manager's interpersonal skills

Reprinted with permission of Sue Canney Davison and the publisher. First published in *Journal of Management Development* (MCB University Press), 13(2), 1994, pp. 81-90.

and contribute to creating a company-wide network. However, they can also bring increased communication difficulties, interpersonal conflicts, and substantially higher costs. When do the costs outweigh the benefits? Do some mixes of nationalities work together better than others? In reality, the exact mix of nationalities is seldom chosen; it emerges as a by-product of the task. Most people are chosen because they have the necessary country knowledge, responsibilities, or technical expertise to complete the task. The extra expense is a constraint the team has to work within. Some teams are having difficulties, while other teams are very successful; what is the difference? Companies need to know and learn.

There are lessons for the managers who create the teams, there are considerations about working at geographical distances, and there are lessons for the team members and leaders.

CREATING AND MANAGING AN INTERNATIONAL TEAM

Choosing the Right Mix of People

As with any team, the first task is to choose people who incorporate, as a group, the skills necessary to complete the task. In an international team, there is also a need for a common working language and sufficient shared goals. There are the added dangers of vested national interests and historical regional competitiveness.

Removing the Constraints

The next most important and difficult tasks are to "bust the bureaucracy" and to find an adequate budget. International teams benefit the company as a whole and tend to threaten individual fiefdoms. If country managers need to be persuaded to second one of their best people for a few years, help from higher up in the organization may need to be called in. There are also part-time teams that meet every month or so. They often run in addition to and parallel with the work that the individuals are paid, evaluated, and promoted for. Extra finances need to be found to support the extra costs that the geographical distances will create. When a manager starts looking for appropriate people, a common retort from other country managers is, "So long as I do not have to pay the airfares and it doesn't interfere with the work they are already doing here, yes, they can join your team; in fact they may learn something."

Assessing the Costs of the Geographical Distances

A geographically dispersed team needs to develop a realistic balance between joint team meetings and the work done in between. At the beginning it is important for the team to meet each other in order to agree on what they are doing and to meet later in the project to argue and review decisions. Sharing information and implementing action, although possible from a distance, is not successful. One manager who was put in charge of a team that had never met, but dialogued over fax, phone, and e-mail, had a nervous breakdown. Effective group techniques can shorten team meetings, and e-mail and computer networks can improve and lighten communication between meetings, but must be bolstered with face-to-face meetings.

Sharing the Rationale with the Team

After setting the overall objectives, giving a time frame and direction, the overall manager must be available to the team to give advice and remove unforeseen obstacles. Initially this means explaining how and why the team is being set up and its role within the rest of the company. The manager should also make the team aware of possible imbalances and encourage members to work around them.

Appreciating the Influence of Nationality

Nationality, as represented by what passport you carry, is not an important variable in international teams. The importance of national culture is that it can have a moderating influence on a number of other factors, such as attitudes, values, behaviors, expectations, background, and common language fluency. If the team members are representing different countries they can also be affected by the status of the organization within the market, by the size of the market share, by belonging to the acquired company as opposed to the acquirer, or by historical difficulties between one market or function and another.

A European marketing strategy team may be made up of peer marketing managers, each from a different European country operation. The team is balanced in nationalities. However, if the headquarters are in the United Kingdom, is there a subtle weighting, giving the U.K. marketing manager more influence than the others? Is there a subtle hierarchy based on the size of operations in each country? If there is a subgroup of people from the headquarters, will they dominate the others? Innovative ideas often start away from the vested interests and bureaucracy of the center.

Choosing the Right Leader for the Task

Interpersonal dynamics and communication patterns will be more complicated in an international team than in a nationally uniform team. The team leader will need sensitive group management skills and an understanding of the cultural differences at play. Should these "group" skills override technical skills as the criteria for selecting the leader? Both cultural influences and the nature of the task will play a role.

A charismatic multilingual French manager was asked to bring a number of long-established independent European bakery firms under one brand name. He used his many languages and interpersonal skills to cajole, negotiate, persuade, and create ultimatums to bring the team together. His technical baking skills were not called for.

Teams with a coordinating task need a leader with good administrative skills. The leader of a transatlantic R&D team will need a high level of technical research skills as well as administrative and interpersonal skills. Team leaders may also be chosen because they have the highest level of influence to sell the outcomes to the rest of the organization. However, in some instances cultural norms may influence the choice. In Germany and Japan a very high premium is usually put on the leaders' technical skills. That is how they earn the respect of the team. In Italy or Chile the premium can be on the status and influence that the manager holds within the organization.

In choosing a team leader, it is important to remember that the leader must act as a role model. For example, in two existing international top teams, both CEOs dominate the interaction. Both are appreciated for their executive abilities and for turning their respective companies around from negative positions. The Finnish CEO, managing a Finnish/U.K. merger, stresses team spirit, common language, and consensus through debate. He encourages managers to participate in debates outside their areas of responsibility and to tell him when he is wrong. The Italian CEO, managing an Italian/U.S. merger, tends to work one-to-one with a small number of Italian colleagues; the large top-team meeting is a place to share these decisions. The few U.S. managers expected decisions to be made through debate and are disappointed. Although English is the agreed common language, when the argument becomes lively it tends to happen in Italian, and the Americans feel left out.

Taking the Implementation of the Task into Account

Managers creating the teams must also consider the implementation of the teams' findings. In a large international drinks company a task force has been set up to cut costs within an eighteen-month time frame. As it was likely that most of the production cuts would be made in Italy, it was a sensible move to appoint an Italian finance expert to the team; this was the best person to sell the bad news.

Lessons for Managers Setting Up Teams

- Choose the people with the best skills and knowledge to plan and implement the task.
- Assess the costs, double them, and find the money within the organization.
- Remove bureaucratic barriers and, if necessary, seek support higher in the organization.
- Involve the team members' managers in the process. Persuade them to include the team outcomes in the members' performance evaluation.

- Share the reasons why people have been chosen and the possible imbalances that they should be aware of, and work around them.
- Offer training and support in group skills if necessary.
- Explain the influences of national cultures. Offer training and support in using intercultural differences to create value.
- Match the leader to the task and make all the team members accountable for the outcomes.
- Give clear terms of reference, time scales, and direction, and be available if the team needs you.

MANAGING THE GEOGRAPHICAL DISTANCES

In the Finnish case above, although the headquarters are in Finland, only the CEO and the financial controller are based there. The other three top vice presidents were free to choose any European headquarters as their operating base. It works because there is a high level of trust and a very disciplined communication pattern. Every month they have a board meeting at one of the regional headquarters or company offices somewhere in the world. Between meetings they have a telephone conference every Monday to share information. They conduct a very organized set of telephone conferences for the company results every month. The benefit of being geographically dispersed is that the top team is always out in the company, encouraging networking and cross-fertilization and bringing a firsthand knowledge of events to the board meetings.

Only full-time special purpose teams tend to be located together. Otherwise, managers operate as a team from their different bases and meet at regular intervals. The administrative, traveling, and communication costs are likely to have been underestimated. If the company does provide the increased budget, they will expect a special return and very high performance. What is the best use of the teams' time?

Establishing the Team Before Working Apart

The team will need to come together to establish a common orientation and to agree on common objectives and goals. In this initial stage they also need to create a common language and to "get a feel for where each one is coming from," to discover the strengths and weaknesses of the team, and to explore the different expectations around the style and depth of team interaction.

Having established some degree of interpersonal comfort and agreed on their goals, the team can then work at a distance to collect and share information, clarify tasks, and implement the decisions. In some cultures, nothing is taken seriously unless it is written down. In others, people do not feel they have communicated until they have spoken to the person directly, even if they have written to them. Teams may need to agree to do both.

Using the Technology Available

E-mail networks help. At the moment, few transnational teams outside computer companies have effective computer networks. Using an e-mail network speeds up communication and makes it much easier to share, edit, and review large amounts of information. This is especially true if the team needs to share complex three-dimensional computer models developed with computer-aided design programs. Whole models seen from many angles can be sent back and forth for refinement and comment. Eventually, virtual reality will allow people to work at a distance simultaneously on a model design.

If the team needs to review their overall objectives, change their orientation, question values of principles, or renew their strategy, then they will need to meet together again. The risk of misunderstanding across faxes, e-mail, and videoconferencing on value-related issues is very high.

Summary

- *In time together:* Establish objectives, goals, and interim targets; build relationships; resolve differences; make decisions; evaluate and review progress; and, if necessary, change values, policies, and principles.
- *In time apart:* Establish a disciplined and regular system of communication; find and share information; clarify goals; implement agreed-on actions; and update others on progress.

Prepare for joint meetings in advance; send all background reading and information in advance; and anticipate your colleagues' questions and needs.

WORKING WITHIN THE TEAM

Implementing the Team Basics

An international team needs high performance goals, mutual accountability, and an interdependent task, as does any national team. The team basics of clarifying and agreeing on a working method and performance goals, bringing assumptions and differences to the surface, actively listening, and participating are the same. In international teams, applying the basics before rushing to complete the task is all the more important. The differences in expectations and approach are likely to be far higher.

As in any team, the task, the method chosen to complete it, the personalities, leadership role and style, team roles, behavior, emotional links, and timing will all have an impact on the effectiveness of the team. We know from research and experience that culture will have a moderating effect on the decision-making process, learning styles, behavior, attitudes toward status, formality, business relationships, and the task or people orientation of each individual.

FIGURE 4.1. Creating a High-Performance International Team

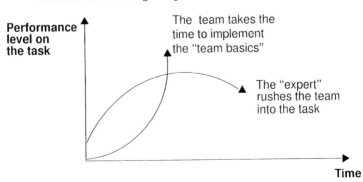

Establishing Cultural or Personal Feedback

People often ask, "Are they like that because of their culture or personality?" Within any culture one would expect a wide spread of individual preferences on the factors outlined above. Research suggests that the effect of culture is to create a statistically measurable national norm on each one. Culture moderates but does not override personality. Experience of different cultures can change the effect of the original culture influence.

The extent to which behavior and expectations are due to the influence of national culture or are a natural part of personality is an ongoing lengthy debate. As yet no line has been drawn. The important point is that in many cultures, feedback, both positive and negative, is very difficult. In international teams, it is much easier to legitimately discuss cultural differences than it is to give feedback on personal differences. Cultural differences can be established as neutral territory. There are combinations of similarities and differences that work easily; there are others that have to be brought up and worked through.

Talking about national culture may not cover all the behaviors that need to be reviewed. One U.S./U.K. team chose a "managerial grid" as a feedback tool. A mixed Asian and European team chose three learning orientations. When one Hong Kong Chinese man got into difficulties, the team suggested that he could act a little less "red" (action oriented) and become more "green" (people oriented). He listened without taking offense or losing face.

Choosing the Working Languages

Most British and Americans do not seem motivated to learn other languages whereas Dutch, Belgian, Chinese, and other people often learn two, three, four, or more. Often, because of the lack of choice, the common business language chosen is English. This can allow the English and Americans to dominate, often by speaking incomprehensible colloquial English instead of the second-language business English that has developed in the business world.

It can work the other way also. Subgroups can use side discussions in other languages to build up alliances. Second-language English speakers are sometimes accused of using language as an excuse to not participate. Leaders can work around this by asking each person to share his or her view. Other team members can be encouraged to translate for them; in extreme cases outside translation facilities can be offered. There seem to be different sensitivities around speaking a foreign language. Finns, Japanese, and Germans tend not to speak unless they know exactly what they are talking about and can express it perfectly. The French are stereotyped as not appreciating or listening to anything but perfect French.

Demanding that only one language is spoken can also exclude people. Many words have no exact translation or can mean various things in different languages. Where the language differences are extreme, such as between Chinese and English, teams have sometimes agreed to allow side discussions in subgroups in their own languages in order to check their mutual understanding. They have then paraphrased their discussion and shared it with the whole team in a common language.

Obviously the more common languages there are among the team, the easier it is to explain details and check understanding. When the top executive team of an Italian subsidiary based in France presented and discussed their company in German to the German company they were buying out, it compensated for months of trust building. When teams have built up trust, they often begin to enjoy the multiplicity of languages and meanings and have fun with them.

The team and team leaders must work to encourage tolerance of and interest in the language differences. It is important to legitimize asking for clarification and repetition and to encourage people to explain the same thing two or three different ways from the beginning. The leader needs to give time, especially at the beginning, for everyone to express themselves and be disciplined about regularly summarizing and checking understanding to keep a balance of participation. This builds up the group cohesion that allows the team to pick up speed without losing people.

Balancing the Participation

Do team members feel free to interrupt each other? Culture can strongly modify a person's tendency to talk (or gesture) along with someone for support (an Italian trait), to interrupt and talk over someone (an American and increasingly British trait), or to wait for a space to speak or to be asked for an opinion (an East and South East Asian trait and usual for a nonfluent common language speaker). In English the subject, verb, and object are usually at the beginning of the sentence and the rest is secondary information. This allows impatient English speakers to interrupt each other freely without losing too much of the overall meaning. On the other hand, in German, Hindi, and Chinese, the verb (and tense) is at the end of the sentence. In Japanese the custom is to build up to the main point rather than putting it at the beginning. A Japanese expressed having "learned to put the point at the front, otherwise they do not hear me." People who feel free to interrupt can dominate those who do not.

Turning Intercultural Conflict into Creativity

Cultures also have very different ways of resolving conflicts. These range across "shoot first, make up later," argue it out on the facts, use a neutral third-party arbitrator, listen to the elders, or use a mediator whose job it is to negotiate, cajole, and persuade the two sides to work together. The team needs to find out what works for its particular mix of people. Different tools and methods can be tried. In cultures that avoid open conflict, the idea that contentious debate can also be creative and not personal may need to be explored. For example, Honda has introduced *wayagaya* creative debate groups to find better solutions to a wide range of problems on the shop floor.

It is unlikely that a team that avoids conflict will reach a high performance level. Surfacing and working through conflicting differences is not the same as accommodating each other. In one joint consortium the two managing directors, one a charismatic autocratic Frenchman and the other a democratic participative German, sat back to back in the same office. They learned to accommodate each other, but did not bring up and resolve their differences. The consortium has failed, pulled apart by different interests and skills.

The team can also anticipate key moments in the task when cultural differences are likely to come into play. In strategic planning, for instance, there is likely to be little difficulty in individuals finding and collecting the necessary information and coming together again to share it. The conflict is likely to arise at the point where the group has to decide how to develop the information into an argued plan. It is also the point where the team needs all the creative ideas it can find. The team can take time out to brainstorm using group techniques such as Metaplan, Hexagons, and Groupware. One high-level team chose this time, as the debate was getting heated, to brainstorm at high volume in the squash courts. As a result, they channeled their conflict creatively.

Making Sure None of the Team Members Are Left Out

Some team members often become excluded. Suggestions are ignored; a team member is left out when the group splits into smaller groups; people are not given time to explain what they mean in a foreign language. Subtle and unsubtle prejudices about the levels of education and expertise between international and regional officers, between people from "developed" and "developing" countries, or between men and women, distort the balance of the team.

Individuals or subgroups can also be left out of the decision-making process. A team may have opted for decisions based on consensus. When the very different positions of the members become apparent, a workable solution can seem impossible. At this point a team needs to find, or create, some common thread to build on. Instead, what often happens is that the team will persist in arguing about their differences. In frustration, individuals will start building alliances with the people who seem at least part similar. Gradually, more and more members join the alliance out of frustration and the remaining few outsiders give up in despair. No synthesis of differences has been found and some of the team are left resentful. The decision-making process has to be conscious and agreed on by everybody.

It takes discipline, courage, and sensitivity to confront the often unconscious forces that exclude some people from the process. It can be a high risk. High-performance international teams have consciously taken those risks or have just been incredibly lucky.

Lessons for Those Participating in and Leading International Teams

- Start slowly and end faster; if you start fast you may not end at all.
- Use outside help if necessary to establish group and intercultural skills at the beginning. Create a common language for

giving feedback, bringing up cultural differences, and talking about the group's interaction. Learn group brainstorming skills such as Metaplan and Hexagons if they are relevant.

- Someone, the leader or a team member, needs to encourage meaningful participation from all members, keep a visual record of what is being said, regularly summarize and check consensus and understanding, and keep track of time.

- The leader or facilitator must also be prepared to use intuition and insight to bring up and confront the underlying differences and prejudices that are causing tension or excluding a team member.

- Develop a decision-making process that avoids unconscious alliances and allows everyone to participate.

- Build in time for discussing and reviewing the overall group process. This increased awareness is an essential ingredient of high performance.

Differences in attitudes, values, behavior, experience, background, expectations, language, and location create far more complex dynamics in international teams than most national ones. These teams have become an integral part of the survival and growth of most international companies. They are challenging, frustrating, costly opportunities for participants to learn and grow. There are no universal formulas for success. The task is to use the similarities and differences and the dynamics that these can set up and to turn them to the group's advantage. If the team members have developed a high level of emotional security, can laugh, joke, question, and play devil's advocate with each other while completing the task, then it has done well.

A high-performance international team will have also accessed all its resources. It will have continuously reviewed and questioned how effectively the team interaction has been molded to fit the task. Digging into the differences has a high risk. It can also yield new and unthought-of solutions to the task at hand and move the company one step nearer to being an effective global network.

Examples come from doctoral research at London Business School and research conducted with D. Hambrick, C. Snow, and S.

Snell for the international consortium of executive development and research.

FURTHER READING

Hofstede, G., *Cultures and Organizations: Software of the Mind,* McGraw-Hill, New York, 1991.

Johansen, R., Sibbett, D., Benson, S., Martin, A., Mittman, R., and Saffe, P., *Leading Business Teams*, Addison Wesley OD Series, Reading, MA, 1991.

Katzenback, J. R. and Smith, D. K., *The Wisdom of Teams*, Harvard Business School Press, Boston, 1993.

Trompenaars, F., *Riding the Waves of Culture: Understanding Diversity in Business,* The Economist Books, London, 1993.

PART II:
DEVELOPING THE GLOBAL
EXECUTIVE

In Part I we presented a basic rationale for learning in global organizations. Global organizations must engage in anticipatory learning: learning that is participative, future oriented, and considers all groups and cultures to have information worth sharing. A model to enable managers to invest in a powerful future for their global organizations was suggested. Specifically, we presented chapters that provided assistance in (1) analyzing cultural differences between the home and host countries within a global organization; (2) developing the ability to manage globally competent people by developing a global or transnational human resource management function; and (3) extending and maintaining global organizational learning through cross-functional teams.

In Part II, we discuss the important task of developing the global executive. In Chapter 5, Keys and Bleicken present a model for selecting appropriate management training methodology, based on the three contingencies—strategies, competency of managers, and cultural differences of the countries involved. The methods of international management development are placed in an ascending order of competencies needed (See Table 5.1 of Chapter 5). Chapters describe several of the unique and involved international management development methods: a culture-general assimilator, global scenarios and cases, and action learning. A case study of an intercultural management development program is presented in Chapter 9 by Gancel and Perlo.

In Chapter 6, Gutman reviews the traditional advantage of cases utilized in international management development, but also shows how cases are being written within organizations to present futuristic scenarios suitable for training and planning. The chapter looks forward to Part III, and suggests ways in which anticipatory and organizational learning may be initiated for individuals and their organizations. According to the author, the use of scenarios and cases provides managers and planners with deeper understanding of the national and international forces affecting their business and its future.

In describing a culture-general assimilator (Chapter 7), Brislin explains the research approach used to develop 106 incidents that capture experiences, feelings, and thoughts virtually all travelers encounter. These incidents were written to illustrate eighteen themes or commonalities that the developers felt were central to an understanding of cross-cultural experiences. The culture-general assimilator is not intended to replace specific cultural learning required of persons about to travel to other countries but makes an understanding of the process easier.

The review of action learning presented by Louise Keys in Chapter 8 chronicles the development and use of one of the more effective team learning approaches of the past fifty years. The approach is so simple that its beauty and potential are often overlooked. Teams of managers share projects and problems, commit to meeting frequently, and assist each other with completing projects—or solving problems; but, most important, they commit to reflecting on the learning that can be gleaned from these projects. Action learning has been used extensively in the United Kingdom and throughout Europe, but only recently has it found its way to North America, largely through General Electric contacts in Europe.

Noel Tichy of the University of Michigan became acquainted with Action Learning while serving as Director of Executive Education at GEC and began a global leadership program at his university. Harvard Business School, famed for the case approach to learning, has recently begun using action learning, led by Michael Porter, well-known strategic management expert. Action learning is another transitional management learning approach that not only allows individuals to learn, but encourages learning across and vertically within organizations.

Gancel and Perlo, in Chapter 9, describe several of their intercultural management training programs based in Paris. Their case discussions conclude with a rather complete description of a project to develop business relations between Russian and Western European industrialists. Gancel and Perlo note that the change required to go from a planned economy to a market economy is so great that to succeed it is essential for Russians to have immediate industrial and commercial business dealings with Westerners. Their case also illustrates many of the principles this text presents for learning across cultures and for initiating organizational learning. The Gancel and Perlo decision to pair the Russian trainees with managers from several Western companies in the same industry was successful in improving communications and providing cross-cultural participants some common ground. Gancel and Perlo conclude with a perceptive admonition for dealing with cross-cultural training. "For learning to take place, consideration and respect are two essential ingredients."

Chapter 5

Selecting Training Methodology for International Managers

J. Bernard Keys
Linda M. Bleicken

The record in the United States for training expatriates has been inadequate to support the corporate competitiveness required in today's global environment. Studies suggest that approximately 30 percent of overseas assignments are mistakes (Black, 1988; Harvey, 1989; Schwind, 1985; Tung, 1987). Some of these mistakes no doubt derive from poor selection of expatriates, but many of them are due to insufficient or inappropriate training. Baker (1984) found, as have earlier studies (Lanier, 1979; Tung, 1981), that fewer than 25 percent of an MNC *Fortune 1,000* sample offered predeparture training; those doing so provided only superficial programs, usually of one to five days in length. To ensure appropriate training, a model for managers accepting international assignments is needed that will allow the proper knowledge, skills, and performance abilities to be selected and taught. This chapter will propose such a model and will provide information about the effectiveness of possible teaching methodologies for categories of contingencies an expatriate might face.

A MODEL FOR MANAGEMENT TRAINING FOR INTERNATIONAL ASSIGNMENTS

In a relatively early model developed for training personnel for overseas assignments, Tung (1981) proposed that organizations con-

Reprinted with permission of J. Bernard Keys and Linda M. Bleicken and publisher. Previously published in *Journal of Transnational Management Development* (The Haworth Press, Inc.), 1(2), 1994, pp. 5-27. All rights reserved.

sider the degree of similarity between the native and host countries as well as the degree of interaction required with the host culture when designing individual training programs. Others building on this model have added length of training time required and level of rigor desired for the trainee (Mendenhall, Dunbar, and Oddou, 1987). These classifications, however, are based on training methodology rather than the competency desired for the expatriate, the criterion which should be the starting point for training selection. Black and Mendenhall (1989) present a model based on training rigor, modeling processes, and training methods. Their model provides excellent depth in discussing situational factors, but it fails to provide the accompanying research literature on training methods.

In Table 5.1, we present a more complete contingency model for international management development, and explain how the various contingencies might affect the choice of training methodology for an individual parent-company manager. This chapter will emphasize training method strengths and weaknesses as they relate to the dimensions of the model, based on the desired competency for the manager. Also, more emphasis will be given to the assignment and tasks of the manager to be trained than in earlier models.

Briefly, a model for training managers for overseas assignments is contingent upon three elements: level of cultural difference between home and host country, strategic assignment and amount of interaction desired within the host country, and level of competency existing and desired of the trainee. These elements are the basis of three propositions that may guide the design of an appropriate training program for international assignments.

Proposition 1: The level of cultural difference between the home and the host countries will determine the degree and type of cross-cultural preparation required of the trainee.

Culture, as defined by Terpstra and David (1991, p. 6), is the "learned, shared, compelling, interrelated set of symbols whose meanings provide a set of orientations for members of a society." The extent to which the "set of orientations" differs between a home and host country is a critical factor in the design of a complete international training program. This distinction could initially be made by using a classification such as the four main dimensions used by Hofstede (1980, 1987) to distinguish national cultures—individualism-collectivism, uncertainty avoidance, power distance, and masculinity-femininity. Alternately, countries to be visited may be categorized for training purposes on Ronen and Shenkar's (1985) eight cultural clusters: Anglo, Arab, Far Eastern, Germanic, Latin American, Latin European, Near Eastern, and Nordic. For example, using Ronen and Shenkar's classification, it is obvious that cross-cultural training required for an American manager assigned to Japan is likely to be much more extensive than for one traveling within an Anglo cluster. As an organization gathers specific information about a country by utilizing feedback from returning expatriates, classifications of competencies required can be sharpened.

Proposition 2: The organization's international strategy and the amount of interaction required within the host country will determine the degree and type of international management training required.

In recent years, U.S. firms have realized the need to link behavioral training (domestic or international) with the strategic plans of the organization (Bolt, 1985; Graham and Mihal, 1986). It is important to consider that not every person assigned internationally will be scheduled for the same degree of interaction with the host country. Some will be placed in positions of minimal interaction while others may enter into heavy negotiations or even day-to-day managerial interaction with host country nationals. Managerial activity will vary on the basis of a company's products, overseas sales activity, and overseas production activity (Peterson and Mueller, 1989).

Several other factors related to organizational strategy may also influence the level of expatriate training required. First, size of the firm may dictate the appropriate training strategy. Small or medium-sized firms may prefer a relatively entrepreneurial strategy and training format in contrast to the more traditional strategy and training offered by larger, professionally managed firms (El-Namaki, 1990). Second, the length of the assignment and degree of integration of the manager within the host country should be considered. Relatively long assignments that entail close integration with home country nationals will naturally require higher levels of cross-cultural training (Mendenhall and Oddou, 1985). Third, managerial

TABLE 5.1. A Contingency Model for International Management Training

STRATEGIC ASSIGNMENT AND AMOUNT OF INTERACTION
DESIRED WITH HOST COUNTRY

(Task) LOW	MODERATE	HIGH
Minimal or no interaction with members of host country	Considerable interaction with members of host country	Extensive interaction with members of host country

Level of Competence

Performance
Project Learning
Language Proficiency
Maintaining Informed Status
Networking
Business Practices
Managerial Skills
Market Entry
Ability to Learn
Critical Thinking

Teaching Mode
Levels

11	Field Experiences	
10	Microcultural Experience	
9	Action Learning	
8	Complex Behavioral Simulation	

BETWEEN HOME AND HOST COUNTRY
HIGH

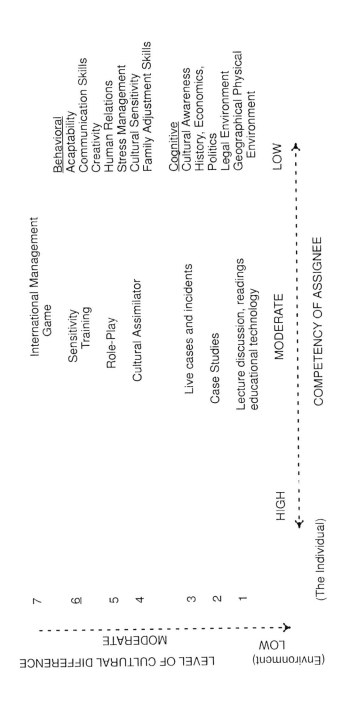

7

6

5

4

3

2

1

(The Individual)

International Management
Game

Sensitivity
Training

Role-Play

Cultural Assimilator

Live cases and incidents

Case Studies

Lecture discussion, readings
educational technology

HIGH   MODERATE   LOW

COMPETENCY OF ASSIGNEE

Behavioral
Acaptability
Communication Skills
Creativity
Human Relations
Stress Management
Cultural Sensitivity
Family Adjustment Skills

Cognitive
Cultural Awareness
History, Economics,
Politics
Legal Environment
Geographical Physical
Environment

MODERATE

LOW
(Environment)

LEVEL OF CULTURAL DIFFERENCE

skills that are well suited for the domestic environment may require modification for the multinational environment (Hofstede, 1987). For example, supervising a multicultural workforce may require specialized cultural or language training not needed for managing in the home-country setting. Finally, since successful adjustment of family members has been shown in many studies (Black, 1988; Lanier, 1979; Pinder and Schroeder, 1987) to influence expatriate success, training for family members may also be an important consideration. Assignments that include families should be distinguished from assignments that require no family consideration.

Proposition 3: The degree of existing competency or competency desired in technical as well as adaptive skills areas will determine the type and level of training required.

Competency as defined by Albanese (1988, p. 66) is "a skill and/or personal characteristic that contributes to effective managerial performance." A common error in the selection of expatriate managers is to use home country managerial success and competency as the sole criterion for overseas assignment. To discuss levels of competency it may be useful to examine what some have suggested as the ideal international manager.

An early survey by Hays (1974) of expatriate managers ranked job ability factors including technical skills, organizational ability, and belief in mission most important to success. Second in importance was the ability to deal with local nationals and cultural empathy. An adaptive and supportive family was ranked third and was weighted higher by the expatriates than language ability or other remaining factors. Not unexpectedly, research suggests that "confidence in one's ability to accomplish the purpose of the overseas assignment and possessing the necessary technical expertise to do so seem to be an important part of expatriate adjustment" (Mendenhall and Oddou, 1985, p. 41). Therefore, an engineer, MIS manager, or transportation specialist on overseas assignment must understand technology simply because such knowledge provides confidence, and because less staff, both superior and subordinate support, is often available overseas.

One of the most important skills that effective international managers must learn when working abroad is the ability to cope with stress and cultural fatigue that can overwhelm the expatriate and his or her family (Murray and Murray, 1986). Culture shock results when the expatriate is bombarded with thousands of unfamiliar stimuli, causing his or her process of selective perception to break down (Adler, 1991). The most severe culture shock is often experienced by managers who are quite effective at international work and therefore immerse themselves more heavily in the culture (Ratiu, 1983). The most competent international managers arc seen by their peers as adaptable, flexible, open minded, and capable of communicating well with host nationals (Hammer, Gudykunst, and Wiseman, 1978; Ratiu, 1983). Also, they appear to possess the ability to interrelate home and host country cultural variables, to adapt managerial responsibilities to fit local conditions, and to recognize the importance of local customs and conditions. Competent international managers understand the interrelationship between technology and social relationships and maintain a global rather than a home-or-host country strategy (Finney and Von Glinow, 1988). The manager proficient at this level has mastered what Terpstra and David (1991, p. 47) call "the backstage culture—the subtle, insider's view of how things work around here. . . . "

A THEORETICAL BASE FOR TRAINING METHODOLOGY

In developing a model for international management training, it is essential to draw upon developed models or theories of learning and behavior. First, as shown by Lewin (1935), appropriate training design will recognize the influence of the environment. Lewin's classic formula, $B = f(P,E)$ or "behavior is a function of the person and the environment," reminds us that appropriate training is contextually based. The level and type of skill development must be tailored to the situation within which the trainee will function. Second, the stepwise learning progression proposed by psychologists such as Hebart and Piaget (Hilgard and Bower, 1966) suggests that training should progress in relation to the level of knowledge or competency possessed by the learner at each stage of the process. Third, in recent years, Kolb (1984) and his associates have proposed that learning occurs in an experiential cycle. Kolb's learning cycle model suggests that work experience acts as a source of learning. He proposes that experience-based learning that occurs in a progression—reflective observation, abstract conceptualization, active experimentation, and concrete experience—is likely to provide the most effective levels of skill development.

More recently, Baba's (1989) contingency model for domestic training in industry has drawn upon past theories and has provided a starting point for our international competency model focused on training methodology. Baba divided management development into three stages—knowledge, skills, and competence—and suggested that effective training depends on an understanding of the environment in which it is conducted.

The model discussed in this paper is based on developed theory and draws on the international studies discussed. We suggest the competencies to be achieved by expatriate training are a more comprehensive version of Baba's (1989) three stages:

- *Cognitive competency*—the acquisition of knowledge and facts about cultures, including such factors as history, economics, politics, business practices, sensitive areas, and family relations.
- *Behavioral competency*—the ability to adapt to diverse conditions, to communicate in other cultures, to scan the country environment capably, to show skill at human relations in another culture, and to manage stress effectively.
- *Performance competency*—the ability to perform well in the assigned business or organizational tasks in another culture including the appropriate technical and managerial skills, the ability to be creative at adaptation while engaging in critical thinking, positional understanding and learning on the job, and the ability to develop networks and support systems for accomplishing the tasks at hand.

The model shown in Table 5.1 is currently untested but draws on the research and theory described above. Most learning theories (e.g., Piaget, Kolb, and Baba) suggest transformations of learning that are hierarchically based, and this is reflected in the current model. The model indicates the level of cultural difference between the home and host countries on the left vertical scale. The levels of this scale correspond to the levels of teaching likely to be required by the trainee or the organization. For example, to the extent the level of cultural differences between home and host country is low, there is likely to be a need for relatively less complex training (e.g., lectures, case studies, or incidents). As cultural differences become more extreme, however, higher-level training methods may be needed (e.g., behavioral simulations, microcultural experiences, or field experiences). Levels of competence progress on the right vertical axis from a relatively low level of cognitive skill (the ability to understand) to the higher level of performance competency. This vertical scale essentially defines benchmarks for levels of competency needed by the management trainee and thus denotes methodologies that can be employed individually or on a cumulative basis.

Understanding that both the competency of the assignee and the amount of interaction desired with members of the host country affect the level of training or competency desired, these factors are positioned on the lower and upper horizontal axes, respectively. These are two independent scales, each of which affects development needs in a different direction. Competency is plotted along the bottom horizontal scale, and suggests that less training is needed for the more competent international manager. On the upper horizontal axis, higher task interaction is plotted to the right and lower to the left, suggesting a lower need for training when interaction is likely to be infrequent. The two scales have inverse impacts on the level of training likely to be required; there is no direct or causal relationship intended between these scales.

MANAGEMENT DEVELOPMENT METHODS

A perennial challenge has been for writers to go beyond identification of competencies for the international manager and to define specific training strategies necessary to assure expatriate competence. Most models in the literature have focused on cross-cultural training to the exclusion of international managerial performance and positional training. Further models dealing with the development of expatriates have simply listed possible teaching methods to be used but have not reviewed the research regarding the efficacy of these methods. This section of the chapter reviews the research available for each method, both from domestic studies and, when available, from research evaluating the methods when used for international training.

Diagonally and across to the right in Table 5.1 are presented various types of training methodologies. These are arranged in an ascending stairway with the least complex and least demanding at the bottom and the most complex at the top. It is anticipated that training methodology selection will be cumulative. Cognitive competencies will usually be developed before behavioral competencies are attempted, for example. The growth of international business programs in colleges and universities presumes that some useful international training can be of a general nature and non-country specific (Beck, 1988; Wolniansky, 1990). As these programs expand, participants in predeparture training and on-the-job training will be expected to possess more general knowledge of international management.

DEVELOPING COGNITIVE COMPETENCIES

Lecture, Discussion, and Educational Technology

Cross-cultural training often consists of cognitive training through reading assignments and country or environmental briefings. Such training is valuable for developing an awareness of cultural differences, but it fails to teach the nuances of behavior in a foreign culture (Bogorya, 1985; Hall, 1973, 1981). Burke and Day (1986), in a systematic review of a large number of research articles, found positive learning effects associated with the lecture method from studies dominated by lower-level learning of basic facts, concepts, and skills. The attitudinal, conceptual learning of values, usually necessary for intercultural training, is not generally achieved through this method.

Moving to international training research, Early (1987), in a comparative evaluation of lecture versus role-play simulations, found both imparted the required skills and neither proved superior at skill development. In this case, the skill training was scheduled immediately before departure by future expatriates, which suggests that the effectiveness of lecture methods may be moderated by the immediacy of need for information, making timing and methods vital to cross-cultural development. In a study reviewed more completely in the section Role-Play and Sensitivity Training, Gudykunst, Hammer, and Wiseman (1977) found lecture methods less effective than a combination of experiential methods in preparing participants for adjustment to a foreign culture.

Cases and Case Incidents

Although various writers have suggested the use of cases and case incidents for intercultural training (e.g., Bogorya, 1985), studies rarely distinguish between international and domestic cases. A review of largely anecdotal research suggests that cases offer a realistic scenario of the manager's world, provide a means for connecting theory with practice, and foster positive learning (Berger, 1983; Keys, 1989; Osigweh, 1986-87). However, they offer little of the immediacy found in real-world decision making (Andrews and Noel, 1986) and fail to foster double-loop learning or provide for transfer of learning (Argyris, 1980). Traditional cases appear to have greater application in our model for international strategic and operational training than for intercultural training.

Social learning theory suggests that cross-cultural training is effective when it increases trainees' confidence in their ability to act within a foreign culture, increases relational skills, or improves the ability to accurately perceive models of the way in which other people view the world (Black and Mendenhall, 1990). In cross-cultural training the lecture, discussion, cases, and other forms of information dissemination and discussion may be useful at levels 1, 2, and 3 of Table 5.1, but they are not likely to bring about frequently needed behavioral or attitudinal change (levels 4-6). For this type of training impact, experiential methods will probably be required (Dechant, 1990).

DEVELOPING BEHAVIORAL COMPETENCIES WITH EXPERIENTIAL METHODS

As one moves from the cognitive to the performance level of learning, learning becomes increasingly hands-on, experience-based, and discovery oriented. Experiential learning is not simply learning from experience, but often vicariously by means of exercises and simulations. This type of learning generates involvement and interest, is active rather than passive, includes an integration of thought and action, involves two-way communication, and is problem-centered (Kolb, 1984). It closely approximates the natural way in which natives learn their own culture by experiencing a variety of situations and involvements. A number of writers have called for experiential techniques in cross-cultural training (Bogorya, 1985; Crump, 1989; Edge and French, 1986; Tung, 1987). Research suggests that a combination of lecture and experiential methods are more effective than training through lecture or cognitive methods alone (Gudykunst, Hammer, and Wiseman, 1977). However, experiential exercises are value laden and may be suitable for one culture and not another. For example, a training program was developed in Beijing by Lindsay and Dempsey (1985) to teach Chinese management trainees Western management techniques. During the program, the Chinese participated readily in group discussions but shunned the decision-making exercises, probably because of their desire to avoid public conflict (Latham, 1988). Therefore, it is important not only to select an effective training method, but one that is suitable for the culture for which training is designed.

Cultural Assimilators

One training methodology developed exclusively for international training is the cultural assimilator. It includes intercultural incidents gathered from research with expatriates, developed in problematic form, and assembled with programmed choices. Incorrect answers include branching paths to provide self-teaching feedback and to lead the participant back to a correct choice. These incidents should be carefully screened by a jury of experts with experience in the country of question (Fiedler, Mitchell, and Triandis, 1971).

Various researchers have empirically tested a cultural assimilator and have achieved positive results in training participants to function effectively in situations involving members of another culture (Albert, 1983; Fiedler, Mitchell, and Triandis, 1971; Worchel and Mitchell, 1972). They cite as strengths of the cultural assimilator its empirically derived critical cultural information, its ability to actively engage participants, and previous demonstrations of its effectiveness in training persons in intercultural social and task situations.

Although cultural assimilators are usually targeted for a specific country, Brislin and his colleagues have assembled what they call a "general cultural assimilator" designed to train participants in cultural awareness (Brislin et al., 1986). It includes 106 critical incidents derived from a number of cultures and eighteen essays that accompany the incidents and integrate points made with them. The essays are organized into eight categories including host customs, interaction with hosts, settling in, tourist experiences, work, family, school, and returning home.

Role-Play and Sensitivity Training

Although a cultural assimilator can be a very useful introduction to intercultural skill development, cultural assimilators are not truly experiential until extended to incorporate role play exercises. Role-play simulations are used extensively at the Japan-American Institute of Management Science (JAIMS) in Honolulu, Hawaii, sponsored by Fijitsui and by companies providing training to prepare Japanese expatriates for departure for international assignments (Crump, 1989; Edge and Keys, 1989). The "Contrast American" role-play exercise is also reportedly very useful for developing cultural self-awareness (Gudykunst, Hammer, and Wiseman, 1977).

Two empirical studies for role-play in intercultural settings were found in the literature. U.S. Navy personnel scheduled for assignment to Japan were trained by two methods: lecture (factual briefing) and a combination of role-play using the BaFa BaFa Simulation and field trips. The experiential methods produced trainees who were better adjusted to the Japanese culture (Gudykunst, Hammer, and Wiseman, 1977). However, another study concluded that role-play (also the BaFa BaFa Simulation) was no more effective for skills training than a lecture for preparing employees for an international assignment. In the latter study, role-play was preferred by participants over lecture. Both lecture and role-play proved effective at enabling participants to acquire behavioral skills with a positive effect on adjustment as expatriates in South Korea (Early, 1987).

Similar to many other training methods, role-play effectiveness may depend on subtle combinations of supporting techniques and skillful implementation. Enrolling multicultural participants in a training session, such as the JAIMS program described above, is often cited as a method of increasing the effectiveness of role-play and other experiential methods in intercultural skill training.

When role-play sessions and other experiential methods utilize heavy interpersonal participant interaction in an unsupervised fashion, followed by extensive debriefing, we call the program "sensitivity training." Organizations such as the comparative workshops at the University of Pittsburgh and the Center for International Executive Training in Paris, France, have used sensitivity training extensively as an intercultural learning technique. Empirical research on the value of sensitivity training in domestic settings, although somewhat dated, indicates that the method is effective at changing short-term attitudes and behavior and in reducing prejudice, but little is known about its long-term effects (House, 1967; Stock, 1964).

Language Proficiency

Debate continues over whether foreign language proficiency is necessary for international managers (McIntyre, 1991). From a 1984 survey of 600 U.S. MNCs, Baker (1984) learned that only 20 percent require languages for overseas assignment, although 36 percent believe that the second language facility is necessary and important. Terpstra and David (1991, p. 23) observe that "the vocabulary of each language reflects the primary emphases and technology of the culture." These writers quote Whorf (1956, p. 13) who suggests that "the structure of the language one habitually uses influences the manner in which one can understand his environment. The picture of the universe shifts from tongue to tongue."

Finney and Von Glinow (1988, p. 20) affirm that an international manager must be proficient in the host country language, especially if one is to understand and manage a workforce. They substantiate their point by noting that "a society's language is a door which opens onto the values, beliefs, and cultural strategies controlling the behavior of its members." One group of international training experts suggests that "survival-level" language training is necessary at the cognitive level of competency, moderate language training is necessary at the behavioral level, and extensive language training is necessary at the performance level (Mendenhall, Dunbar, and Oddou, 1987). Certainly at some point in the country integration scale and the country diversification scale, language training will be necessary. As with many complex cultural factors, the newly acquired language is more effective if used within the context of the host country culture in laboratories or in work-oriented activities.

DEVELOPING PERFORMANCE COMPETENCIES

Learning occurs within the task or work setting or in a situation similar to the context of the real thing we call "performance-oriented learning." Although mastery of performance in international settings necessitates cross-cultural training, it also requires other types of training as well. In this section we discuss several more complex experiential training methods including international management games, complex management simulations, and on-the-job learning experiences.

International Management Games and Simulations

A business game refers to a learning laboratory composed of a case study of an industry, a company history, and a computerized model that allows competitive business decisions to be made and financial results to be returned. Variations of games and simulations are used extensively in 86 percent of the business schools in the United States and are found in over 4,000 U.S. corporate training programs (Faira, 1989). Simulations that deal with a total company operation, provide decision variables in marketing, production, and finance, and thus require a strategic emphasis for total organizational performance are called total enterprise games or simply management games (Keys, 1987).

International Management Games are used extensively at such well-known international training centers as the American (Thunderbird) Graduate School of International Management, the Japan-American Institute of Management Science (JAIMS), Georgetown University, and the University of Southern California. In Europe, 150 management teams participate in the *Markstrat* competition (Larreche, 1987); in Singapore and Malaysia a game is administered by the Singapore Institute of Management (Keys, Edge, and Pang, 1989) and international competitions have been conducted throughout the Arab nations. Research indicates that games provide meaningful, lifelike roles for participants and reward intelligent, rational, and well-planned executive-type decision making (Keys and Wolfe, 1990).

Empirical studies of management game learning outcomes, most often compared with case-taught classes, have generally found positive learning outcomes for both methods, but superior learning has been attributed to game-taught classes (Keys and Wolfe, 1990; Wheatley, Hornaday, and Hunt, 1988). A study, vital to the evaluation of the higher levels of our model, found both cases and a game imparted factual knowledge equally well. The game, however, was superior in teaching conceptual knowledge (Wolfe and Guth, 1975), the kind of knowledge necessary in international environments. Several games have been written for this purpose and would seem to benefit from some of the same characteristics suggested by domestic game research (Barker, Temple, and Sloan, 1988; Hinton and Smith, 1985; Keys and Wells, 1992; Keys, Edge, and Wells, 1992; Thompson and Stappenbeck, 1990; Thorelli and Graves, 1989). Klein, Fleck, and Wolfe (1994) provide an excellent review that evaluates the coverage of international games.

Although little research is available on the use of games in international education and training, anecdotal support for their validity as a training environment has been positive and suggests that games provide effective environments for intercultural as well as strategic management training, especially when participants from different cultures are included on the same team (Edge and Keys, 1990; Edge and French, 1986). Klein (1984) found that an international business class of students learned more about comparative advantage, direct foreign investment, product adaptation, product life cycle, social custom and needs, and technology transfer from an international game than did a control group which either played a domestic simulation game or received lectures on these subjects.

Total enterprise games show promise as competency-training environments for high-involvement managerial roles in a host country because of the strong cultural and historical carryover to game-play. Patterns of business in other countries can be taught experientially by such programs, and company-specific strategies and plans may be incorporated into a management game. By including participants from multiple cultures, complex work-related issues may be simulated and dealt with in a business-oriented context. This produces the opportunity for a multitude of realistic role-play encounters within a goal-oriented and environmentally rich context (Edge and Keys, 1990).

Complex Behavioral Simulations and Microworlds

Recently, in-basket simulations have been combined with total enterprise cases to form what are called "complex behavioral simulations." These simulations link strategic behavior with individual behavior and incorporate more role and positional identification than the total enterprise games discussed previously (Haley and Stumpf, 1989; Lombardo, McCall, and DeVries, 1976). During these simulations, managers are placed in roles ranging from president to plant manager. They prepare for their roles by reading annual reports, job descriptions, and a set of memos supposedly just written or just received. Numerous problems and issues are imbedded in the information provided to participants who work in an office-like setting. The idea is to bring out a manager's natural behavior as it would occur on the job, a rationale required of effective intercultural training programs. Extensive trainer- and self-assessment follows a round of simulation (Kaplan, 1986). Complex behavioral simulations appear to offer potential for training in interpersonal behavior and leadership processes, and a number of these include simulated international business environments (Dunbar and Stumpf, 1989; Dutton and Webster, 1988; Mullen and Stumpf, 1987).

Recently, management simulations called microworlds have been custom designed to teach entire organizations to become "learning organizations" through team learning, organizational strategies, and collaborative as well as competitive activities. Like the complex behavioral simulation, microworlds are introduced by in-basket roles of participants. Unlike the more generalized behavioral simulation with its emphasis on leadership training, however, microworlds reflect more extensively such factors as organizational dynamics and organizational performance. Some microworlds have been designed to develop global managers who can build a unifying microculture, rather than simply develop cultural diversity (McBride, 1992).

On-the-Job Learning

Contrary to popular opinion, on-the-job learning is the best teacher only if the manager is skillful at learning from the job. Consequently, many management consultants and writers have argued that the most important management skill is the ability to learn (Carnevale, 1986: Dechant, 1990; McCall, Lombardo, and Morrison, 1988). This argument seems even more valid in overseas settings, given the frequent nontransferability of management skills (Hofstede, 1980). "Learning to learn internationally" may be the first step in learning from on-the-job experiences.

In interviews with 250 young executives, representing thirty-five different nationalities, Ratiu found that the most effective internationals described their approach as "considerable observation and listening, experimentation and risk-taking, and, above all, active involvement with others" (Ratiu, 1983, p. 141). This section will discuss three types of on-the-job learning that can enhance these competencies: action learning, microcultural experiences, and field experiences.

Action Learning

One of the most intense on-the-job learning experiences is that of action learning, a technique used extensively in intercultural training in Europe. Action learning is usually organized by assigning projects to team members (sets) who then share their projects as real cases to be analyzed by the set. It is a combination of on-the-job project learning, team and interpersonal relations, and case analysis. It serves well as task-oriented learning for an intercultural mix of employees from the same organization (Beck, 1988; Mumford, 1987). A typical action learning program might consist of a set of middle managers or executives from one company, with diverse backgrounds, ages, and functional expertise, working on real projects within their MNCs.

Though empirical research about action learning effectiveness in international programs was not found, extensive accounts of its use are available, all of which stress the linkage of strategic plans by joint participation by senior managers from a variety of companies (Braddick, 1990). General Electric (GE) has used action learning to address actual business issues with executive teams from the United States visiting in Europe (Bolt, 1989). It was reported that this trip provided "GE executives with hands-on experiences in the complexities of conducting business in the international arena and . . . also provide[d] European operations with inputs from GE's best people" (Bolt, 1989, p. 47). However, U.S. firms often reject action learning because of the long time frame necessary to develop projects and intercompany programs and the fear of sharing competitive information (Marsick, 1990).

Microcultural and Field Experiences

Temporal and Burnett (1990) warn against what they call the "deep-end" approach of throwing a manager or executive into the international marketplace without sufficient training. These writers note that "the global marketplace is a changing, paradoxical, confusing and ambiguous area in which to operate, and the demands placed on managers who have to manage in such an environment are not catered for in the traditional structured systems of management development" (Temporal and Burnett, 1990, p. 58).

Many companies include various types of field experiences and on-the-job learning for employees assigned overseas work. Most large U.S. cities include some microculture centers that mirror cultures to be found overseas. A one-week assignment in such an area can be a very useful and risk-free method of sensitizing employees to the overseas culture (Tung, 1981).

McCall and his colleagues (1988), in their landmark book *The Lessons of Experience,* provide a framework for executive development that includes applications to both domestic and international settings. Concepts they cite as most frequently learned from experience include: "finding out one's shortcomings," "accepting responsibility," "finding situations where learning new things is essential," "finding ways to get help and support" and "asking questions and seeking advice." Employees working abroad can learn managerial skills, tolerance for ambiguity, multiple perspectives (diplomacy), and increased tolerance for diversity (Brislin, 1979). One survey showed that managers consider their most meaningful lessons to be those learned about their own values and feelings. The factors that describe these changes clustered in four areas: influencing others, visioning, enhancing political acumen, and relationship forging (Dechant, 1990).

One consultant suggests that on-the-job learning is more productive when a learning diary or learning logbook is maintained by the participant (Bogorya, 1985). Intercultural situations and incidents can be recorded daily and analyzed each evening.

SUMMARY AND CASE APPLICATION
OF THE TRAINING MODEL

A number of recently developed programs suggest applications of teaching models similar to the contingency model presented in Table 5.1. First, the University of Michigan's Global Leadership Program uses a number of the training methods described above but focuses on action learning in its global leadership program. This program is performance-oriented, and it trains managers in all areas of competency: cognitive, behavioral, and performance. Participants are fast-track managers from sponsoring companies, grouped in teams of six. Teams are initially given country briefings and scheduled for an industry visit (cognitive). Teams are organized in an intercultural mix incorporating members from various countries and spend a week in an Outward-Bound program on Maine's Hurricane Island. During this period, team cohesiveness is built and some behavioral skills are enhanced through interaction with teammates of other nationalities. Teams also begin laying a foundation for worldwide performance by building a global world model and critiquing their own firms on a global scale. As a capstone experience and performance competency builder, the teams visit three different countries, establish contacts, and develop networking for their companies back home (O'Reilly, 1993).

A second example that reinforces our thinking about contingency models is the Japan-American Institute of Management Science, which operates two management development programs throughout the year, the American Management Program (AMP), and the Japan Management Program (JMP). Students from Japan study American management, and students from the rest of the world study Japanese management for five months. Also, students study traditional courses but with emphasis on a management model that contrasts the Western emphasis on functional skills with the circular generalist skills of the Eastern culture. In both programs students from Japanese and Western cultures are brought together in teams for a number of experiential laboratories, using as a centerpiece a multinational management game. Around the computerized simulation are built role-plays and other experiential exercises (Edge and French, 1986; Edge and Keys, 1990). The AMP students study Japanese language and live with Japanese counterparts who are, in turn, studying English. The emphasis in this program is on cross-cultural behavioral skills. However, graduates also are placed in three-month internships—the Japanese in some Western setting and the Western students in Japan. This dimension of the program allows progress on the performance dimension of the model.

Most training programs that fall in the right-hand extremes of the cultural difference scale, the left side of the competency scale, and the extremes of cultural difference between the host and home countries will require integrated international training programs. Companies or programs choosing to use the model in Table 5.1 need not exhaust all levels or methods of training. Generally, the contingency model follows the development of cross-cultural training from less-intense cognitive training to more-intense performance training. One or more of the training methods can be selected depending on the needs determined by the model. For inexperienced expatriates assigned to countries with cultures very different from their native country, and targeted for assignments with a heavy community interaction on a long-term basis, or training for various international assignments, all levels of training shown in the contingency model will most likely be required, and most if not all training methodologies will be necessary. Perhaps most important for management development and human resource managers, the model with its listing of training methods, and the accompanying literature, provides a handy reference to training methodology likely to provide strength for the competency desired.

RECOMMENDATIONS FOR FUTURE RESEARCH

Although there is evidence that the model described in this chapter is representative of some specialized training programs, future research should be conducted to determine the extent to which the model reflects training as it occurs among multinational firms. This research should utilize interviews with training managers of Fortune 500 and Global 1000 organizations as the basis for the development of a survey instrument. The instrument could then be distributed to training heads of multinational organizations. Feedback from such a study can help researchers and practitioners in several ways. First, it will help researchers to identify the breadth of training currently being delivered by multinationals. Second, assessments of the effectiveness of training methods used by both U.S.-based and foreign-based multinationals is likely to help in the design of future training. This knowledge may be useful in developing customized organizational training uniquely tailored to an organization's strategy and the skill levels of its employees. Third, an assessment of training practices will help to identify learning gaps so that training methods can be suggested to effectively fill these gaps.

Finally, future research should also seek to expand our understanding of the process of learning. Through interview and questionnaire research, an examination of the ways in which international managers learn may be performed.

REFERENCES

Adler, N. J. (1991). *International Dimensions of Organizational Behavior.* Boston: PWS-Kent Publishing Company.

Albanese, R. (1988). Competency-based management education. *Journal of Management Development, 8* (2), 66-76.

Albert, R. (1983). The intercultural sensitizer or culture assimilator: A cognitive approach. In D. Landis and R. Brislin (Eds.), *Handbook of Intercultural Training* (pp. 2-15). Elmsford, NY: Pergamon.

Andrews, E. S., and Noel, J. L. (1986). Adding life to the case study method. *Training and Development Journal, 40* (2), 28-29.

Argyris, C. (1980). Some limitations on the case method: Experiences in a management development program. *Academy of Management Review, 5* (2), 291-298.

Baba, V. V. (1989). Management development: A contingency perspective. *Journal of International Management, 6* (1), 37-47.

Baker, J. C. (1984). Foreign language and predeparture training in U.S. multinational firms. *Personnel Administrator, 29* (1), 68-70.

Barker, J. R., Temple, C. S., and Sloan, H. M. (1988). *WISE: The International Simulation Exercise for Management Development.* Lexington, MA: Authors.

Beck, J. E. (1988). Expatriate management development: Realizing the learning potential of overseas assignment. In F. Hoy (Ed.), *Academy of Management Best Papers Proceedings,* (pp. 112-116). Athens, GA: University of Georgia.

Berger, M. A. (1983). In defense of the case method: A reply to Argyris. *Academy of Management Review, 8* (2), 329-333.

Black, J. S. (1988). Work role transitions: A study of American expatriate managers in Japan. *Journal of International Business Studies, 19* (2), 277-294.

Black, J. S. and Mendenhall, M. (1989). A practical but theory-based framework for selecting cross-cultural training methods. *Human Resource Management, 28* (4), 511-539.

Black, J. S. and Mendenhall, M. (1990). Cross-cultural training effectiveness: A review and a theoretical framework for future research. *Academy of Management Review, 15* (1), 113-136.

Bogorya, Y. (1985). Intercultural training for managers involved in international business. *Journal of Management Development, 4* (2), 17-25.

Bolt, J. F. (1985). Tailor executive development to strategy. *Harvard Business Review, 63* (6), 168-176.

Bolt, J. F. (1989). *Executive Development: A Strategy for Corporate Effectiveness.* New York: Harper & Row.

Braddick, B. (1990). Learning Together: Practical Lessons in Partnership in Management Development. *The Executive Learner.* Special issue of *The Journal of Management Development, 9* (4), 16-22.

Brislin, R. W. (1979). Orientation programs for cross-cultural preparation. In A. J. Marsella, G. Tharp, and T. J. Giborowski (Eds.), *Perspectives on Cross-Cultural Psychology* (pp. 287-304). Orlando, FL: Academic Press.

Brislin, R., Cushner, K., Cherrie, C., and Yong, M. (1986). *Intercultural Interactions: A Practical Guide.* Beverly Hills, CA: Sage Publications.

Burke, M. J. and Day, R. R. (1986) A cumulative study of the effectiveness of managerial training. *Journal of Applied Psychology, 71* (2), 232-245.

Carnevale, A. P. (1986). Training—today and tomorrow. *Training and Development Journal,* June, 34-37.

Crump, L. (1989). Japanese managers-western workers: Cross-cultural training and development issues. *Management Development in Japan.* Special issue of *The Journal of Management Development, 8* (4), 48-55.

Dechant, K. (1990). Knowing how to learn: The neglected management ability. *The Executive Learner.* Special issue of *The Journal of Management Development, 9* (1), 40-49.

Dunbar, R. L. M. and Stumpf, S. A. (1989). Trainings that demystify strategic decision-making processes. *Journal of Management Development, 8* (1), 36-41.

Dutton, J. E. and Webster, J. (1988). Patterns of interest around issues: The role of uncertainty and feasibility. *Academy of Management Journal, 31* (3), 663-675.

Early, P. C. (1987). Intercultural training for managers: A comparison of documentary and interpersonal methods. *Academy of Management Journal, 30* (4), 685-698.

Edge, A. G. and French, M. (1986). Management development at the Japan-American Institute of Management Science. *The Journal of Management Development, 5* (4), 51-68.

Edge, A. G. and Keys, J. B. (1989). Executives in transition at the Japan-American Institute of Management Science. *Executive Development, 2* (1), 32-34.

Edge, A. G. and Keys, J. B. (1990). Cross-cultural learning in a multinational business environment. *The Journal of Management Development, 9* (2), 43-49.

El-Namaki, M. S. S. (1990). Management training for small and medium scale industries: A cross country analysis of characteristics, constraints, and catalysts. *Journal of Teaching in International Business, 1* (3,4), 29-51.

Faira, A. J. (1989). Business gaming: Current usage levels. *Management Development Review.* Special issue of *The Journal of Management Development, 8* (2), 58-65.

Fiedler, F. E., Mitchell, T., and Triandis, H. C. (1971). The cultural assimilator: An approach to cross-cultural training. *Journal of Applied Psychology, 55* (2), 95-102.

Finney, M. and Von Glinow, M. A. (1988). Integrating academic and organizational approaches to developing the international manager. *Journal of Management Development, 7* (2), 16-27.

Graham, J. K. and Mihal, W. L. (1986). Guidelines for designing management development programs. *The Journal of Management Development, 5* (5), 57-65.

Gudykunst, W. B., Hammer, M. R., and Wiseman, R. L. (1977). An analysis of an integrated approach to cross-cultural training. *International Journal of Intercultural Relations, 1* (2), 99-110.

Haley, U. C. and Stumpf, S. A. (1989). Cognitive trails in strategic decision-making: Linking theories of personalities and cognitions. *Journal of Management Studies, 26* (5), 477-497.

Hall, E. (1973). *The Silent Language.* New York: Doubleday.

Hall, E. (1981). *Beyond Culture.* New York: Anchor Books.

Hammer, M. R., Gudykunst, W. B., and Wiseman, R. L. (1978). Dimensions of intercultural effectiveness: An exploratory study. *International Journal of Intercultural Relations, 2,* 382-393.

Harvey, M. (1989). The other side of foreign assignments: Dealing with the repatriation problems. *Columbia Journal of World Business, 17,* 53-59.

Hays, R. D. (1974). Expatriate selection: Insuring success and avoiding failure. *Journal of International Business Studies, 5* (1), 25-37.

Hilgard, E. R. and Bower, G. H. (1966). *Theories of Learning* (3rd ed.). New York: Doubleday.

Hinton and Smith. (1985). *Strat-plan.* Englewood Cliffs, NJ: Prentice-Hall.

Hinton, R. W. and Londo, E. (1992). Learning to manage strategically: Prescription for a changing world? *Developing Strategic Leaders.* Special issue of *The Journal of Management Development, 11* (6), 13-24.

Hofstede, G. (1980). *Culture's Consequences: International Differences in Work-related Values.* Beverly Hills, CA: Sage.

Hofstede, G. (1987). The applicability of McGregor's theories in Southeast Asia. *Journal of Management Development, 6* (3), 9-18.

House, R. J. (1967). T-group education and leadership effectiveness: A review of the empirical literature and a critical evaluation. *Personnel Psychology, 20,* 1-32.

Kaplan, R. E. (1986). What one manager learned in the Looking Glass and how he learned it. *Journal of Management Development, 5* (4), 37-45.

Keys, J. B. (1987). Total enterprise business games. *Simulation & Games, 18* (2), 225-241.

Keys, J. B. (1989). Teaching middle managers to think like executives. *Executive Development, 2* (1): 2-5.

Keys, J. B. and Wells, R. (1992). A global management development laboratory for a global world. *Journal of Management Development, 11* (1), 4-11.

Keys, J. B. and Wolfe, J. (1990). The role of management games and simulations in education and research. *Journal of Management, 16* (2), 307-336.

Keys, J. B., Edge, A., and Pang, J. (1989). The National Management Game at the Singapore Institute of Management. *Executive Development, 2* (2), 8-9.

Keys, J. B., Edge, A. G., and Wells, R. A. (1992). *The Multinational Management Game: A Global Simulation.* Homewood, IL: Irwin.

Klein, R. D. (1984). Adding international business to the core program via the simulation game. *Journal of International Business Studies, 15* (1), 151-159.

Klein, R. D., Fleck, R., and Wolfe, J. (1994). The role for management games in internationalizing the business school curriculum. *Journal of Management Education, 17* (2), 159-173.

Kolb, D. A. (1984). *Experiential Learning: Experience as the Source of Learning and Development.* Englewood Cliffs, NJ: Prentice-Hall.

Lanier, A. (1979). Selecting and preparing personnel for overseas transfer. *Personnel Journal, 58,* March, 160-163.

Larreche, J. C. (1987). On simulations in business education and research. *Journal of Business Research, 15,* 559-571.

Latham, G. P. (1988). Human resource training and development. *Annual Review of Psychology, 39,* 545-582.

Lewin, K. (1935). *A Dynamic Theory of Personality.* New York: McGraw-Hill.

Lindsay, C. and Dempsey, P. (1985). Experience in training Chinese business people to use U.S. management techniques. *Journal of Applied Behavioral Science, 21,* 65-78.

Lombardo, M., McCall, M., and DeVries, D. (1976). *Looking Glass.* Greensboro, NC: Center for Creative Leadership.

Marsick, V. (1990). Experience-based learning: Executive learning outside the classroom. *The Executive Learner.* Special issue of *The Journal of Management Development, 9* (1), 50-60.

McBride, M. (1992). Management development in the global village: Beyond culture—A microworld approach. *Journal of Management Development, 9* (1), 50-60.

McCall, W. M. Jr., Lombardo, M. M., and Morrison, A. M. (1988). *The Lessons of Experience: How Successful Executives Develop on the Job.* Lexington, MA: Lexington Books.

McIntyre, D. J. (1991). When your national language is just another language. *Communication World, 8* (6), 18-21.

Mendenhall, M. and Oddou, G. (1985). The dimensions of expatriate acculturation: A view. *Academy of Management Review 10* (1), 39-47.

Mendenhall, M., Dunbar, E., and Oddou, G. (1987). Expatriate selection, training, and career-pathing. *Human Resource Management, 26* (3): 331-345.

Mullen, T. P. and Stumpf, S. A. (1987). The effect of management styles on strategic planning. *Journal of Business Strategy, 7* (3): 60-75.

Mumford, A. (1987). Helping managers learn to learn. *The Journal of Management Development, 6* (5), 49-60.

Murray, F. T. and Murray, A. H. (1986). SMR Forum: Global managers for global businesses. *Sloan Management Review, 27* (2), 75-79.

O'Reilly, B. (1993). How executives learn now. *Fortune, 127* (7), 52-58.

Osigweh, C. A. B. (1986-87). The case approach in management training. *The Organizational Behavior Teaching Review, 11* (4), 120-133.

Peterson, M. F. and Mueller, R. (1989). University and in-house management education of multinational business and bank employees. *Journal of Teaching in International Business. 1* (1), 47-75.

Pinder, C. C. and Schroeder, K. G. (1987). Time to proficiency following transfers. *Academy of Management Journal, 30,* 336-353.

Ratiu, I. (1983). Thinking internationally: A comparison of how international executives learn. *International Studies of Management and Organization, 8* (1-2), 139-150.

Ronen, S. and Shenkar, O. (1985). Clustering countries on attitudinal dimensions: A review and synthesis. *Academy of Management Review, 10* (3), 435-454.

Schwind, H. (1985). The state of the art in cross-cultural management training. In R. Doktor (Ed.), *International Human Resource Development Annual* (pp. 7-15), Alexandria, VA: ASTD.

Stock, D. A. (1964). *T-Group Theory and Laboratory Method.* New York: John Wiley.

Temporal, P. and Burnett, K. (1990). Strategic corporate assignments and international management development. *The Journal of Management Development, 9* (5), 58-64.

Terpstra, V. and David, K. (1991). *The Cultural Environment of International Business.* Cincinnati: South-Western Publishing.

Thompson, A. A. and Stappenback, G. J. (1990). *The Business Strategy Game: A Global Industry Simulation.* Homewood, IL: Irwin.

Thorelli, H. B. and Graves, R. L. (1989). *INTOP Classic PC.* Bloomington, IN: Indiana University.

Tung, R. L. (1981). Selection and training of personnel in overseas assignments. *Columbia Journal of World Business, 16* (1), 68-78.

Tung, R. L. (1987). Expatriate assignments: Enhancing success and minimizing failure. *The Academy of Management Executive, 1* (2), 117-125.

Wheatley, W. I., Hornaday, R. W., and Hunt, T. G. (1988). Developing strategic management goal-setting skills. *Simulation and Gaming, 19,* 173-185.

Whorf, B. L. (1956). *Language, Thought, and Reality.* New York: Wiley.

Wolfe, J. and Guth, G. (1975). The case approach vs. gaming in evaluation. *Journal of Business, 48* (3), 349-364.

Wolniansky, N. (1990). International training for global leadership. *Management Review, 79* (5) 27-28.

Worchel, S. and Mitchell, T. R. (1972). An evaluation of the effectiveness of the cultural assimilator in Thailand and Greece. *Journal of Applied Psychology, 56,* 472-479.

Chapter 6

Creating Scenarios and Cases for Global Anticipatory Learning

John A. Gutman

This chapter focuses on the development and use of cases and scenarios for anticipatory learning and provides background on new advances in the field. The examples mentioned here demonstrate that a key component of anticipatory learning depends on spurring participants to acknowledge and reshape their mental models of the future. By using the types of scenarios and cases discussed in this chapter, individuals and organizations can improve their preparation for the future around the world and can understand the recurring systemic patterns that organizations confront.

Building on work at the Stanford Research Institute and at Royal Dutch/Shell, Pierre Wack, Arie de Geus, and Peter Schwartz have publicized the practices of Shell and other organizations to create coherent, logical scenarios about various ways that the future may develop. For some organizations, these scenarios can be applied in future-oriented cases. In addition, traditional cases can be supplemented by computer-based simulation models that incorporate the principles of system dynamics. However, before scenario planning, future-oriented cases, and simulation models can be championed as a means to improve managers' mental models, a set of issues surrounding anticipatory learning programs in international organizations needs to be confronted.

Abridged, edited, and reprinted from "Creating Scenarios and Cases for Global Anticipatory Learning," with permission of John A. Gutman and publishers. First published in *American Journal of Management Development* (MCB University Press), 1(3), 1995, pp. 37-43.

REVIEW OF ANTICIPATORY LEARNING
PROGRAM ISSUES

As an area of research and application, anticipatory learning is increasingly being used to encourage organizational change and to encourage learning by organizations and individuals. As noted by Fulmer, "Anticipatory learning is both future oriented and participative. Instead of considering what has worked in the past, it tries to anticipate creative solutions to problems which have not yet emerged." It "addresses both the long-term consequences of present actions and the best ways to deal with a future environment" (Fulmer, 1994, p. 21).

Programs to spur anticipatory learning vary by industry and by type of organization, and orientations chosen by senior managers and HR executives depend on the objectives ascribed to the programs. Of course, programs must be developed with consideration for current organizational strategies, ongoing initiatives within the organization, and internal roadblocks that the programs will confront. At the outset, some specific questions need to be answered: With the time and money allocated to the program, can expectations be met, or do expectations need to be modified at the start? Who are the champions of the program and how do their status, perspectives, and agendas influence the content and visibility of the program?

Given the variety of expectations for anticipatory learning, program objectives can vary. Four potential examples follow. Alpha Company chooses a focus on anticipatory learning for senior managers as part of a plan to invigorate its top leadership (Tenaglia and Noonan, 1992). Beta Gmbh encourages marketing planning teams to use anticipatory learning in order to prepare for a significant change in the market environment (Millett, 1992a). At Gamma NKK, human resources and operations functions could develop skills in anticipatory learning, given impending changes in the labor pool available to build the company's products. At Delta et Cie. S. A., anticipatory learning could be the pole around which the company reshapes its work processes.

In implementing anticipatory learning programs, senior managers must determine if they should use cases and scenarios written externally or written inside the organization, or if participants should learn by writing their own cases and scenarios. No hard and fast rule applies because the situation of each organization at a given point in time will guide the decision. The decision revolves around the following questions: Is the thrust of the program management development or specific future-oriented problem-solving? How much time is available for training? Have appropriate cases or scenarios already been developed?

To give an idea of how scenarios and cases can be used in anticipatory learning, three examples are detailed:

1. The corporate planning staff formulates broad scenarios of the marketplace ten to fifteen years hence, and groups of line managers use those scenarios as a groundwork for developing specific future directions for the company.
2. Future-oriented cases encourage common "mental models" of the business environment through different levels of the business as middle and senior-level managers develop coherent shared views of the future.
3. A broad group of managers are exposed to system dynamics concepts through existing computerized "microworlds" that elicit important characteristics of the skills and orientations to be fostered for the future.

SCENARIO PLANNING

The scenario planning techniques developed at Shell in the 1970s first received international prominence when Pierre Wack (1985a, 1985b) and Arie de Geus (1988) wrote articles for the *Harvard Business Review.* Confronted by oil markets in turmoil in the 1970s, it was important that Shell be prepared to react to a wide variety of options in the coming decades. By assiduous study of important social, political, and economic trends around the world, the scenario planners at Shell were able to develop a set of scenarios (usually three to four) about how the oil market would unfold. Significant but little-known factors affected the future for Shell: the political situation among OPEC nations and the economic interactions bubbling through what was then the Soviet Union. Given Shell's business interests in over 100 countries, the scenarios developed by Shell Group Planning in London served as a tool for communicating and perfecting views about the future of the oil business to managers in its decentralized subsidiaries and affiliates around the world (Wack, 1985a).

Scenario planning has its theoretical roots in the tradition of military planning that has evolved over centuries (de Geus, 1988). Herman Kahn's scenarios for the Defense Department in the 1950s and 1960s are a prominent example. Futurists at the Stanford Research Institute (now SRI International), Peter Schwartz's early home, also publicized the techniques (Schoemaker, 1993).

Scenario planning is more than just another set of analytical techniques from consultants. Wack, de Geus, and Peter Schwartz all point to the equally important, *cognitive* side of scenario planning: it enables a group of managers to develop common "mental models" about their business and its environment.

This blend of analysis and intuition mirrors Mintzberg's comments about the duality of analysis and intuition needed for successful planning (Schoemaker, 1993). Wack describes the combination well:

> Scenarios deal with two worlds: the world of facts and the world of perceptions. They explore for facts but they aim at perceptions inside the heads of decision makers. Their purpose is to gather and transform information of strategic significance into fresh perceptions . . . [You have an impact when the work] reaches the microcosms of decision makers, obliges them to question their assumptions about how their business world works, and leads them to change and reorganize their inner models of reality. (Wack, 1985a, p. 140)

In *The Art of the Long View*, Peter Schwartz (1991) elaborates on his Shell experiences. The aim of his book is to teach the art of creating scenarios. The process as a whole demands hard thinking and a willingness to challenge one's own assumptions. Experience shows that it is important to suspend disbelief—to try to believe in a future that you think is *not* going to happen.

Although the word "scenario" is used extensively in current parlance, under Schwartz's usage, it actually refers to a specific set of "plots" in which a few significant elements have been exaggerated in order to be emphasized. "Scenarios are stories that give meaning to events." Like myths, when developed by a group of managers and supported by others, scenarios become universally believed stories about the past and future (Schwartz, 1991).

Three successive stages of analysis precede the development of specific plots. Together, "driving forces, predetermined elements, and critical uncertainties give structure to our exploration of the future." The first step is to identify *driving forces* influencing the area of concern; society, technology, economics, politics, and the environment are initial areas to look for driving forces. By their nature, driving forces like demographics or cultural values cannot be changed, but at least they must be recognized. Second, *predetermined elements*, e.g., slow-changing phenomena, constrained situations, and inevitable collisions—like federal budget impasses between defense expenditures and social spending   need to be highlighted. Third, the *critical uncertainties* derived from the predetermined elements need to be pinpointed. Examples might include the expected pattern of real incomes for senior citizens or children's literacy rates.

After these three stages of analysis, plots can be developed that explain the situation. The three most common types of plots are Winners and Losers (a zero-sum game), Challenge and Response, and Evolution. A set of plots interweave to create a scenario. Three scenarios can reasonably capture likely pathways for the future.

Overall, several warnings are appropriate. First, it takes a long time to become good at creating scenarios. Part of the process is to review why previous versions did or did not develop as forecasted. Second, some of the most important changes in the environment are gradual changes that are difficult to perceive. For instance, Schwartz (1991) highlights a little-seen driving force, The Global Teenager, a reflection of the high birth rates and decreased infant mortality in the third world. Third, although uncertainty about the future cannot be eliminated, scenario planning can structure and provide boundaries around the uncertainty (Schoemaker, 1991).

Fourth, scenario planning will be difficult to implement in backward-looking companies or at companies in which senior management believes that it or experts have all the answers. The image of managerial competence that managers hold for themselves and for others is based upon assurance and knowledge about the present and the future. An admission that the future is unknown, a key tenet of scenario planning, implies holes in the image of managerial competence, a difficult position for managers to accept (Baily and Wilson, 1995).

The preponderance of work on scenarios has emphasized broad-brush views with focus on macro trends. These could be termed "framework scenarios." In addition, scenarios can be used to evaluate specific strategic issues, markets, or investments. These can be termed "decision scenarios" (Duncan and Wack, 1994).

Other scenario planners use a more technical and quantitative approach with more explicit probabilistic and quantitative analysis. Several organizations use PC-based models to structure their process; often this approach appeals to technology-driven firms or those with an engineering culture. Representative organizations include the Battelle Research Institute and The Futures Group (Millett and Randles, 1986). For large consulting firms such as SRI International (Millett, 1992b), scenario planning can be marshaled from a larger set of tools as appropriate to meet a variety of client needs. On the other hand, Peter Schwartz's organization, the Global Business Network, and Northeast Consulting Resources (Mason, 1994) use scenario planning as the lynchpin of their consulting practices.

Through using these techniques, managers and planners participate in developing a deeper understanding of the national and international forces affecting their businesses in the future. In the process, the managers' mental models become more coherent and consistent. Thus, scenario planning is designed for organizational learning, and the concurrent individual learning by managers is a beneficial by-product. Case studies, on the other hand, are designed for individual learning, and additional organizational learning often occurs at the same time.

CASES

Recently, case studies have begun to change in two ways in order to become more relevant to current business situations. First, cases are being utilized to shape directly the future of organizations by challenging received wisdom about the evolution of the business environment. Second, cases are being supported by computer-based system dynamics models to give insight into real-world situations.

In business schools and executive education programs from INSEAD to Thunderbird, cases enhance the analytical skills of students and provide a framework for teachers to lead participative class discussions. Commonly, cases develop understanding of the perspective of general managers on issues such as organizational strategy and structure, human resources, marketing dilemmas, and new product development. The case method encourages a high level of involvement and the interactive development of applied analysis as a case leader elicits responses from a group. These advantages of the case method are now being taken to a new level with future-oriented case studies and cases supported by computer simulation models.

Future-Oriented Cases

In future-oriented cases, the material is brought alive by making it relevant to the specific problems a national or global organization needs to solve. First, participants challenge the conventional wisdom of how an industry will grow. Discussion, background research, and expert advice draw out the slow-moving trends that affect the business and demonstrate important ways in which an industry will differ in the future. For example, in preparing "Johnson & Johnson 2002," case writers conducted over 100 interviews in six countries to assess key issues in Johnson & Johnson's businesses and to reflect global challenges and possible discontinuities.

Second, participants focus on how actions by their own organizations help to create and mold the future. Managers begin to realize that it is within their ability to influence the external environment. In these situations, case leaders need to capture the existing wisdom of the group. At the same time, it is important not to be limited by the group, but to move beyond its initial level of understanding.

The third benefit of future-oriented cases is the least tangible, but it also has the greatest relevance for molding anticipatory learning inside an organization. Under the tutelage of good case leaders, managers of diverse functions develop a common understanding of the future environment they face. This common understanding has been called a "microcosm" or a "mental model" by the formulators of scenario planning. By forging shared mental models, managers can lay the foundation for more effective organizational coordination and for improved readiness for impending change.

Over a three-year period ending in 1995, the top 700 managers from over 100 Johnson & Johnson companies in 60 countries participated in an anticipatory learning program built around the "Global Health Products 2002" case. At first, people thought that the case was too optimistic and that change and technology would not evolve as quickly as presented in the case. By the end of the three-year period, however, participants began to say that the speed of change was too conservative.

At least three reasons can explain the difference in opinion. First, the pharmaceutical and medical equipment industries underwent very rapid change in the first half of the 1990s as third-party payers focused on cost containment. Second, the initial participants were from senior management, which is often slower to change its viewpoints. Third, many of the later participants were from non-U.S. subsidiaries, and they felt that the case reflected too much of a U.S.-based view of the future.

The business trends in the case were primarily extrapolations of current orientations. In retrospect, as a reflection of the organization's thinking at the start of the three-year period, these trends did not break the mold sufficiently. Overall, although the specific plan described in the case was less than 100 percent correct, the process of working through a view of the future with other participants was invaluable. The involvement from the middle layers of Johnson & Johnson increased the sense of participation in deciding the future direction of the organization, and the process moved certain issues from "not-considered" or "inactive" to the "active" set (Cyert and March, 1992).

Future-oriented cases, although similar to scenario planning, differ in one fundamental way. While scenario planning is often used by a planning group working in a staff capacity to learn for the organization as a whole, cases are a familiar management development tool that spur learning by individuals and foster common mental models across a broad spectrum of management.

CONCLUSION

The importance of robust mental models for economic success is increasingly recognized. Douglas North, 1993 Nobel Prize Laureate in Economics, used his acceptance speech as a chance to stress the importance of mental models as a component of the productive functioning of the economy and organizations (North, 1994). Scenario planning, future-oriented cases, and computer-based simulation models all encourage participation and foster learning for the future. In choosing these methods, senior executives can be sure that managers' mental models will be challenged and strengthened and that the dynamic nature of anticipatory learning will have a carryover effect into day-to-day tactical and strategic management.

In closing, a few general caveats are in order:

1. In preparing programs for anticipatory learning, issues about program objectives and content must be resolved at the outset. Be sure there is clarity about what objectives the programs are designed to accomplish, e.g., organizational learning, individual learning, initiation of change, or increased awareness.
2. Do not be limited by the existing wisdom of the group. Most executives find it difficult to project themselves into the future. Envisaging a slightly implausible future is the challenge.
3. Once managers have developed new visions of the future, try not to get locked into them. Managers need to remain flexible and to be prepared to react as the environment changes in unexpected ways.

REFERENCES

Baily, Michael and Ian Wilson (May, 1995). *Personal Conversation.* Northeast Consulting Resources and SRI International.

Cyert, Richard M. and James G. March (1992). *A Behavioral Theory of the Firm,* Second Edition. Cambridge, MA: Blackwell: 32, 45.

de Geus, Arie (1988). "Planning as learning." *Harvard Business Review,* 66 (6), November-December: 70-74.

Denzau, Arthur and Douglas C. North (1993). "Shared mental models: Ideologies and institutions." Washington University working paper.

Duncan, Norman and Pierre Wack (1994). "Scenarios designed to improve decision making." *Planning Review,* 22 (4), July-August: 18-25, 46.

Forrester, Jay W. (1961). *Industrial Dynamics.* Cambridge, MA: Productivity Press.

Forrester, Jay W. (1992). "Policies, decisions, and information sources for modeling." *European Journal of Operational Research,* 59:42-63.

Fulmer, Robert (1994). "A model for changing the way organizations learn." *Planning Review,* 22 (3), May-June: 21.

Graham, Alan K., John D. W. Morecroft, Peter M. Senge, and John D. Sterman (1992). "Model-supported case studies for management education." *European Journal of Operational Research,* 59:158-162.

Isaacs, William and Peter M. Senge (1992). "Overcoming limits to learning in computer-based learning environments." *European Journal of Operational Research,* 59:183-196.

Mason, David H. (1994). "Scenario-based planning: Decision model for the learning organization." *Planning Review,* 22 (2), March-April: 6-11.

Morecroft, John D. W. (1984). "Strategy support models." *Strategic Management Journal,* 5:227.

Millett, Stephen M. (1992a). "Battelle's scenario analysis of a European high-tech market." *Planning Review,* 20 (2), March-April: 20-23.

Millett, Stephen M. (1992b). "Los Angeles 2007: Implications of a scenario analysis for energy forecasting." *Planning Review,* 20 (3), May-June: 38-39.

Millett, Stephen M. and Fred Randles (1986). "Scenarios for strategic business planning: A case history for aerospace and defense companies." *Interfaces,* 16 (6), November-December: 64-72.

Nicholls, J. A. F. (1990). "People Express management flight simulator." *Social Science Computer Review,* 8 (3), Fall:465.

Nicholls, J. A. F. (1990). "The People Express flight simulator—a unique tool for management instruction." *Syllabus for the Macintosh,* January/February, (9): 6-7.

North, Douglas C. (1994). "Economic performance through time." *American Economic Review,* June:359-368.

Schoemaker, Paul J. H. (1991). "When and how to use scenario planning: A heuristic approach with illustration." *Journal of Forecasting,* 10: 550,557.

Schoemaker, Paul J. H. (1993). "Multiple scenario development: Its conceptual and behavioral foundation." *Strategic Management Journal,* 14 (3), March: 192-213.

Schoemaker, Paul J. H. and Cornelius A. J. M. van der Heijden (1992). "Integrating scenarios into strategic planning at Royal Dutch/Shell." *Planning Review,* 20 (3), May-June: 41-46.

Schwartz, Peter (1991). *The Art of the Long View.* New York: Doubleday Currency: 30-123. In the book, Schwartz describes his assignments for Shell, Weyerhauser, Smith & Hawken, and Pacific Gas & Electric and explains the mechanisms behind scenario planning.

Senge, Peter M. (1990). *The Fifth Discipline: The Art and Practice of the Learning Organization.* New York: Doubleday Currrency: Chapter 17.

Senge, Peter M. and John D. Sterman (1992). "Systems thinking and organizational learning: Acting locally and thinking globally in the organization of the future." *European Journal of Operational Research,* 59:137-150.

Sterman, John D. (1989). "Misperceptions of feedback in dynamic decision making." *Organizational Behavior and Human Decision Processes,* 43: 301-335.

Sterman, John D. (1992). "Teaching takes off: Flight simulators for management education." *OR/MS Today*, October:40-44. These games and others are available through Professor John Sterman, Sloan School of Management, MIT, 30 Wadsworth Avenue, Cambridge, MA 02142.

Sterman, John D. (1994). "Learning in and about complex systems." *System Dynamics Review*, 10 (2-3), Summer-Fall:291-330.

Tenaglia, Mason and Patrick Noonan (1992). "Scenario-based strategic planning: A process for building top management consensus." *Planning Review*, 20 (2), March-April: 12-19.

Wack, Pierre (1985a). "Scenarios: The gentle art of reperceiving." *Harvard Business Review*, 63 (5), September-October: 73-89.

Wack, Pierre (1985b). "Scenarios: Shooting the rapids." *Harvard Business Review*, 63 (6), November-December: 140.

Chapter 7

A Culture-General Assimilator: Preparation for Various Types of Sojourns

Richard W. Brislin

INTRODUCTION

The cross-cultural training materials described in this chapter (published in a second edition as Cushner and Brislin, 1996) were designed to be useful in a wide variety of orientation programs regardless of the countries in which people will live or the roles they will assume (e.g., businessperson, international student, diplomat). Further, the materials were designed to be applicable to training programs aimed at improving communication and facilitating interaction among members of different ethnic groups within any one country. Since the basic unit of these materials is the critical incident, and since the materials were designed following suggested guidelines for culture assimilator development (Fiedler, Mitchell, and Triandis, 1971; Albert, 1983), we are calling the result a "culture-general assimilator."

RATIONALE FOR MATERIALS DEVELOPMENT

The basic assumption behind the development of a generally applicable set of training materials is that there are extensive com-

Reprinted with permission of author and publisher. From Richard W. Brislin, "A Culture-General Assimilator: Preparation for Various Types of Sojourns," in R. M. Paige (Ed.), 1993, *Education for the Intercultural Experience*, Yarmouth, ME: Intercultural Press, pp. 281-299.

129

monalities in the experiences of people who interact with culturally different others. These commonalities occur despite differences in the exact jobs people have or despite differences in the exact place where the intercultural interaction takes place. In preparing a broad overview of the wide range of issues and problems involved in cross-cultural encounters (Brislin, 1981), I was struck by the similarities in the intercultural interaction literature even though the material was gathered from very different parts of the library. There are sections of the library where materials on international students can be found, another section concerned with the experiences of businesspeople, another on interpreters and translators, another on Peace Corps volunteers, still another on diplomats, and so forth. There were also materials in other sections of the library on interaction among citizens of one country, such as research reports on the adjustment of immigrants or the experiences of teachers and students in recently desegregated schools. Yet upon studying these materials, we found that the experiences of people are very similar. For instance, all have frustrations while trying to communicate with culturally different others. All have to make adjustments in familiar, habitual patterns of behavior to interact effectively with others. All observe behaviors which are difficult to interpret, and all experience confrontations with their prejudices. Further, looking at the encounters in a positive light, all people have the potential to grow and to develop as a result of their cross-cultural experiences.

To digress just slightly, these commonalities may explain why people who have interacted extensively with people from other cultures frequently form friendships with each other (Useem and Useem, 1967). These friendships occur even when the cultures they experienced were different and they have no roles in common. For instance, a former Peace Corps volunteer in India may develop a friendship with a businessperson who worked in Sweden, and both may have extensive interaction with a social worker who works with refugee communities. A well-known principle in the study of interpersonal relationships is that similarity leads to attraction (Bryne, 1971). The similarity in the experiences of people who have had extensive intercultural interaction is the commonalities under discussion throughout this chapter.

Given the assumption of commonality, it was thought that a set of materials could be developed which deal with the experiences, feelings, and thoughts that are typically encountered during cross-cultural interactions. There would be a number of potential benefits. One is that there could be more communication across the specialist roles of people who work with the various types of participants in cross-cultural interaction. Examples are social workers who design job programs for immigrants, international student advisors, Peace Corps trainers, and personnel officers in multinational corporations. Another benefit is that if commonalities could be pinpointed, they could form the basis for identifying widely shared concepts which all professionals in intercultural communication would know and use. One reason why the study of intercultural communication and cross-cultural orientation has not advanced as fast as it might is the relative paucity of widely shared concepts. With few shared concepts, there is little possibility for serious conversations about, or for in-depth analysis of, people's cross-cultural experiences. If professionals, in their discussions and presentations, go beyond the few relatively well-known ideas such as culture shock (Oberg, 1958), U- and W-shaped adjustment curves (Gullahorn and Gullahorn, 1963), and cultural differences in the use of time and space (Hall, 1959, 1966), they have to be very careful to ensure that their audience is familiar with their terminology. Another benefit is that the identification of commonalities allows the participants in cross-cultural training programs to develop a framework which assists them in interpreting their forthcoming experiences. Often, participants in orientation programs complain that while the material presented was interesting and the staff well prepared and concerned, the content was hard to organize in their minds (Ptak, Cooper, and Brislin, 1995). So much is presented that too great a burden is placed on information-processing skills and on the ability to remember specific facts. If the orientation program can be organized around a framework consisting of the feelings, thoughts, and experiences which people will almost surely have, then participants are likely to bring newfound knowledge to their cross-cultural encounters rather than to leave the knowledge at the training program site (Bhawuk, 1990).

THE CULTURE-ASSIMILATOR FORMAT

The format chosen for the development of the training materials was that of the culture assimilator (Fiedler, Mitchell, and Triandis, 1971), also called the "culture sensitizer." Of all the various cross-cultural training techniques, the culture assimilator has been subjected to the largest number of empirical research studies (see Albert, 1983; Cushner, 1989; Cushner and Brislin, 1996 for reviews). In the past, culture assimilators were designed for people from one specific and named country who were (1) about to live in another specific and named country, or (2) about to interact with a specified minority group their own country. For example, assimilators have been designed for citizens of the United States about to live in Thailand and for white, middle-class company employees about to interact in the workplace with newly hired African Americans. In an assimilator, there are approximately 100 incidents involving miscommunication and/or problematic interaction among members of different cultural groups, alternative explanations of the incidents, and discussions about the appropriateness of each alternative. Learning takes place as participants in a training program choose one or more of the alternative explanations and then find out the reasons for the correctness or incorrectness of their choice(s). Evidence exists (Malpass and Salancik, 1977) to suggest that participants benefit from reading discussions of all the alternative explanations, both those that they choose as correct and those that they implicitly or explicitly label as incorrect. "Correctness of choice" is determined by a validation procedure in which members of the host or target culture give their judgments concerning the various explanations for any one incident. In the two examples mentioned above, the validation process would involve Thai nationals and African-American workers, respectively.

In the development of the culture-general assimilator, 106 incidents were written which attempted to capture experiences, feelings, and thoughts which virtually all sojourners encounter. These incidents were written to provide concrete examples of eighteen themes (to be discussed later), or commonalities, which the developers felt were central to an understanding of cross-cultural experiences. These incidents can also be grouped according to eight categories that reflect the social context of the cross-cultural interactions, or the obvious subject matter of the incidents. These categories can also provide the basis of various sessions within a longer training program.

host customs	the workplace
interactions with hosts	the family
settling in	schooling
tourist experiences	returning home

The more subtle, and perhaps more important, aspects of the incidents are discussed as the eighteen themes are introduced and explained. The distinction between the eight categories and the eighteen themes might be confusing. Basically, the eight categories allow the 100 to be grouped into units which are familiar to workshop participants. The eighteen themes examine the underlying, more subtle aspects of the incidents, and these themes are very frequently not part of participants' vocabulary and thinking prior to the cross-cultural training program. One of the major assumptions of the culture-general assimilator is that if these eighteen themes are understood, they provide an effective framework for the sophisticated analysis of people's actual intercultural experiences subsequent to the training program.

For the development of a culture-general assimilator, the people who would constitute the validation sample could not be from any one country. Rather, the reasoning was that since a culture-general assimilator should be able to assist in preparing people no matter what their role and no matter where they will be interacting, then the validation sample should reflect this diversity. For this project, then, a validation sample consisting of sixty people was chosen with the following characteristics:

1. All had lived in another country for two years or more or had extensive interaction with minority groups within their own country for a similar period of time.
2. All had (or have) jobs which necessitated extensive interaction with culturally different people; for example, Peace Corps volunteers, teachers in overseas schools, diplomats, overseas busi-

nesspeople, social workers involved in programs for refugees, international students, immigrants, and so forth.

3. All were interested in reviewing their cross-cultural experiences and bringing them to bear on the assimilator materials, as shown by their willingness to volunteer the six to eight hours necessary to read and make judgments about the 106 critical incidents.

In addition, all members of the validation sample were over twenty-five years of age, ranging up to seventy-one, with an average age of forty-two. All continents except Antarctica were represented in the list of places where the people had lived. There were thirty-two females and twenty-eight males. Twenty-eight members of the sample had published articles in professional journals concerned with cross-cultural training and/or communication.

More details on the nature of the validation sample's task can be found in the introductory chapter to the cultural-general assimilator (Brislin et al., 1986; Cushner and Brislin, 1996). Briefly, based on the responses to the appropriateness of the explanations for each of the incidents, 100 of the 106 original incidents were clear, unambiguous, and led to a consensus with respect to correct explanations. Thus the final culture-general assimilator is based on these 100 validated incidents (Brislin et al., 1986). The second edition (Cushner and Brislin, 1996), has 110 validated incidents, and this is the edition referred to in the rest of this chapter.

Examples and Advantages of Critical Incidents

The best way to introduce these training materials is to examine and to discuss one of the 110 incidents. The decisions made at various points concerning the training materials should be clearer if they are applied to a specific case. In an actual training program, participants would read the following incident, ponder the question, and judge the adequacy of all the alternative explanations. It is best to judge the adequacy of all the alternatives since successful cross-cultural communication involves rejecting incorrect explanations as well as making appropriate conclusions.

LEARNING THE ROPES

Henry Connor had been working in a Japanese company involved in marketing cameras. He had been in Japan for two years and was well respected by his colleagues. In fact, he was so respected that he often was asked to work with new employees of the firm as these younger employees learned the ropes. One recent young employee, Hideo Tanaka, was assigned to develop a marketing scheme for a new-model camera. He worked quite hard on it, but the scheme was not accepted by his superiors because of industry-wide economic conditions. Henry Connor and Hideo Tanaka happened to be working at nearby desks when the news of the nonacceptance was transmitted from company executives. Hideo Tanaka said very little when he heard. That evening, however, Henry and Hideo happened to be at the same bar. Hideo had been drinking and Henry overheard him vigorously criticize his superiors at work. Henry concluded that Hideo was a very aggressive Japanese male and that he would have difficulty working with him again in the future.

Which alternative provides an accurate statement about Henry's conclusion?

1. Henry was making an inappropriate judgment about Hideo's traits based on behavior that he observed.
2. Since, in Japan, decorum in public is highly valued, Henry reasonably concluded that Hideo's vigorous criticism in the bar marks him as a difficult co-worker.
3. Company executives had failed to tell Henry and Hideo about economic conditions, and consequently Henry should be upset with the executives, not Hideo.
4. Henry felt that Hideo was attacking him personally.

Rationales

For Alternative 1, Trainees Would Read:

This is the best answer. When observing the behavior of others, a very common error is to draw conclusions about the traits or qualities of those others. Here those judgments (called attributions) are that

Hideo is aggressive and hard to work with. There is much less tendency to take into account the immediate factors in the situation which could also cause the behavior, such as the frustration upon hearing bad news. Interestingly, if Henry had been asked to interpret his own behavior had he gotten angry, he would undoubtedly have said something like, "Well, wouldn't you be angry if a plan you had worked hard on ended up being rejected?" In addition, vigorous behavior in bars is an acceptable outlet in Japan. People are not supposed to make permanent conclusions about others based on the "bar behavior" they see. But in analyzing the behavior of others, there is much less tendency to take into account such immediate factors of the situation or social context. This error—making trait judgments about others and not taking situational factors into account—has been called the fundamental attribution error (see Ross, 1977; Gilbert and Malone, 1995) and is probably more prevalent in cross-cultural encounters, since there is so much behavior that is new and different to sojourners. When abroad, sojourners often make more attributions about people and events than they would in their own countries. Even though Henry has been in Japan for two years, there will still be many new experiences that call forth judgments or attributions from him.

For Alternative 2, Trainees Would Read:

Certainly a common observation about Japan is that decorum is highly valued. Yet people do become angry and upset. Rather than jumping to a conclusion, it is usually better to go beyond the common observation or stereotype (in this case the frequently noted value placed on proper decorum) and to analyze in more detail the specific instance. If a person has been exposed only to the common observation, then he or she is ill prepared for behaviors (which will inevitably be encountered on a long sojourn) that are at odds with the general observation. An important point is that vigorous behavior in bars is an acceptable outlet in Japan. Permanent conclusions should not be made based on "bar behavior," Japanese hosts tell us. Please choose again.

For Alternative 3, Trainees Would Read:

Henry and Hideo, if they are capable professionals, should know about industry-wide conditions on their own. While Hideo might be expected to take into account these conditions before his reaction to the nonacceptance of his plan, a highly abstract and nonimmediate thought like "industry-wide conditions" rarely wipes out the frustration of seeing hard work leading to no visible reward. Please choose again.

For Alternative 4, Trainees Would Read:

This could be part of the interpretation. There is a strong tendency on the part of people, upon seeing the negative behavior of others, to wonder if they somehow were involved. Since Henry had been working with Hideo, such feelings would be natural. During cross-cultural experiences, this tendency is probably stronger. Since Henry and Hideo have not worked together long and are still learning things about each other, Henry is not going to be able to readily interpret all of Hideo's actions. Since he is not intimately knowledgeable about Japanese culture after two years there, he will be motivated to wonder even more if he is somehow personally involved. Because of felt personal involvement, any of Henry's final conclusions will be even more intense. There is another explanation which focuses on a mistake Henry could be making in his thinking. Please choose again.

A striking fact about the incident is that even though it was designed for a culture-general assimilator, it deals with behavior taking place in a specific country. Indeed, this is true for all 110 incidents—they take place in specific countries, although in different countries for different incidents. There are a number of reasons for choosing to specify settings. One is that the critical incidents are much more interesting to read if the settings are noted, characters created, a plot line developed, and conclusions reached involving a misunderstanding between people from different cultural backgrounds. In pretest work with training participants, people were uncomfortable if a more general setting was indicated, such as "an Asian country." People asked, "Which one?" Another reason is that specifying the exact country sometimes helps people to choose correct responses or to eliminate inappropriate responses. Actual cross-cultural interaction involves figuring out problems and trying to discover the reasons for communication difficulties in specific other cultures. Knowing the exact place where the assimilator incident takes place adds an air of specificity and reality to the exercise. In the case of countries like Japan, readers, even though they have not lived there, often have some knowledge of the culture because of the country's frequent mention in the popular press.

Consequently, the choice was made to create incidents which take place in a specific country. A very important point, however, is that correct responses to the 110 incidents rarely demand knowledge of a particular aspect of the country's culture. In the above incident, for example, there are two good explanations (numbers 1 and 4), but neither involves an aspect of culture or behavior specific to Japan. Rather, the correct explanations, as well as the discussions of the incorrect alternatives, involve issues typical of any extensive cross-cultural interaction. In this incident, these issues include (1) over-reacting to colorful incidents, (2) the trait-situation distinction, (3) the fundamental attribution error, (4) avoiding stereotypes (Jussim, Eccles, and Madon, 1996), (5) acceptable outlets for aggressive feelings, and (6) feeling personally attacked. These are the sorts of issues which could be discussed in any training program where these materials are used.

In creating the 100 incidents, the developers tried to appeal to people's basic interest in human relationships. A major complaint about many cross-cultural training programs, voiced by both participants and trainers, is that the materials have little meaning for the participant. Given that participants have not had much cross-cultural experience prior to training, material depicting life in another culture often seems irrelevant. Of course, trainees see the relevance after some actual cross-cultural experience, but this fact does not help the administrators of preexperience (usually called predeparture) training programs. The developers of the culture-general assimilator attempted to tackle this problem by creating incidents in which the characters have problems to which the trainees can relate. In the incident presented above, for instance, the assumption was made that everyone, at one time or another, has been tempted to react too quickly to colorful incidents, or has felt personally attacked by someone else. Trainees can thus relate to the characters in the incidents and learn about cross-cultural interaction by analyzing how these common human experiences are played out when people are interacting across cultural boundaries.

There are other advantages to materials based on critical incidents. The incidents, since they depict real people attempting to make a good cross-cultural adjustment, are inherently interesting. Workshop participants want to know what happened to the people depicted in the incident. Readers of this chapter, for instance, would undoubtedly be frustrated if there were no analysis of the four alternative explanations for the critical incident reviewed above. Further, the incidents capture problems which the participants will actually experience during their cross-cultural interaction. Any of the critical incidents can form the basis of role-play scenarios, should workshop participants want to play out the encounters during the orientation program and then discuss their reactions. Of course, such an approach would take place only in workshops where the administrators are comfortable and experienced with this more active approach to cross-cultural orientation (see Landis and Brislin, 1983; Bhawuk, 1990; and Brislin and Yoshida, 1994) for discussion of various approaches to orientation). Much information about cross-cultural experience comes out of discussions of the incidents. Participants learn such information relatively painlessly as they attempt to discover whether their choices regarding correct and incorrect alternatives match the analyses of the experienced, sixty-member validation sample. Finally, participants can retain a copy of the 110 incidents and explanations so that they can be referred to after the workshop so as to help in the interpretation of their actual cross-cultural encounters.

THE THEMES AROUND WHICH THE ONE HUNDRED INCIDENTS WERE DEVELOPED

As discussed previously, a major assumption is that there are commonalities in people's cross-cultural experiences. To explore these commonalities in the 110 critical incidents, eighteen themes were identified which are central to understanding people's cross cultural interactions. These eighteen themes were gathered in the development of several publishing projects designed to provide broad and extensive treatment of both cross-cultural interaction and cross-cultural orientation programs (Brislin, 1981; Landis and Brislin, 1983), and longer discussions can be found in those sources. These eighteen themes provide a framework for the analysis of specific experiences people have during their cross cultural interaction. The eighteen themes themselves are grouped according to three broader categories: emotional experiences, knowledge areas, and the bases of cultural differences.

Emotional Experiences Brought About by Encounters with Cultural Differences

1. *Anxiety.* Since people will encounter many unfamiliar demands, they will be anxious about whether or not their behavior is appropriate.
2. *Disconfirmed expectancies.* People may become upset not because of the exact set of situations they encounter in the host culture, but because the situations differ from those which they expected.
3. *Belonging.* People want to feel accepted by others and want to feel at home, but they often cannot, since they have the status of outsiders.
4. *Ambiguity.* The messages people receive in other cultures are often unclear and give little guidance for decisions about behavior that is acceptable to their hosts.
5. *Confrontation with one's prejudices.* People discover that previous attitudes which they learned during their socialization in their own cultures simply are not useful when interacting in another culture.

Knowledge Areas Which Incorporate Many Specific Cross-Cultural Differences and Which Sojourners Find Hard to Understand

6. *Work.* Many cultural differences are encountered in the workplace, such as attitudes toward creative effort and the proper relationship between on-task time and social interaction.
7. *Time and space.* Varying attitudes exist regarding the importance of being on time to meetings, as well as to the proper space people maintain when interacting with each other.
8. *Language.* Perhaps the most obvious problem to overcome in crossing cultural boundaries is that of language differences. Attitudes

toward language use, and the difficulties of learning language as it is actually spoken rather than from a book, are part of this knowledge area.

9. *Roles.* As a result of being socialized in their own cultures, sojourners are accustomed to a set of generalizations regarding who plays what roles or performs what sets of related behaviors. Examples of roles are the family provider, the boss, the volunteer, the leader, and so forth. Large differences exist with respect to the occupants of these roles and how they are enacted in other cultures.

10. *Importance of the group and the importance of the individual.* All people act, at times, out of their individual interests and at other times, out of their membership in groups. The relative emphasis on individual and group allegiances varies from culture to culture. This dichotomy is also called "individualism-collectivism" (Triandis, Brislin, and Hui, 1988).

11. *Rituals and superstitions.* All cultures have rituals to meet the needs of people as they cope with life's everyday demands, and people in all cultures engage in behaviors that outsiders can easily call superstitious.

12. *Hierarchies: Class and status.* The relative importance placed on class distinctions and the markers of high versus low status differ from culture to culture. The amount of power people have is related to their status.

13. *Values.* People's experiences with such things as religion, economics, politics, aesthetics, and interpersonal relationships become internalized. Understanding these internalized views, called values, is critical in cross-cultural adjustment.

The Bases of Cultural Difference, Especially Concerning How People in Different Cultures Think About and Evaluate Information

14. *Categorization.* Since not all pieces of information can be attended to, people group bits of information into categories for more efficient organization. People in different cultures place the same individual elements into different categories (e.g., who is a friend, what a good worker does), causing confusion for people accustomed to another set of categories. Stereotypes are categories that deal with people.

15. *Differentiation.* One result of increased interest in, or importance of, a certain knowledge area is that more and more information is differentiated within that area so that new categories are formed, for example, the kinds of obligations which accompany various types of interpersonal relationships or the ways one overcomes red tape. If outsiders do not differentiate information in the same manner as hosts, they may be treated as naive or ignorant.

16. *In-group/out-group distinction.* In-group refers to people with whom interaction is sought. Out-group members are held at a distance and are often the targets of rejection. People entering another culture have to be sensitive to the fact that they will often be out-group members and that there are some behaviors associated with in-group membership in which they will never participate.

17. *Change and growth, as well as the possibility for self-improvement, involve new learning styles.* Even though people desire change and improvement, the style in which they best learn new information differs from culture to culture and often from person to person.

18. *Attribution.* People observe the behavior of others and make judgments about the causes of that behavior. These judgments are called attributions. The same behavior, such as a suggestion for how a proposal can be improved, may be judged as helpful in one culture but insulting in another.

Each of these eighteen themes is examined in five or six of the critical incidents. In addition, there are essays on each of these themes which pull together and expand the various ideas which were introduced in the discussions of the 110 incidents.

USES FOR A CULTURE-GENERAL ASSIMILATOR

The culture-general assimilator can be used in a number of ways and with various types of workshop audiences. It should be mentioned that this assimilator is not intended to replace culture-specific training. Take the example of people about to travel to other countries. There will always be a need for specific information about a country for those sojourners about to go to live there. For instance, if I were about to accept an assignment in Saudi Arabia, I would want to have detailed information about limits which will be placed on my behavior, support groups, avocations or interests which I can and cannot pursue, working conditions, key aspects of the culture which sojourners find difficult to understand, legal sanctions for misbehavior, the impact of American military presence, and so forth. But even in such a program, to prepare people for life in one country, a culture-general assimilator can play a complementary role to the culture-specific training. This and other uses of the general package will now be discussed. For convenience, the examples will be drawn from the experience of sojourners living abroad, though examples could also be drawn from different ethnic groups within the same country.

Culture-Specific Training

At times, financial considerations will work against a culture-specific program. There may not be enough people going to any one other country to make such training possible. For instance, study-abroad students at a university often fan out to a large number of different countries. The person in charge of training, such as the study-abroad coordinator or the international student advisor, may not have the funds for culture-specific training corresponding to each destination. At times, people (e.g., military personnel, business-people) know that they will be going abroad, but don't know until the last minute their exact country of assignment. In such cases, a culture-general assimilator can be very useful.

Even in cases where there are a large number of workshop participants going to one country, the culture-general materials can be helpful. For example, the general assimilator can provide an outline of what might be covered in culture-specific training, which is sometimes implemented by asking people who have lived in the specific country to talk and/or to lead sessions. But what do they talk about, and what is the content of their sessions? Although these resource people undoubtedly know a great deal, they sometimes have a difficult time deciding what to say and how to organize the presentation. But if they do go through the list of eighteen themes and examine the 110 incidents, they will undoubtedly be reminded of important specific information which they can cover. For example, they might be reminded about key problems in understanding the in-group/out-group distinction (Theme 16) in that country or specific work attitudes which sojourners should know about (Theme 6). Such resource people may also be able to modify some of the incidents slightly so that they are exactly applicable to the specific country. For instance, with minor modifications the full incident presented above can be used for culture-specific training designed for most Asian countries.

In longer training programs, the general assimilator can be used for sessions devoted to experiencing extensive cross-cultural inter-action, while other materials can be used in sessions devoted to preparing for life in the specific country. One caveat has to be mentioned. If the materials are to be used as part of culture-specific training, participants must have some intellectual interest in the eighteen themes and in the potential generalizability of the 110 incidents. They must find it intriguing to examine the incidents and themes and make modifications so that they can apply the ideas to their own cross-cultural experiences. If trainees are looking only for specific advice that they can use tomorrow in their own precise jobs within their specific communities, then the culture-general assimilator is not the best material to use.

Professionals Who Work with a Multicultural Clientele

There are many professionals who deal with so many different cultural groups that a general training approach is most appropriate for workshops designed to develop their cross-cultural skills. Ex-amples of such professionals are international student advisors, counselors who see clients from many different ethnic groups, teachers in multicultural school districts, social workers, college professors who attract students from different countries, and per-sonnel officers in multinational organizations that send business-people to various countries. Workshops designed around preparing for extensive cross-cultural interaction are more appropriate for the training needs of these professionals than are culture-specific orientation programs. In addition, some people who are typically thought of as having experiences in one country actually have expe-riences in several. Businesspeople in multinational organizations may be sent on troubleshooting trips to offices in several countries. Students on study abroad programs live in one specific country but often travel to others during vacation breaks and as part of their return trips to their own countries.

College Students

Professors face a problem in teaching courses in the broad area known as international studies (Spodek, 1983)—cross-cultural psychology, intercultural communication, international economics, transnational political organizations, multicultural education, and so forth. The problem is that the typical college student has had little cross-cultural or international experience. Many college students find attempts to introduce concepts such as the influence of culture on behavior overly foreign, dull, or irrelevant. The exceptions to the rule are students who have had a cross-cultural experience, such as former Peace Corps volunteers or participants in one of the youth exchange programs (e.g., Experiment in International Living, AFS International, Youth for Understanding). Professors have long applauded the interest and performance of such students in internationally oriented courses. One possibility is to use the culture-general assimilator with college students to determine if it can substitute for an actual cross-cultural experience. As mentioned previously, the incidents were written so that all readers could relate to them, given the basic concerns in human relationships being examined. The importance of culture is introduced in the discussion of each incident, so readers learn about cultural differences (and similarities) as they work through the assimilator.

Even though the lack of extensive cross-cultural experience among students is decried, many if not most have had some contact, however limited, with people who are culturally different. At times, the incidents will remind students of an encounter which they had previously not thought about, such as the presence of an international student in one of their classes or a chat with a minority-group peer. The assimilator, then, may draw out experiences which students had not thought important at the time they occurred. After learning about the importance of culture, students may become more interested in their internationally oriented coursework. It should be mentioned, however, that these curriculum suggestions have not yet been empirically verified. Recent research at the East-West Center involves testing the suggestions in undergraduate courses.

Two research projects have explored the use of the culture-general assimilator in undergraduate college classes. In both studies, the research design included randomly selected experimental groups, whose members studied assimilator incidents, and control groups, whose members studied other material related to the goals of their course. Broaddus (1986) found that students using the assimilator developed greater empathy for people from cultural groups other than their own. Combining the culture-general assimilator within a cooperative group-learning framework, Ilola (1989) found that students were able to identify the underlying issues involved in intercultural difficulties after working with assimilator incidents and essays. They also showed much more sophistication in analyzing personal incidents from their own lives. In both studies, students exposed to the culture-general assimilator were better able to solve new intercultural problems to which they had not been exposed during their classroom instruction. Both studies also documented student enthusiasm for use of the culture-general assimilator as one of their texts. In a related study that again had experimental and control groups formed through random assignment, Cushner (1989) found that teenage students participating in an exchange program in New Zealand benefited in various ways from the analysis of the culture-general assimilator incidents and essays. They demonstrated better adjustment to a new culture, were more efficient at identifying reasonable outcomes when dealing with problems and were able to identify the means to achieve those outcomes, increased their understanding of the dynamics that mediate intercultural interaction and adjustment, and could apply that understanding to personal incidents in their own lives

Returning Study-Abroad Participants

There are several seriously underused resources on college campuses which, if better marshaled, could improve the institutions' international orientation efforts. One is the presence of international students (Mestenhauser, 1983; Paige, 1990). Another is the presence of returned study-abroad participants. Often, there is little attempt to build upon students' international experience during their remaining time in college (e.g., during the senior year if study abroad was for the junior year). Consequently, returning students are both ignored and underutilized. A frequent complaint is that "no one is interested in hearing about anything I learned." In some cases, the benefits of the cross-cultural experience are undoubtedly lost due to the lack of follow-up attention.

Sometimes students could do more on their own, but their cross-cultural experiences are unintegrated, poorly understood, or confusing. Presenting them with the culture-general assimilator after their experiences may help them to integrate what they have learned. The eighteen themes, for instance, may provide a conceptual map which allows an organizational framework for their specific experiences. This after-experience recommendation follows from one of the more interesting points in the research literature on cross-cultural training: training can be more effective for people who have already had some cross-cultural experience (O'Brien, Fiedler, and Hewlett, 1971). The probable explanation is that experienced trainees can better relate to the workshop offerings. They have experiences which make the training materials interesting, relevant, and meaningful. In the case of the culture-general assimilator, experienced readers should find stimulation in comparing their own experiences with those depicted in the 110 critical incidents and determining if the concepts presented in the assimilator aid in integrating their previously disparate thoughts and feelings.

CONCLUSION

By working through the materials in the culture-general assimilator (Cushner and Brislin, 1996), people can prepare themselves to become more effective when working in cultures other than their own. People become exposed to both typical intercultural experiences by examining 110 critical incidents and learn to put these and other incidents into a framework based on eighteen themes. A major goal of training is for people to learn to use these eighteen themes, since trainees will later be able to interpret *their own specific* intercultural experiences according to a helpful framework. The type of intercultural analysis provided by the framework can provide a helpful language, or a helpful set of concepts, that people can use when dealing with difficulties that are brought on during their intercultural interactions. This language, or set of concepts, allows discussions of differences that do not threaten people since the focus is on cultural differences and recurring issues in intercultural interactions, not on the qualities and traits of individuals.

REFERENCES

Albert, Rosita (1983). "The intercultural sensitizer or culture assimilator: A cognitive approach." In Dan Landis and Richard Brislin (Eds.), *Handbook of intercultural training,* Vol. 2. Elmsford, NY: Pergamon, pp. 186-217.

Bhawuk, D. P. S. (1990). "Cross-cultural orientation programs." In Richard Brislin (Ed.), *Applied cross-cultural psychology.* Newbury Park, CA: Sage.

Brislin, Richard (1981). *Cross-cultural encounters: Face-to-face interaction.* Elmsford, NY: Pergamon.

Brislin, Richard, Kenneth Cushner, Craig Cherrie, and Mahealani Yong (1986). *Intercultural interactions: A practical guide.* Beverly Hills, CA: Sage.

Brislin, Richard, and Tomoko Yoshida (1994). *Intercultural communication training: An introduction.* Newbury Park, CA: Sage.

Broaddus, Darrell (1986). "Use of the culture-general assimilator in intercultural training." Doctoral dissertation, Indiana State University, Terre Haute, IN.

Bryne, Donn (1971). *The attraction paradigm.* New York: Academic Press.

Cushner, Kenneth (1989). "Assessing the impact of a culture-general assimilator." *International Journal of Intercultural Relations,* 13:125-126.

Cushner, Kenneth, and Richard Brislin (1996). *Intercultural interactions: A practical guide* (2nd ed.). Thousand Oaks, CA: Sage.

Fiedler, Fred, Terence Mitchell, and Harry Triandis (1971). "The culture assimilator: An approach to cross-cultural training." *Journal of Applied Psychology,* 55: 95-102.

Gilbert, Daniel, and Patrick Malone (1995). "The correspondence bias." *Psychological Bulletin,* 117: 21-38.

Gullahorn, John, and Jeanne Gullahorn (1963). "An extension of the U-curve hypothesis." *Journal of Social Issues,* 19 (3): 33-47.

Hall, Edward T. (1959). *The silent language.* Garden City, NY: Doubleday.

Hall, Edward T. (1966). *The hidden dimension.* Garden City, NY: Doubleday.

Ilola, Lisa Marie (1989). "Intercultural interaction for preservice teachers using the culture-general assimilator with a peer interactive approach." Doctoral dissertation, University of Hawaii, Honolulu.

Jussim, Lee, Jacquelynne Eccles, and Stephanie Madon (1996). "Social perception, social stereotypes, and teacher expectations: Accuracy and the quest for the powerful self-fulfilling prophecy." In Mark Zanna (Ed.), *Advances in experimental social psychology,* Vol. 28, pp. 281-388. San Diego, CA: Academic Press.

Landis, Dan, and Richard Brislin (Eds.) (1983). *Handbook of intercultural training* (3 vols.). Elmsford, NY: Pergamon.

Malpass, Roy S., and Gerald R. Salancik (1977). "Linear and branching formats in culture assimilator training." *International Journal of Intercultural Relations,* 1: 76-87.

Mestenhauser, Josef (1983). "Learning from sojourners." In Dan Landis and Richard Brislin (Eds.), *Handbook of intercultural training,* Vol. 2. Elmsford, NY: Pergamon.

Oberg, Kalvero (1958). "Culture shock and the problem of adjustment to new cultural environments." Washington, DC: Department of State, Foreign Service Institute.

O'Brien, Gordon, Fred Fiedler, and Tom Hewlett (1971). "The effects of programmed culture training upon the performance of volunteer medical teams in Central America." *Human Relations,* 24: 209-231.

Paige, R. Michael (1990). "International students: Cross-cultural psychological perspectives." In Richard Brislin (Ed.), *Applied cross cultural psychology.* Newbury Park, CA: Sage.

Ptak, Cynthia, Joanne Cooper, and Richard Brislin (1995). "Cross-cultural training programs: Advice and insights from experienced trainers." *International Journal of Intercultural Relations,* 19: 413-436.

Ross, Lee (1977). "The intuitive psychologist and his shortcomings: Distortion in the attribution process." In L. Berkowitz (Ed.). *Advances in experimental social psychology,* Vol. 10. New York: Academic Press.

Spodek, Howard (1983). "Integrating cross-cultural education in the postsecondary curriculum." In Dan Landis and Richard Brislin (Eds.). *Handbook of intercultural training,* Vol. 3. Elmsford, NY: Pergamon.

Triandis, Harry, Richard Brislin, and C. Harry Hui (1988). "Cross cultural training across the individualism-collectivism divide." *International Journal of Intercultural Relations,* 12: 269-289.

Useem, John, and Ruth Useem (1967). "The interfaces of a binational third culture: A study of the American community in India." *Journal of Social Issues,* 23 (1): 130-133.

Chapter 8

Action Learning: Executive Development of Choice for the 1990s

Louise Keys

At General Electric, teams chosen from the top 3,500 executives, are engaging in a nontraditional executive education program referred to as "action learning." At Harvard University, Michael Porter is using action learning to teach teams competitive strategy. The University of Michigan is enrolling companies in its international executive education action learning program. Action learning represents a new and revolutionary type of organizational learning that is erupting in U.S. companies today, as they seek to both teach and learn from their managers. Although this concept is new to the United States, globally speaking action learning is not new. It was introduced by Reg Revans and first referenced as early as October, 1945, in a report on the British coal mining industry. In the report Revans recommended the establishment of a staff college for the industry in which field managers would be encouraged to learn with and from each other using group review to find solutions to their immediate problems.

Since the British coal industry was nationalized, action learning took on another form in the coal mines, where the men who man-

Reprinted with permission of Louise M. Keys and publisher. First published in *Journal of Management Development* (MCB University Press) 13(8), pp. 50-56. Excerpts from Reg Revans, "What is Action Learning?" Reprinted with permission of author and publisher. First published in *Journal of Management Development*, 1(3), 1982, pp. 18-25.

aged the mines met at the mine sites and discussed problems and solutions they had observed. From the questions they learned to ask, they wrote their own handbook for running a coal mine (Revans, 1982).

WHAT IS ACTION LEARNING?

Revans captures the spirit of action learning with the following perceptive statement:

> When, in an epoch of change, tomorrow is necessarily different from yesterday, and so new things need to be done, what are the questions to be asked before the solutions are sought. Action learning differs from normal training (education development) in that its primary objective is to learn how to ask appropriate questions in conditions of risk, rather than to find the answers to questions that have already been precisely defined by others—and that do not allow for ambiguous responses because the examiners have all the approved answers. (Revans, 1982, p. 65)

Since its modest beginning in 1945, action learning has developed a constituency of practitioners throughout the world, generally traveling along the paths of British influence to Australia and Canada, and to the United States via U.S. firms with European units.

However, action learning generated little worldwide interest until 1975, when Sir Arnold Weinstock encouraged the General Electric Company to try action learning. The General Electric experience mentioned previously developed as a result of GE contacts in Europe.

To understand more clearly Revans' approach one must understand his learning theory. Learning, he suggests, consists of two interrelated components. The first is programmed knowledge (P), which is the traditional component called knowledge and often transmitted through books and lectures. The second component is questioning insight (Q), which is based on experience, or historical evidence, and creativity, and assists us in resolving problems for which solutions have previously been ascertained. Q is required when facing problems like many in the world today for which no historical solution exists (Jones, 1990). Revans constantly admonishes managers who possess the experience, not professors or consultants, to exercise leadership on Q. In action learning, the latter are relegated to assisting in managing the learning process and to offering supplemental knowledge that might expedite Q. Action learning teaches participants to "act themselves into a new way of thinking, rather than think themselves into a new way of acting" (Lawrie, 1989, p. 59).

A protege and a client of Revans have succinctly captured the steps in the classical action learning process (Lewis and March, 1987):

- The learning vehicle (must be) a current live problem owned by the individual manager. . . .
- The set teams must consist of several managers, each bringing their own problems. Often a mix of age, experience, ability, and diversity of work area is sought for each team.
- The set members learn from other members as they meet periodically to discuss problems at scheduled meetings and to test plans in the field.
- There are few, if any, planned inputs of knowledge or skill training (P).
- Often a set advisor (a professor or consultant) is present throughout the life of each team.
- The client(s), often top executives, agree to attend an evaluation meeting and listen to the results of the teams.

TRADITIONAL APPROACHES TO ACTION LEARNING

Since the early days in which action learning was developed by Revans, many variations of the classical system have been developed and implemented. As is usually the case, many companies and consultants have adopted the concept, often incorporating a few changes, and frequently giving it a new name, such as "live cases," "operating cases," "management action groups," "project-based development," "activity training," and so on.

Prudential Assurance

Prudential Assurance Company, England, is an example of a company that introduced a program of action learning in 1979, as a general management course for their 400 district managers. The program begins with a 1½ day action learning program, in which Prudential participants present problems of their choice to client groups (top executives) through the use of a "mind map" referred to as "the spider." This is essentially a pictorial representation of the team member's problem, designed to communicate it visually through the use of flip charts. Presentations by the participants initiate an "informed contract" with the client executive and are accompanied by detailed action plans for the first month of the program.

Prudential participants are also introduced to the "manager's learning diary," a short set of recorded notes and comments about problems learned from listening to team (set) members, as well as conclusions and response feelings of the participants (Lewis and March, 1987).

The presentations at Prudential are organized around five basic questions (Lewis and March, 1987):

- Where did I start?
- What have I done?
- What have I achieved?
- What have I learned?
- Where do I go from here?

Sri Lanka Institute

The Sri Lanka Institute of Development Administration (SLIDA) in Colombo adopted several action learning projects in 1988, following a British-sponsored visit by Reg Revans. A number of variations of action learning were adopted in response to the suggestions of Revans, which included (Jones, 1990):

1. A familiar problem in a familiar situation;
2. A familiar problem in an unfamiliar situation;
3. An unfamiliar problem in an unfamiliar situation, and
4. An unfamiliar problem in a familiar situation.

In one variation each participant was attached for ten days to a corporate division other than his employing division, to attack a problem in the host division. The movement away from familiar territory forced action learning members to ask basic probing questions and generated an independent point of view that could be characterized as questioning insight.

The action learning success story in Sri Lanka is significant due to its success in the persistent cultural bias of a society that includes a deep respect for authority figures—teachers and traditional knowledge experts.

UNIQUE ACTION LEARNING ADAPTATIONS

Strategic learning adaptations of the traditional approaches to action learning projects have developed in the past decade. Their designs, although similar in nature to the Revans model, have undergone adaptations in construction and integration with traditional management development approaches, in an effort to build upon programs already in place in companies.

TRW—Linking Strategy and Behavior Through Management Development

In recent years organizations have insisted that management development programs be linked to corporate strategies. These programs are expected to do more than cause managers to behave better. They are expected to enable executives to take actions that will accomplish corporate goals. TRW has adopted action learning precisely for this reason. A recent program focusing on the TRW value of customer satisfaction affirmed that participants, in order to meet their needs, can show great creativity in modifying the general structure of a project (Clover, 1991).

International Management Centers: An MBA Program Based on Action Learning

The International Management Center in Buckingham, England, conducts an open program, internationally, based almost exclusively on action learning (Caie, 1987). Managers select numerous projects throughout their years of matriculation on the way to an MBA or doctorate. These projects are completed and "written up" for credit. Professors drawn from an international pool provide some lectures, but more often play the role of set advisors. The program boasts 500 MBA graduates and lists as sponsoring organizations a number of Fortune 500 firms. Most programs have been conducted in Europe, Australia, and Southeast Asia (Margerison, 1988).

The Swedish Management Institute (MiL)

One organization that appears to have bridged the gap between strategic action learning and traditional management development approaches is the Swedish Management Institute (MiL). They host action learning programs of thirty to forty days duration, over nine-month periods, that intersperse seminars with action learning projects (Marsick, 1990). Their original "flagship" program includes managers from seven or more companies. MiL uses three learning tracks including projects, seminars, and the executives' personal jobs.

Some seminars prepare participants for project work and stimulate reflection about projects. Others include special topics of interest to client companies, such as cross-cultural team building or international market analysis. Each action learning track must have a sponsor, either one large company with many units, or a consortium of companies. The three learning tracks are coordinated within a common theme chosen by the sponsoring company or consortium. For example, a company engaged in a corporate merger might choose a common theme such as "creating a corporate culture." Related seminars would cluster around this theme and participants would be encouraged to bring their related personal problems to the program. Slots are left open for emerging problems that expand the theme as it develops.

At MiL the resource person in action learning projects is more likely to be a visiting manager from another company, an actor, or an artist. Every attempt is made to generate previously unasked questions. Such questioning usually results from conversations with persons from totally different occupations or from companies with different cultures. For this reason action learning experts usually recommend the inclusion of participants from different backgrounds—education, age, gender, ethnicity, experience, and functional specialties—who can share multiple viewpoints.

The General Electric and the University of Michigan Action Learning Programs

Similar to the Swedish Management Institute program, and perhaps building on this model, are the General Electric and University of Michigan programs of action learning.

General Electric

At General Electric, action learning problems are identified by the company's top executives, such as CEO Jack Welch or heads of major divisions. Sample questions posed in the past are: "What is the market for GE financial services in India?" "How can GE serve the automobile industry better?" "How does GE stack up against foreign competition such as Electrolux, Toshiba, and Asea Brown Boveri?" These are clearly problems to which answers are yet unknown (O'Reilly, 1993, p. 54).

GE teams take executive action to conduct research internationally, assisted by the information gathering skills of consultants and business school professors. Results are presented to the client executives who chose the question. Projects at GE are chosen so that they can be completed in a four-week period. This facilitates implementation of training but loses some of the learning that comes from long-term projects (Marsick, 1990).

The University of Michigan Global Leadership Program

After becoming acquainted with action learning while visiting General Electric as Director of Executive Education, Noel Tichy returned to the University of Michigan to establish a global leadership program using the concept (Galligan, 1990). Global sponsor companies were recruited, along with host countries Russia, Brazil, India, and China. The sponsor companies invested development monies and agreed to participate in action research projects. They also provided advisory group members for the program. Participants were fast-track company managers, grouped in teams of six, with the scheduled project of developing strategies for entering various international markets (O'Reilly, 1993). Teams chose countries to study and profile and visited three of them to become acquainted and establish contacts and develop networks.

The global leadership program adds to action learning the unique element of cross-cultural team development, through the enrollment of team members from countries throughout the world. Cross-cultural team building is fostered prior to group travel overseas. The mixed-nationality teams are also given country briefings and scheduled for an embassy visit. Other projects before going offshore include the task of building a global world model and critiquing team members' firms on a global scale. The cohesiveness of team members is accelerated by requiring they spend a weekend in an Outward-Bound program on Hurricane Island, Maine (Galligan, 1990).

Masato Murakami, general manager of human resource planning for Sony Corporation, reflected retrospectively on his experience in the program.

> I still have a very strong impression of the five weeks I spent in the global leadership program last summer . . . The most valuable part of the program for me was to spend five weeks getting to know people from various companies. I was able to see how a person from GE operates differently from a person from AT&T. (Galligan, 1990, p. 63)

Contrary to traditional wisdom about brief visits for international management development, Joel Beck, VP of U.S. Manufacturing, Bell Worldwide Information Systems, felt the teams "met the real movers and shakers." His response to the experience was, "I came away with an in-depth insight into the thinking of government ministers, heads of large corporations and financial institutions" (Galligan, 1990, p. 63).

Of course it should be noted that insight and understanding are still not "action"; therefore the global leadership program stops one step short of the classical action learning equation. Perhaps the investment is too large and the planning required too lengthy to expect participants to actually launch a new international initiative as part of an executive development project. Nevertheless, Reg Revans would probably be displeased with the lack of closure in these projects.

Harvard Business School

The programs at GE and Michigan have been very successful and seem to be influencing executive development at the best-known business program in the world, the Harvard Business School. At Harvard, the executive program, led by Michael Porter, links the classroom to the workplace with an action learning program in competitive strategy. Porter bases his course on the premise that "education is not truly valuable unless it is translated into action" (Jubilerer, 1991, p. 17). Dean Lorsch has acknowledged that Harvard is considering more extensive use of action learning in addition to the well-known and widely accepted Harvard Case Method.

SUMMARY

Action learning is a truly unique organizational learning process that requires an instructional mind-set usually absent in traditional instructors. Action learning is growing in acceptance around the world. As with the case method, it was designed as a managerial learning process, but if projects and teams are selected appropriately, and designed with teams from the same organization, it offers excellent opportunities for promoting strategic organizational learning. Significantly, two processes are taking place inside action learning groups, as evidenced by successes at General Electric and Prudential. Team members are resolving problems, the solutions to which are passed to clients and are themselves learning processes and information valuable for future problem-solving episodes; but more important, the body of institutional knowledge and the pace of institutional learning is accelerating in user organizations.

REFERENCES

Caie, B. (1987). Learning in style—reflections on an action learning MBA programme. *The Journal of Management Development, 6* (2), 19-29.

Clover, W. H. (1991). At TRW executive training contributes to quality. *Human Resources Professional*, 3 (2), 16-20.

Galligan, P. (1990). Execs go global, literally. *Training & Development Journal*, 44 (8), 58-83.

Jones, M. L. (1990). Action learning as a new idea. *Journal of Management Development*, 9 (5), 29-34.

Jubilerer, J. (1991). Action learning for competitive advantage. *The Journal of Private Sector Policy*, 15 (9), 16-19.

Lawrie, J. (1989). Take action to change performance. *Personnel Journal*, 68 (1), 58-69.

Lewis, A. and March, W. (1987). Action learning: The development of field managers in the Prudential Assurance Company. *The Journal of Management Development*, 6 (2), 45-57.

Margerison, C. J. (1988). Action learning and excellent in management development. *Journal of Management Development*, 7 (5), 43-53.

Marsick, V. (1990). Experience-based learning: Executive learning outside the classroom. *Journal of Management Development*, 9 (4), 50-60.

O'Reilly, B. (1993). How execs learn now. *Fortune*, 127 (7), 52-58.

Revans, R. W. (1982). What is action learning? *Journal of Management Development*, 1 (3), 64-75.

Chapter 9

Case Studies of International Management Development

Charles Gancel
Alison Perlo

Internationalization is a key component of success for companies today. It opens new markets and allows for the exchange of new technologies, skills, and expertise. Nonetheless, with internationalization comes increased competition. Given the confrontation of different corporate and national cultures, and different communication and management styles, managers who are effective within their home markets must add new skills to maintain excellence in competitive international markets.

Inter Cultural Management Associates (ICM) has extensive experience in developing skills for international managers. ICM develops approaches based on the specific needs of individual companies; in this chapter are descriptions of some of the training programs and services developed in the past. Each skill described is a module that can be combined with others to develop a program that will reach objectives. ICM will train managers for each module, or train trainers to do so.

ICM has helped international companies with management development since 1983. Clients include Banque Nationale de Paris, BP, BSN, Ciments Français, EDF International, Kodak, Steelcase-Strafor, and Schlumberger. The ICM approach addresses three critical aspects of management development in an international context:

Edited and reprinted with permission from Charles Gancel and Alison Perlo, "Inter Cultural Management Associates (ICM)," and publisher. First published in *Journal of Management Development* (MCB University Press), 14(5), 1995, pp. 15-27.

1. Assessing a situation
2. Guiding the implementation
3. Training key players

NEEDS ANALYSIS FOR INTERNATIONAL TRAINING

First, ICM defines the key management skills and styles essential for managers in the organization to succeed in implementing the business objectives of the company. Second, they access the current skill level and managerial style. Third, they identify the gaps between current and desired skill levels. Completion of these three steps allows the setting of training program objectives and content.

ICM's approach links international management development to the needs of the business by including senior executives, management, and at times customers, in determining strategic development needs. Through interviews, on-the-job analysis, questionnaires, or workshops with top management, they develop a profile of the management culture and skills deemed essential for the company's success.

Using this information, the present skill level in the organization is measured and compared to the desired management culture and skills. Self-assessment questionnaires, focus groups, and structured as well as unstructured interviews determine where the gaps or weaknesses lie. From this analysis are identified concrete objectives and target populations for future training programs.

PROGRAM DESIGN AND DEVELOPMENT

ICM's goal is to design a program that creatively meets training objectives. All key players are involved, including top management, to ensure that the program design responds to international client needs and to build "ownership" for the program in all stakeholders. The consultancy works to determine the skills to be developed, the appropriate programming of the sessions, and the most effective pedagogical approach. They also develop the materials, in particular a company course manual. This manual helps integrate into an organization's culture the skills deemed essential for a company's success.

ICM coordinates programs and helps in finding the particular expertise necessary to meet objectives. It identifies key players, trainers, participating senior managers, and guest speakers and briefs them on program objectives, and on their roles. It then conducts evaluations to determine the effectiveness of program in order to make any necessary changes in the design and delivery. ICM evaluates each module and program by getting feedback from both trainers and participants. A subsequent evaluation is done a few months after the program has been completed when participants have returned to their workplace, to measure performance improvement.

TRAINING FOR TRAINERS

The program length and content depend on the program objectives and the needs of the trainers. ICM's approach assumes that good trainers and coaches must be "trainable and coachable." Therefore, in the train-the-trainers programs, ICM builds skills in giving and receiving constructive feedback, developing clarity, and optimal approaches to differing learning styles. For some programs the trainers being trained will first experience the program as a participant and then review it as a trainer. In this way they get firsthand experience of the content from the participant's point of view and of the strength of the methodology. As necessary, an ICM consultant can cofacilitate the programs with the trainers initially and organize skill-building sessions to provide additional coaching. Varied methodologies are used, including formal lectures, role plays, discussions and tasks in small groups, exercises and presentations, and personalized feedback.

CULTURAL AWARENESS

Managers from various cultural backgrounds must work and manage people internationally. ICM's goal is to deepen participants' sensitivity to the impact culture can have on daily life, interpersonal relations, and international management practices. Also, ICM provides guidelines for a better understanding of cultural differences. Finally, ICM plans what individuals can do to manage misunderstandings and facilitate adaptation to different communication and management styles. Cultural Awareness usually includes a two- to three-day program providing general preparation for understanding and dealing positively with cultural differences in values, attitudes, customs, and behaviors. Varied methodology is used including presentations, films, guest lecturers, exercises, and case studies.

INTERNATIONAL NEGOTIATION

International Negotiation is a two- to three-day program that can be general or country-specific. The sessions combine presentations on how culture influences negotiation (for example, negotiator selection criteria, concern with protocol, nature of persuasive arguments, basis of trust, risk-taking propensity, etc.) and extensive negotiation practice based on a model for negotiating effectively and for building long-term relationships. The negotiations are filmed, so that in addition to analysis by the consultants and feedback from the other participants, each person can evaluate his or her own strengths and weaknesses in negotiating. ICM can develop cases specific to a company's situation.

Varied methodology is used including presentations, exercises, films, role-plays, case studies, negotiations, and personalized feedback.

CONSULTING
IN A MULTICULTURAL ENVIRONMENT

Managers working in an international context are often called on to work as internal or external consultants. They must build the specific skills in communication, methodology, and client relations essential to success in selling and delivering consulting services. ICM assists in developing an approach to effecting change in client organizations by involving key players and building consensus. Programs range from two to five days depending on client needs and objectives. These seminars focus on the influence and communications skills essential for internal consultants working in a decentralized international company and for consultants who manage projects financed by international financial institutions such as the World Bank.

A varied approach is geared to program objectives: intensive skill-building using role-plays and situations from the participants' jobs, guest case studies, and videotaping for in-depth reviews.

COMMUNICATION
IN AN INTERNATIONAL CONTEXT

Communication in an International Context is a highly intensive two- or three-day program, which uses material and situations from the participants' jobs so that skills can be immediately applied. Programs can be developed to prepare participants to communicate with a specific culture. Preplanning meetings with participants ensure that the program is adapted to their specific needs. An approach involving intensive feedback, building on strengths to help participants develop their most effective personal style through role-plays and private videotape reviews, is utilized.

EXPATRIATE PREPARATION

Expatriate Preparation helps participants become familiar with a new country and gain understanding of the expatriation process in order to prepare as well as possible for departure, the adaptation abroad, and the return home. It also helps the family being expatriated become aware of the particular challenges involved in expatriation and the steps to take for an effective transition to the new environment. The expatriate preparation program is a way to brief participants on the differences in national, corporate, and functional cultures for the mission. This is a two- to five-day program for future expatriates and/or their spouses and children. The content varies depending on the needs of the participants, and the country and project in question. Varied methodology is used including formal lectures, presentations by previous expatriates, films, role-plays, authentic documents, discussions and tasks in small groups, and question and answer sessions with the client.

MANAGING INTERNATIONALLY

Managing Internationally is designed for managers leading international teams or projects. It aims to build the specific skills needed for transnational managers to be successful in leading, motivating, and maximizing effectiveness in an international context. The program is divided into four different skill groupings. These skill groupings can be put together to form an integrated training program or used separately to meet a specific need. All programs are geared to the specific needs of each client.

Providing Leadership in an International Environment

For Providing Leadership in an International Environment, ICM develops leadership programs suited to the company and national cultures. These programs focus on building the skills essential to getting results by motivating people, setting direction, delegating appropriately, and increasing flexibility. Programs vary from intense, one-to-one coaching sessions to sessions for groups spread out over several months.

Appraising and Coaching Staff

The Appraising and Coaching Staff programs focus on developing skills managers need to maximize the performance of their teams by assisting people in their professional development. By learning to give constructive performance appraisals and ongoing supportive feedback, managers create an atmosphere conducive to continual improvement and high standards of excellence.

Coordinating International Projects

This module, Coordinating International Projects, helps participants to communicate effectively and manage information flow and exchange in an international context. By building on role complementarity for increased team effectiveness and strength, managers learn how to develop common working methods for better decision making and team cohesion.

Developing International Networks

In the Developing International Networks module managers learn how to build productive working relationships on a world scale. By reinforcing their influence skills, they are able to gain commitment and actions from those whom they do not necessarily know or see often and over whom they have no hierarchical authority.

AN APPLICATION BY ICM MANAGEMENT TRAINING IN RUSSIA: TRAPS AND GAPS

This section describes a training program proposed by Western countries to help ease the transition of Russian industry from a planned economy to a market economy. We will first highlight the potential problems of introducing Western-style training programs in Russia identified by ICM and then describe the program developed to overcome these traps and gaps. We then discuss what we consider a critical success factor for training programs today: industrial involvement.

At the end of 1992, ICM conducted an extensive series of interviews in Moscow and visited several industrial installations for the textile and clothing industries. This investigation allowed ICM to get a clear picture of the current situation and to evaluate the gaps between European practices and those in use in Moscow. The study provided crucial information about participant expectations and helped ICM develop not only the content but also the approach and methodology for the training program.

The content and approach of Western management training programs are consistent with corporate objectives and reinforce the roles of managers in a competitive environment. ICM assumes that the participants know and understand their missions and roles and that they master certain concepts (economic viability, competition, decision making, etc.). This presumption cannot apply in Russia, where these notions are often misunderstood, given that Russian managers were trained in a different system. ICM quickly discovered that it was not faced with managers who lack training, but with managers whose training was obsolete. Although ICM has encountered this situation in Western industry, it has never existed to the extent found in Russia.

The Challenge of Training

For the trainer, the challenge is not simply to teach, but to replace one acquired body of knowledge (that was valid in the old system) with another, new body of knowledge. This is extremely difficult since the actual development of a market economy is still in embryonic stages in Russia and has been slowed down by the instability of Russian society. The trainer is facing the challenge of a deeply rooted system. The trainer has to persuade the participants to abandon the convictions and practices on which they have built their careers, and to adopt others for which they have no reference points, little trust, and little concrete proof of effectiveness.

After all, in their old system, the Western concept of profit was considered suspect. Today, still, the idea of seeking profit connotes something unethical. What had been considered immoral suddenly becomes moral, and this raises the question of what is acceptable and what is not. Unfortunately, the legal system is still too embryonic to provide credible answers. Thus, there are no guiding principles for the moral dimension of corporate practices. The trainer finds him- or herself in this new and difficult position of training participants in notions that they can accept theoretically but that they question morally.

In addition to adjusting moral vision, the Russians need to acquire new concepts that can only take on meaning with real social change. Talking about "market segmentation," for example, is difficult in a society that formerly refused to acknowledge this concept and still does not have a segmented market in the Western sense of the word. If you ask Russian managers in the clothing industry who their target population is, they all give more or less the same reply: "Our client is an average Russian man or woman of average income"—in other words, a nonsegment. It is clear that the notion of market segmentation, even if understood intellectually, will not affect company decisions until it becomes a reality in Russian society itself.

Major Differences

Unfortunately, numerous Western trainers between 1991 and 1993 made the assumption that Russian managers perceive their role and that of the company as being like those of their Western counterparts. This has led to misunderstandings and inefficiency in the training programs that have been used. The Russian concepts of "mission and organization" are a logical extension of the planned economy they knew for so long. The wave of privatizations and the evolution toward a market economy have not yet brought about serious structural adjustments. For example, production remains the driving function of companies. The integrating of purchasing, sales, distribution, marketing, and so on into the notion of product development is slow to occur and is further hindered by the general lack of social organization.

For example, the Russians have tried to concentrate all activities for production and sales within specific regions. Since industries do not know how to source raw materials and distribute products on a country-wide scale, proximity gives a feeling of control. The inefficiency of the banking system, hyperinflation, and demands for prepayment make financial management and the extension of credit almost impossible.

Human resource management to a great extent still fulfills a sort of feudal village role (or "social sphere"), responsible for health, transportation, food, lodging, and family services for the personnel. One of the textile managers who was questioned on his business priorities said that he could not find any more pigs for his company's breeding area. The majority of his time was spent handling this problem. The Western view that a human resource manager's role concerns training and development is unknown.

Clearly the Russians have not yet made the transition from a production and social mission to an economic mission. This change is neither understood nor fully accepted and certainly is not operative. The organization of the company as well as the roles of the people who work there are still determined by the old production and social mission. Many of the company managers said that their corporate mission was to "provide clothing for Russian children."

The Managing Director's Role

ICM asked the company heads to describe their roles and how they spend their time. Russian executives spend only 10 percent of their time on the activities that take up 80 percent of a Western executive's time. The 90 percent left over is spent looking for raw materials, handling litigation with clients, and taking care of the activities in the "social sphere." The Russian manager must handle a permanent state of crisis.

Consequently, the competencies needed for a Russian director to succeed in the old system are very different from those required for success in a market economy. ICM identified three types of such traditional competencies: technical, political, and social.

Technical Competencies

The technical competencies required correspond to those necessary in the West for a factory manager. The Russian director, especially in the textile industry, has received only technical training, centered on production and on the ability to execute a plan.

Political Competencies

This concerns the "little black book" executives have that allows them to pull the necessary political strings to help their company obtain supplies, investments, distribution, recruitment, and so forth. It is naive to believe that these competencies are no longer necessary. Many of the people who held key positions in the old political network continue to exert power and still have their hands in business dealings. The ability to reach the right person at the right time constitutes a vital competency for doing business in Russia today. It is important to understand that this dimension is not just a by-product of the old system. According to some, it is a fundamental value of Russian culture and, as such, is not about to disappear quickly.

Social Competencies

Social competencies involve the ability to take care of personnel and their families. In the privatization phase, during which many company directors had to get elected by their shareholders (the personnel for the most part), these competencies were key. One of the company directors told ICM that she had been elected essentially because the personnel thought of her as their mother and felt that she would take good care of them.

One can now better understand why management training based on Western concepts corresponds only slightly to the expectations and needs of Russian managers who are trying to push the change process ahead. Western management concepts have remained pure theory, as the Russian environment has provided only minimal ground for concrete application and learning. ICM decided to look for the answers by involving Western industrialists who are seeking Russian business partners in the program. By helping Russian managers break out of cultural and economic isolation, we also help them to confront the reality of the Western market and to apply the new concepts and skills learned during the seminars. If we only discuss the notion of quality in the classroom, for example, it remains totally theoretical. However, when the Russians consider the requirements of Westerners who delocalize some of their activities to Russia and accept or reject orders on the basis of "quality," they very quickly see what "quality" means and how you get it. In the cases ICM observed, the Russians have subsequently been able to make the changes necessary to meet Western standards.

Program

ICM's project was launched at the end of 1992, beginning with the audit described above. The seminars were developed after the audit and were run for the first time in the fall of 1994. The program was designed to be run many times over a period of several years in order to include a critical mass of executives in the industry. It differs from programs previously offered in Russia in four important ways:

1. It targets a specific branch of industry: textile and clothing.
2. It involves European textile and clothing industries on an operational level. They took the initiative for the development of this project, and they manage it with the European Commission within the framework of the Commission's TACIS program.
3. Its content, pedagogy, and methodology were developed only after the in-depth examination of the daily challenges Russian industrialists currently face, the general evolutionary trend of this particular branch of industry, and of the lingering impact of the business practices used before 1991.
4. It goes beyond management training per se and aims at developing business relations between Russian and Western European industrialists in order to support the Russians and to provide a context where the new skills they develop during the seminars can be immediately applied.

Target Population

The target population of this program was executives of companies in the textile and clothing industries. The participants were all members of the executive committees, within their companies.

Program Objectives

- Create a pool of managers who thoroughly understand the role, organization, and management of a company in a market economy.
- Develop the competencies needed to implement this management role in a market economy (these competencies were not required in a planned economy and therefore not taught).
- Trigger the development of business relations between Russian industrialists and their Western counterparts.
- Maintain ongoing evaluation of the potential of this Russian industrial sector in order to continue supporting its restructuring process.

Seminar Design

During the audit phase, ICM identified five priority areas for learning and developed five seminar modules in 1993. These were based on the following principles.

- Involve consultants and specialists from several European countries.
- Develop seminars with a five-day format.
- Provide the pedagogical materials in Russian.
- Run the seminars in Moscow.
- Form a two-person pedagogical team for each module consisting of a Western trainer and a Russian trainer. The Western trainer is the module manager and head trainer. The Russian trainer ensures understanding and builds a bridge between Western and Russian cultures. ICM was very aware that if cultural differences were not taken into account, they could sabotage the training process and the transfer of knowledge and skills.

- Provide opportunities for exchange between Russian and Western executives of the textile and clothing industries during the seminars and later during the internships.

The Seminars

Each five-seminar program was held over a period of three months, given that company directors can rarely be absent from their offices for more than two weeks at a time. The five modules are described as follows:

Change Management. The extreme instability and disruption of Russian society as well as the privatization process and the resulting efforts to set up new, interindustrial relations mean that Russian managers have to lead rapid change processes inside and outside their companies. None of the Russian managers had received training that could help them face the situation they are in today. This module was designed to provide them with change management tools to help them master the change process.

Financial Management. The basic tools for managing finances used in a market economy were irrelevant in the Soviet planned economy system and as such were never taught. Competencies in this field are clearly lacking. This seminar provided the executives with concepts and tools to monitor and control their budget, costs, cash flow, and so on.

International Trade Fairs. Trade fairs provide an initial contact with the international market and industry. The Russian industrialists already participated somewhat in trade fairs, but the results of their efforts were quite often disappointing. Working with them on the preparation, participation, and follow-up of fairs was a concrete way of bringing out the marketing concepts necessary to succeed in a competitive market.

Product Development Cycle. Previously, the Russian industrialists were cut off from the market and its expectations. They simply had to respond to the centralized dictates of the ministries. Their role was limited to production; there was little room for creativity. What is more, they gave little thought to price setting, as they were in a system that foresaw no real sanctions for financial loss. This seminar addressed their current need to develop products according to identified market needs in a cost-effective way.

International Raw Materials Market. Just as the companies were cut off from the market and from distribution, they were also cut off from sources of raw materials. Raw material supply was to a great extent organized and controlled by centralized institutions. The breakup of the Soviet Union cut Russia off from its habitual sources of materials (Uzbekistan, Tajikistan, etc.). Russian companies now must turn to international sources. This seminar familiarized Russian managers with the international raw materials market and how it is organized, who the key players are, and how it works.

Participant Selection

With the help of Russian partners, ICM first identified possible companies. It then selected an initial 120 potential participants from the executive committees of these companies. Afterward ICM conducted individual interviews with these executives and chose the first forty participants.

The biggest challenge was to manage the selection process to form a coherent group of participants without being influenced by political pushing and pulling, which has often played a significant role in the way participants are selected for training programs.

In an effort to increase impact after the program, ICM tried to select at least two people from each company. In this way, they could share on two sets of shoulders the heavy task of transferring knowledge and skills from the program participants to the others in the company and also create support for new ways of doing things within the company.

Internship

A major point emerging from the interviews was that the Russian managers were hungry for contacts with European firms. The internship part of the program responded to this and also constituted an innovation in the kinds of training generally available in Russia.

The seminars were followed by a one-month internship in a European company. Ten groups of four managers, each group accompanied by an interpreter, was sent to a specific company. Each group was managed within the host company by a "tutor" from the human resource department. ICM prepared the tutors for this role.

The internships allowed the participants to experience a Western company firsthand, and to apply the management concepts and skills practiced in the modules. They also provided the opportunity to pursue the initial contacts made with Western counterparts during the seminars.

Each team was given a specific project to work on by their European host company. In this way, the Russian managers were able to take on more ambitious projects than if they were each working alone, and the Western companies benefited from having this team of Russian experts examine some aspect of their business that they wanted help or information on. Once back in Moscow, the Russian project teams had a work session to share the experience and knowledge gathered from their work in Europe.

Involving the Industry: A Critical Success Factor

Involving the industry from the very onset of the ICM program had two major consequences: it promoted credibility and led to potential partnerships.

Credibility

Many of the Russian directors ICM met had already received training in Western programs set up since 1989. Their evaluation of these programs was harsh: "of very limited use in the Russian context." They considered the direct involvement of people in the industry in the ICM program a very positive change. The Western industrialists from prestigious textile and clothing companies who came to the seminars to give lectures and spend time in discussions brought credibility and added value that was recognized by all the Russian industrialists. It gave them the unexpected chance to meet with their Western counterparts and to learn from them directly.

Russian industrialists' interest in participating in the ICM program was overwhelming. Given the despair that exists in Russian industry, this motivation was key.

Potential Partnerships

It is obvious that the Russians are seeking international business possibilities, either through export, outward production traffic

(OPT), or direct investment. Their main objective is to get some of the work (especially in the clothing industry) currently subcontracted to companies in Southeast Asia. Their participation in the program, which allowed them to meet with Western industrialists, provided a unique opportunity for them to pursue this objective.

ICM's position is that the change required to go from a planned economy to a market economy is so great that to succeed it is essential for Russians to have immediate industrial and commercial business dealings with Westerners. In the clothing industry, those Russian companies that have set up subcontracting or OPT with Western partners have made the most spectacular progress.

Getting Beyond Cultural Models

Does a typical Western manager exist? If you sit a German, an American, a British, and a French manager around a table and start asking them questions, you quickly wonder. Unfortunately, quite often this notion of a "Western model" has pervaded training programs in Russia, and it has been a source of problems. Russian directors can be quite critical of the inconsistencies within the Western system that they fought against for so long!

Choosing one branch of industry allowed ICM to concentrate on a particular field and avoid generalities. When people of one industry speak to others of the same industry, they find themselves on common ground, which provides an immediate basis for communication. The ideological separation then becomes easier to bridge.

Management Training or Change Management?

The change process undertaken by the Russian industry is probably the most extraordinary that any industry has ever known. It is now apparent that ICM's role is not simply to train those Russians who drive the economy, but also to provide them with tools to help them master this change process, for their companies and for the Russian economy as a whole. ICM focuses not only on acquiring knowledge, but also on the ability to transform industry structurally as well as culturally. It is for this reason that ICM launched the five-seminar series with a module on managing change. This module draws on some of the change management tools that have been developed in Western companies over the past fifteen years that ICM feels are culturally adaptable. For the training program to contribute to increased individual awareness, the participants must be armed with tools to help them confirm the validity of new ways of doing things within their companies.

Conclusion

One final, important message our interviews allowed us to understand is that we must at all costs avoid a repetition of the "Verdun syndrome." The Russians perceive the events of these past few years as proof of a terrible failure. To add insult to injury, their traditional rival, the West, has not just proven the superiority of its ways of doing things; it also offers training to the loser.

In addition to the extraordinary difficulties they encounter today, the Russians feel that they have lost face precisely where they had felt so strong: industry. These feelings, along with a certain degree of frustration, are always present in the relations that develop between the Western trainers and industrialists and the Russian managers. We must understand this and take it into consideration in our attitude with the Russians. A "we know best" approach will push the Russians to stick more strongly to their positions and create antagonism. For learning to take place, consideration and respect are two essential ingredients.

PART III:
DEVELOPING THE LEARNING ORGANIZATION

Part III of the text begins with a discussion of systems dynamics and organizational learning by Peter Senge and Robert Fulmer (Chapter 10). The chapter describes how organizational role players possess mental models about their organizations that are often superficial. These models must be shared and sharpened through organizational learning—especially through debate and dialogue. A systems dynamics perspective can improve the ability of managers to develop generative learning, learning that enhances the capacity to create the future.

In Chapter 10, the microworld, an interactive simulated environment, is introduced and several microworlds are described. Major challenges are noted that must be addressed to maximize the impact of systems dynamics and microworlds on learning in organizations.

Chapter 11 introduces practice fields for managers and categorizes these developing managerial and organizational learning laboratories into two more refined categories: simuworlds stemming from computerized management game architecture, and microworlds stemming from personnel assessment programs built on the in-basket architecture, often called complex behavioral simulations.

Practice fields for management, such as microworlds and simuworlds, are presented as ideally suited for promoting "big picture" organizational learning and connecting leadership training to the strategies of an organization. They are also useful in overcoming barriers to learning. Examples of how these barriers are overcome in various simulated environments are presented.

Chapter 12, The Multinational Management Game: A Simuworld, by Keys, Wells, and Edge, expands on a computerized management game introduced in Chapter 11. This game is quite realistic and is modeled after the microcomputer industry and several actual companies within the industry. MMG is a game and case combination and therefore includes some of the attributes summarized in Chapter 11 regarding simuworlds, and some of the attributes of cases and scenarios (see Chapter 5). Organizational learning opportunities that usually occur in MMG that are explained in the chapter are summarized below.

- The system dynamics lesson that all corporate functions are interrelated.
- Some systems incorporate reinforcing feedback and some balancing feedback, and some balancing of functional areas is done by organizing properly.
- Effective teams soon discover that they must learn how to develop a resonance or synergy through dialogue.
- How to work with intercultural groups (if diverse teams used).
- How to conduct a regional or country international briefing and incorporate it into a strategic plan.

A number of other learning opportunities, which usually arise for MMG participants, are noted.

Stumpf, Watson, and Rustogi elaborate on two complex behavioral simulations, Foodcorp and Globalcorp, and explain their use in Chapter 13. These simulations are aptly suited for training in behavioral and organizational concepts since they include a formal hierarchy among participants, division of labor, and realistic information contained in expansive in-baskets. A large number of issues is included with which the organization must deal. The simulated organizations are so realistic that participants are "caught up" in the activities and reproduce their real feelings, behavior, and interactions toward organizational and interpersonal problems. Examples of applications in two companies are provided.

Chapter 10

Systems Dynamics
and Anticipatory Learning

Peter M. Senge
Robert M. Fulmer

One of the first contributions of systems dynamics to understanding organizational learning lies in the way managers' mental models might be improved. Recognition of managers' mental models dates from the beginnings of the systems dynamics field (Forrester, 1961, pp. 49-50):

> A mental image or a verbal description in English can form a model of a corporate organization and its processes. The manager deals continuously with these mental and verbal models of the corporation.

Although mental models are rich in detail, they are deficient in critical ways. They focus deeply on particular parts of a business and are superficial regarding other equally important parts. They are predominantly static and do not clearly distinguish assumptions about structure, behavior, and expected outcomes of policy changes. Mental models are largely tacit, expressing themselves as intuitions and "gut instincts" that are difficult to communicate and share.

What is important for organizational learning is not only the mental models of individual managers but mental models that are

---

Abridged and edited with permission of authors and publisher. From Peter M. Senge and Robert M. Fulmer, "Systems Dynamics and Anticipatory Learning." First published in *Journal of Management Development* (MCB University Press), 12(6), 1993, pp. 21-33.

shared among learners. For many critical organizational issues, the fundamental learning unit is not the individual but the team of managers who need one another to take new actions. As Stata puts it (1988, p. 4):

> Organizations can learn only as fast as the slowest link learns. Change is blocked unless all of the major decision makers learn together, come to share beliefs and goals, and are committed to take actions necessary for change.

The systems dynamics perspective parallels the distinction between single-loop and double-loop learning. This is the distinction between adjustments in behavior that occur *within* a feedback structure and *changes in the structure itself*. Within the feedback structure created by existing physical and information flows and operating policies, people are learning in the sense of modifying decisions and actions as new conditions develop. Changes in behavior take place as new information is acted upon within the goals, norms, traditions, and constraints established by current policies. For example, in a manufacturing firm, changes in business conditions lead to adjustments in production rates, changes in material orders, and the hiring and firing of workers. The type of continual learning that occurs within a given structure is what Argyris (1994) would call "single-loop learning." (His classic example of single-loop learning is the adjustments made by a thermostat to maintain a desired temperature.) On the other hand, learning *about* a structure that leads to changes in that structure itself comes very close to the essence of double-loop learning. In this sense, the purpose of systems dynamics has always been double-loop learning.

Another important distinction between levels of learning contrasts *instrumental learning* with *generative learning*. Instrumental learning involves adjustment in behavior as individuals or organizations cope with changing circumstances. It is neither trivial nor guaranteed. Like generative learning, which will be discussed next, instrumental learning is critical to survival and is characteristic of a well-functioning organization that must continually recognize and respond to changes in its environment. By contrast, generative learning enhances the individual's or organization's capacity to create its future. Generative learning involves changes in predominant *ways of thinking*—toward ways of thinking that empower people and organizations to see more and more deeply how their actions can influence their reality.

Once again, the discipline of systems dynamics helps make the notion of generative learning more tangible. Generative learning, which comes from the practice of systems thinking, involves more than simply discovering structures at play. It produces or generates growth in learning capacity as individuals and organizations become systems dynamics thinkers.

Systems thinking, as articulated by J. W. Forrester and his colleagues and disciples at MIT and elsewhere, helps individuals see patterns and helps create the ability to reinforce or change these patterns. Unfortunately, most individuals focus on isolated parts of the systems instead and then wonder why efforts at solving problems or perpetuating success fail. Systems thinking is a discipline for seeing the "big picture." It is a framework for understanding the patterns in interrelationships. Systems thinking is an antidote for the feelings of helplessness that often overwhelm an individual who feels, "It's the system. I have no control." By seeing the patterns that lie behind the events and details, we can actually simplify the world. It is this aspect of systems thinking that can enrich the challenge of seeing the patterns of the present and also in understanding some of the probable evolution of the future.

Several developments in recent years have set the stage for systems dynamics to make a potentially significant contribution to this exciting new field (Senge, 1989). First, there has been steadily increasing attention to involving managers more directly in the modeling process. In early applications of systems dynamics to policy issues, technical experts built models and then wrote reports for managerial decision makers. Relatively little attention was focused on how managers might themselves learn from modeling. The implicit assumption was that the experts did the learning about the system and made recommendations. Managers needed only to be concerned with putting into practice the recommendations of the technical consultants. Effective consulting practice has evolved to the point of "significant client participation" in problem definition, model development, and policy analysis (Senge, 1989). This trend of increasing management involvement in modeling has continued in recent years, aided by new computer software that enables managers to participate more directly in building and simulating models, and in decision-making games based on models (Richmond, 1987).

A second development has been to more clearly understand how prevailing mental models influence strategy and policy design. This is the *future-oriented* part of anticipatory learning. In particular, Morecroft, building on earlier ideas expressed by Forrester, suggests that whenever a new strategic issue confronts policy makers, it initiates a process of "debate and dialogue . . . [that] leads to clarification of the problem or issue and eventually to recommendations for action" (Morecroft, 1988, p. 302). Morecroft suggested that a logical extension of systems dynamics was to develop "microworlds" to enhance the quality of debate and dialogue and to improve strategy and policy.

As a result of these and related developments, we believe system dynamics is beginning to make a significant contribution to the emerging field of anticipatory learning. This chapter attempts to illustrate the nature of that contribution and to discuss some of the new issues and challenges that must be faced if this potential contribution is to be realized.

We are finding that managers can learn to think systemically if they can uncover the subtle interactions that thwart their efforts. This can be done by creating "microworlds" (Senge and Lannor, 1990, p. 64), a term coined by Seymour Papert, MIT media technology professor, to describe an interactive computerized environment that simulates a real-world situation. Managers can use microworlds to expose assumptions underlying their business strategies. Through computer-simulation models such as those discussed in the following paragraphs, microworlds could transform how organizations learn. And they may be a first step in reversing the chronic tendency of companies to focus on the short term and neglect the long term.

EXAMPLES OF MICROWORLDS

In a managerial microworld, a simulation model generates a company's behavior based on interactions in the organization and with its market and competitors. We will summarize three cases of how managers can use computerized systems simulations to clarify their mental models of organizations and anticipate the consequences of following specific strategies.

Siemens Electronics and Allied-Signal Postmerger Simulations

One of the authors had an opportunity to work with two custom-designed microworlds developed, at least partly, in response to postmerger pressures. One of these simulations (Siemens Electronics) is discussed in detail later in this book (see Chapter 11). The other will be briefly described here.

After two major acquisitions (Bendix and Signal), Allied-Signal recognized the importance of integrating the diverse cultures that had been brought together, developing understanding of and support for the new strategic planning process and encouraging more cooperation and teamwork between various groups within the organization. While management development was viewed as an important part of this integrative effort, a customized microworld called Capstone was employed to support these objectives within the middle management ranks of the firm.

While the simulation employed many characteristics in common with "total enterprise" or strategic games, it reflected many of the characteristics of industries with which Allied-Signal competed. It was also designed to reflect the strategic planning process introduced by CEO Ed Hennessy and utilized some of the same forms used by general managers throughout the firm. Four to six teams competed against each other throughout a weeklong learning initiative that included sessions on finance, customer orientation, and strategy. After content sessions, participants were asked to make decisions that provided a practice field for them to test their grasp of concepts and to see the impact of their decisions without costing the company if their decisions were not well grounded. Because participants came from different parts of the company and had diverse educational and functional backgrounds, each team member had an opportunity to be a relative expert in some part of the exercise and to learn from other team members at other decision points. Many of the tensions associated with working in a new environment and having to cooperate with people with other backgrounds and viewpoints were successfully simulated while the competitive feedback kept the learning both engaging and practical.

Few new competitive strategies emerged but much better understanding of existing strategy and the process of planning were engendered by middle managers in all sectors and functions within the corporation.

People Express

Drawing on a Harvard Business School case study, MIT's John Sterman produced a microworld that incorporates key features of that firm (Senge and Lannor, 1990):

- Lower fares affect both established and new travelers.
- Both advertising and word of mouth drive market growth.
- Job rotation and self-managed teams create high employee productivity.
- Employee productivity also depends on experience level, morale, turnover, and, since the employees are all given stock in the company, stock prices.
- Flight availability, fares, service quality, and the range of services offered affect the number of passengers.
- As People Express grows, competitors respond by lowering their own prices.

Teams of two or three players can explore the People Express microworld by drawing up their own growth strategy for the company. The teams make five decisions. Two are strategic choices—the average fare and scope of services to provide. The others are operating decisions made on a quarterly basis—the number of aircraft to add to the fleet, the number of hires, and the money to allocate to marketing. The computer simulates what happens each quarter and presents a summary report. To chart the long-term consequences of its decisions, a team also has access to information on such matters as changing stock prices, employee morale, market research, and fleet size.

By experimenting, players can test hypotheses about why People Express failed. One scenario is to trace the actual company history by following Don Burr's operating strategy. This strategy keeps prices deeply discounted, maintains no-frills service for travelers, expands the fleet and service staff by about 100 percent per year, and markets extensively. As the computer begins to simulate quarterly results, problems appear. The average workweek gradually rises to sixty hours, which makes turnover increase, and the percentage of new employees rises sharply. Service quality erodes, and eventually the number of passengers drops off sharply, along with profits.

The results reveal an inherent inconsistency in the People Express strategy. Management attempted to build a high-commitment, flexible work force, yet it needed to double the number of service employees yearly. More time was required to train and assimilate People Express employees into the company's distinctive human-resource system than was possible given the rapid passenger growth. The result was deteriorating service that drove away many loyal customers. When business turned down, stock prices declined, and morale and service quality fell even further. While the simulation was not developed in time to help People Express avoid disaster, its use today in business schools and management development programs can help participants anticipate and avoid similar problems.

The Claims Laboratory

A third simulation, now used at Hanover Insurance to develop an understanding of claims work, is explained more fully in Chapter 11.

Hanover has used the claims learning lab for more than two years, and virtually all the company's claims managers have attended the sessions. Throughout the lab, managers are encouraged to question their beliefs. They debate about whether connections among certain variables are consistent with their experiences, and they eventually develop their own theories of claims operation. Then the participants develop strategies for improving long-term profitability and predict the outcomes. Finally, they test their hypotheses using the simulation model. This has the effect of improving current and future practice, thus combining maintenance and anticipatory learning.

CHALLENGES OF USING MICROWORLDS

Properly designed and conducted, managerial microworlds can meet both conditions of anticipatory learning. They provide a way of anticipating consequences of contemporary decisions and, by nature, involve a number of people in both the learning process and the opportunity of sharing mental models. The concluding paragraphs of this chapter will identify four major challenges that must be addressed and balances to be achieved in order to maximize the impact of systems dynamics and microworlds for anticipatory learning.

Learning versus Teaching

In traditional systems dynamics, most of the learning goes on in the modeling process. The simulation designers are model builders who, usually with a small number of clients, become involved in developing and testing the basic simulation. Once this group comes to some stage of completion, they arrive at recommendations that they attempt to transmit to the larger organization. At this point, the model or simulation becomes a tool for convincing people rather than a learning tool. Generally, however, the more radical the shift in policy required as a result of the modeling effort, the less "teaching" is likely to be successful in the process of bringing about change.

The objective of microworlds is to include learning in both the development and the utilization of the simulation. The optimal learning experience occurs when large numbers of managers can develop their own insights. While it is possible that learners may arrive at insights other than those originally conceived by the project team, the payoff is well worth the risk. Levels of interest and commitment achieved through this type of learning process will almost always exceed those achieved through a "convincing" process.

Learning versus Winning

The creation of microworlds draws on the discipline of system dynamics along with some aspects of simulation and game theory. Most managers who have experience with microworlds or computer-based simulations remember a competitive situation where the goal was to perform better than another team. This type of mind-set leads to two negative consequences. The first is a creation of a "win-lose" or "us versus them" mentality that tremendously limits the activity considered. Rather than looking for creative solutions, the pressure is to create short-term solutions that gain an advantage over other participants. Learning becomes a by-product of the real objective of beating other people. Although the competitive aspect of simulation can enhance the interest level of the activity, it provides little opportunity for reflection, insight, or genuine understanding about the process. Participants can simply "push buttons" and try to optimize the score with little serious thought about the dynamics of the issues involved. This phenomenon can be called the "video game effect." If the game is "user friendly" enough, participants can speed up the process of trial and error learning without anticipating the outcome or understanding why certain results follow particular decisions. The amount of genuine insight achieved by this "random search learning" strategy is very low.

Learning versus Beating the Computer

Even with the advent of large numbers of computer-literate managers, the role of the computer in the microworld can be problematic. Some successful utilizations of this tool have asked participants to spend the first day or more in understanding their own mental models and formulating strategies to be tested without ever touching a computer. Most managers today still see the computer as possessing greater power as a predicting tool than as a learning device. To make the learning process successful, it is important that managers perceive that the process is about them, their ways of thinking, their strategies. Any problem in understanding the computer or trying to guess the algorithms on which the simulation is based is less important than understanding the dynamics of the original system.

Real World versus Microworlds

While generic computer simulations are useful learning tools that help managers understand some of the relationships in complex environments, care must be taken in customized applications to ensure that the assumptions are actually "a constructed representation of the real world." This is what Donald Schon (1983) called a "virtual world." Often, the creation of a microworld reduces the constraints on experimentation. The pace of action can be varied. Actions that are irreversible in the real world can be reversed or the process tried again. Complexity can be simplified. But this capacity for simplification poses a dilemma. It can improve the ability of participants to focus on the key issues. Unfortunately, this may encourage participants to think more simplistically than the real world can tolerate. True learning involves experimentation and reflection in both the virtual world *and* the real world. No real organizational learning will take place if the experiments and questions are confined to the microworld. Experiments here should lead to tentative hypothesis that require experimentation and data gathering in the real world. In creating the models for a microworld, care must be taken that false economies are not sought by reducing the developmental time so much that the resulting model does not reflect the complex dynamics that must be understood.

CONCLUSION

We believe "microworlds" have the potential to deepen and accelerate anticipatory learning in a wide range of management situations. Researchers at MIT have concluded that microworlds can be developed from a relatively small number of generic structures that seem to occur in many types of business situations.

Well-intentioned policies, decisions, and strategies in complex systems may produce an initial positive outcome. Later consequences, however, may be more costly than the original advantages. By utilizing microworlds created with systems dynamics to help anticipate these consequences, managers and their organizations can discover a new capacity for gaining control of their destinies.

REFERENCES

Argyris, C. (1994). *On organizational learning.* Oxford, UK: Blackwell.

Forrester, J. W. (1961). *Industrial dynamics.* Cambridge, MA: Productivity Press, 49-50.

Goodwin, J. S. and R. M. Fulmer. (1992). Management development at Siemens Electronics: Hitting a moving target. *Journal of Management Development,* 11 (6), 40-45.

Morecroft, J. D. W. (1988). System dynamics and microworlds for policymakers. *European Journal of Operational Research,* 35, 302.

Richmond, B. (1987). *The strategic forum.* Lyme, NH: High Performance Systems.

Schon, D. (1983). *The reflective practitioner.* New York: Basic Books.

Senge, P. (1989). Organizational learning: A new challenge for systems dynamics. Working paper D-4023. Cambridge, MA: Sloan School of Management, MIT.

Senge, P. M. (1990). *The fifth discipline.* New York: Doubleday, 326-332.

Senge, P. M. and C. Lannor (1990). Managerial microworlds. *Technology Review,* July, 64.

Stata, R. (1989). Organizational learning—The key to management innovation. *Sloan Management Review,* Spring, 63-64.

Chapter 11

Microworlds and Simuworlds: Practice Fields for the Learning Organization

J. Bernard Keys
Robert M. Fulmer
Stephen A. Stumpf

Attorneys have "moot court," theater groups and symphony orchestras have rehearsals, and doctors have the practice cadaver. But where—or how—do managers rehearse?

Unfortunately, say Fred Kofman and Peter Senge, managers "seldom practice; they only perform" (1994, p.20). Indeed, management may be one of the few professions in which members attempt to achieve competence without formal practice.

The absence of rehearsal space is especially acute in today's world. With rapid organizational change—spawned by time-based global competition, mergers, acquisitions, and proliferating alliances—learning is being proclaimed the only long-run, sustainable competitive advantage. Reg Revans, creator of the "action learning" concept, gives this idea an edge by suggesting that learning must be equal to or greater than environmental change or the organization will not survive.

Learning in organizations can be perceived as a systems-flow process that requires liberation within both individuals and organizations. Children at play demonstrate this form of learning naturally and spontaneously when the flow process is uninhibited. Organizational life,

Reprinted with permission of American Management Association. All rights reserved. J. Bernard Keys, Robert M. Fulmer, and Stephen A. Stumpf, "Microworlds and Simuworlds: Practice Fields for the Learning Organization," *Organizational Dynamics*, Spring, 1996, pp. 36-49.

however, is often filled with hindrances to learning—what Senge refers to as "learning disabilities." Managers who succeed in removing these barriers will be able to share and enjoy learning in a natural manner.

In a special issue of *Organizational Dynamics*, John Slocum Jr., Michael McGill, and David Lei (1994) identified the pillars that must undergird learning in organizations. They propose that organizational learning must include "strategic intent to learn, commitment to experimentation, and an emphasis on learning from past successes and failures."

Valuable as these concepts may be, they are difficult to initiate without opportunity to practice in a low-risk environment. As Kofman and Senge (1994, p. 24) suggest, "We need virtual learning spaces—what have come to be known at the [MIT] Learning Center as 'managerial practice fields.' "

Management games and simulations are increasingly used to answer this need for "practice fields." As the following discussion reveals, these games and simulations can serve as mechanisms for releasing learning that seems to lie dormant in organizations.

THE EVOLUTION OF PRACTICE FIELDS

Practice fields for the learning organization have developed around two types of architecture. The first, which we call "simuworlds," evolved from competitive business games; the other, called "microworlds," stems from in-basket simulations that were first used in assessment programs.

For three decades, management games have provided middle and lower level managers with vicarious experience at general management. In 1955, the Rand Corporation developed Monopologs, the first organizational simulation, which required participants to perform as inventory managers in a simulated Air Force supply operation. A year later, the first business game, Top Management Decision Simulation, was introduced by the American Management Association. This was followed closely by J. R. Greene and G. R. Andlinger's Business Management Game. By the late 1980s, approximately 5,000 firms were using simulations in their training programs.

Research on the value of games within the strategic management teaching and learning area has shown that games and cases used in combination are more effective than cases or games alone. Additional research revealed that games can create meaningful, lifelike roles, and reward intelligent, rational, and well-planned executive-type decisions. Unfortunately, the tactical complexity of many of the better-known management games continued to expand until their tests of participants' quantitative sophistication was more highly valued than their potential for strategic and organizational learning.

PROVIDING "BIG PICTURE" LEARNING

This need for strategic and organizational learning gave rise to a new breed of computerized general management games. Crafted with new faces and new hearts, these games have been particularly innovative in tracking and simulating real industry competition and actual company case histories, prompting the name "simuworlds." Simuworlds, like their general management predecessors, are built on computerized models and are competitively interactive, factors that distinguish them from the complex behavioral simulations discussed below. They are based on published information about their respective industries and relevant companies, rather than the internal proprietary knowledge that is usually characteristic of microworlds. As with the Fortune 1,000 worlds they mirror, simuworlds usually include an international or global dimension.

Consider two examples: International Operations Simulation (INTOPIA) and the Multinational Management Game (MMG). Both have been used for years in corporate seminars, and both have been extensively modified to simulate firms in the microcomputer industry and to track the historical development of real companies within this industry. They provide experiences in dealing with traditional functions within a learning environment that encourages experimentation. Also, simuworlds provide a laboratory in which participants can overcome the blind spots that develop in the real world. For example, players can observe implementation of planning across all functions of the simulated company, and they see the interrelationships of cause and effect within a compressed time frame.

LEARNING LEADERSHIP
AND STRATEGY IN A MICROWORLD

When chosen carefully from on-the-job activities, in-basket simulations define a manager's role experientially in realistic terms. Used in leadership development programs, they have been found to create intense interest, improved attitudes toward self-development, and more effective transference of concepts into practice. Simulations and games stemming from the in-basket architecture include extensive role and organizational definition and allow participants to examine their leadership styles while addressing strategic plans within teams.

Consider one prototype complex behavioral simulation: Looking Glass, Inc. (LGI), a centerpiece laboratory for The Center for Creative Leadership in Greensboro, North Carolina. LGI was developed by three behavioral scientists through extensive interviews with managers of several glass companies. It has been used successfully for more than two decades to help participants analyze leadership styles and team roles of participants and to conceptualize the ways in which strategy develops—or fails to materialize. LGI's success stimulated the development of other in-basket simulations, including games of the New York University Management Simulation Projects (MSP) Group and the Center for Leadership at The University of Tampa.

Complex behavioral simulations such as these differ from simuworlds in that they focus on individual and collective behaviors observable in the work environment. Similarity of practice setting to performance setting is critical. Just as we would expect a soccer team to exhibit more game-like behavior on an outdoor field than in a gymnasium, so also with these simulations. The microworld achieves its reality through interconnected background information and in-baskets for each role. The play action gives participants a choice of roles based on hierarchical position, product, or functional responsibility, and issues to be addressed. Participation consists of "a day in the life" of a company rather than several years of simulated performance.

Foodcorp International and Globalcorp are representative complex behavioral microworlds. Foodcorp, a food-manufacturing organization microworld, simulates fourteen senior management roles, three levels of hierarchy, and two product groups. Participants work with activities integral to the food processing industry: new product development, consumer marketing, joint ventures, international licensing agreements, and diversification-consolidation.

In comparison, Globalcorp is a diversified international financial services conglomerate microworld with thirteen executive roles focusing not only on corporate strategy development but also on business portfolio management. Unlike the more homogeneous line-of-business situation and cross-functional activity common to Foodcorp, Globalcorp involves active coordination and competition across lines of business.

These simulations mirror top management challenges, including politics, culture, and conflict. They generate dynamic interaction among participants to replicate actual behavior of managers responsible for developing and implementing strategy in an organization. For a summary listing of representative simuworlds and microworlds, see Exhibit 11.1.

REDUCING THE HIGH RISK
OF ORGANIZATIONAL LEARNING

Microworlds used for organizational learning purposes include combinations of both architectures described in the previous section. Some are role-based and rich in organizational scenarios, while others include computer models that define their competitive environment. Most are built on internal interviews and nonpublished, company-specific information. For convenience, we will call these games "customized microworlds." The genesis of many of the customized microworlds is found in the systems dynamics sessions for planners held at the Massachusetts Institute of Technology. (Seymour Papert, MIT media technology professor, coined the term "microworlds.") Typical customized microworlds discussed throughout this chapter include the Siemens Electronics Simulation and the Hanover Insurance Company Claims Adjustment Game. We will also describe a futuristic exercise, called the Merlin Exercise, based on a free-form simulation process.

The primary role of the customized microworld is to enable participants to explore organizational and strategic change alternatives similar to ones planned for their employer, discover weaknesses or reasons for shortcomings, and improve choices. Partici-

EXHIBIT 11.1. Simuworlds and Microworlds for the Learning Organization*

	Architecture	Primary Purpose	Organizational Learning Emphasis
SIMUWORLDS MMG INTOPIA BML Business Strategy Game	Computerized management game	Big picture learning	Horizontal
MICROWORLDS (Complex Behavioral) Looking Glass, Inc. Foodcorp Globalcorp Metrobank Investcorp Landmark Insurance The Northwood Arts Center	In-basket simulation	Leadership/ strategy integration Dynamic interdependencies	Vertical and horizontal
MICROWORLDS (Customized) Siemens Electronics Hanover Insurance People's Express Allied-Signal RAMPLAND SCAMP	Combinations	High-risk learning problems Dynamic interdependencies	Short-term and long-term Vertical and horizontal
OTHER Beer Distribution Game Merlin Exercise	Combinations	Systemic problems Futuristic planning	Horizontal across industry Anticipatory learning

*See references for sources of these simulations.

pants can examine activities and interactions of divisions and subgroups of a company within a compressed time frame and see how these are played out over several iterations of planning. Errors can be made, leadership problems can emerge, and new strategies can be crafted without permanent injury to the participants or the organization. When an organization is engaged in a merger or acquisition or faces other major change requirements, practicing strategy and implementation within a simulation can be a valuable risk-free preparation for the real thing.

OVERCOMING BARRIERS TO LEARNING

In "Communities of Commitment," Senge and Kofman (1993, p. 6) discussed three barriers to creating a learning organization: the fragmentation of problem solving, an overemphasis on competition to the exclusion of collaboration, and a tendency of organizations to experiment or innovate only when compelled to change by outside forces.

The fragmentation problem is prolific and occurs in several shapes and forms.

1. Individuals in each functional specialty see only one aspect of a larger problem, and this fragmentation prevents learning horizontally across the organization.
2. Top management planners fail to perceive the interaction required with lower management levels, and lower management levels fail to conceptualize plans beyond their own functional area. This fragments vertical learning.
3. Strategic planning is frequently truncated by a failure to integrate learning for leadership with strategic planning.
4. Executives often fail to grasp the connections between short-term actions and long-term results. This fragmentation obscures an understanding of cause and effect.

Let us consider how various simuworlds and microworlds are being used to overcome these barriers. Although the illustrations presented focus on one kind of simulation, most simuworlds and microworlds are useful in multiple learning and planning roles.

Overcoming Horizontal Fragmentation

Simuworlds are usually played in a one-week seminar or, alternatively, in segments over a five- to six-week period. Participants assume the roles of CEO and senior vice presidents of marketing, operations, finance, and international. They study the history of the industry in order to engage in top management control of a multimillion-dollar company. They may be given a lackluster company with many strategic and tactical problems. Even when this is the case, the simulation allows the new management team to ride a growth wave to a billion-dollar operation similar to those experienced by such companies as Compaq Computer Corporation or Intel.

During the simulated start-up years, participants spend their time clarifying team roles, developing a viable organization, and learning to use the information processing system. After they have stabilized domestic operations, they may introduce a new upscale product, then progress to exporting, manufacturing offshore, financing in other countries, and ultimately developing an integrated mix of global operations. After seven to ten years of corporate oversight, teams must develop a five-year plan for the future. In some simuworlds, teams are provided industry updates and required to develop realistic strategic plans for the industry, unrestrained by game rules. A major debriefing follows participant presentations of their plans for the future.

Simuworlds provide an opportunity for functional specialists to develop broader learning horizons within the corporate organization. By playing top management roles, participants develop skill in environmental analysis and strategic planning across functions. They gain a broad picture, as if viewed through a wide-angle camera lens, of the patterns of horizontal planning, often initiated by sales and marketing and followed by responses from operations and finance. Moreover, they see the patterns develop within a compressed time frame. By requiring that teams maintain responsibility for corporate-level strategy design and cross-functional strategy implementation, the simulation promotes "big picture" learning.

Overcoming Vertical Fragmentation

When Siemens Electronics acquired Bendix Electronics from Allied-Signal, Siemens executives faced the challenge of integrating the acquired unit into its larger operations. They knew they would need to prepare Bendix managers for a future with new corporate ownership and a greater reliance on team-based decision making. Some Bendix employees had been exposed to a microworld as part of Allied-Signal's core development program, and they suggested use of a similar program. But this situation was different. To meet the current challenge, the microworld would need to stimulate anticipatory learning, that is, learning that anticipates future events and involves key people in the learning process.

Siemens engaged the Burgundy Group to craft a simulation around the business issues that Bendix managers would deal with in the coming decade. The simulation designers chose an industry similar to that in which the company operated, but altered the simulation slightly so participants would not focus on "the way things are." The exercise emphasized two major themes: team-based business planning and group coordination. The class was divided into five product groups plus a headquarters team that oversaw financial strategy for all the manufacturing divisions while developing the plans for launching a new division.

Each team competed with three simulated competitors rather than against other groups of participants. Headquarters was expected to launch a new division involving mini-terminals and to incorporate components from the three existing divisions into the new unit. Participants were asked to analyze their simulated company and, with the help of spreadsheets, develop brief business plans and make tactical decisions to implement the plans. To promote reflective learning, program leaders periodically encouraged participants to "step outside the moment" to observe how they were working together and what progress they had made.

Because of the time pressures in managing resources for the various operating groups, the headquarters group found they were unable to provide adequate attention to the strategically important launch of the new division. Similarly, representatives from actual operating divisions assigned to manage the simulated headquarters developed appreciation for some of the complexities associated with headquarters operations. The exercise replicated many of the problems to be faced by the newly merged organizations within the confines of the one-week simulation.

For further evidence of how such exercises overcome vertical fragmentation, we look briefly at a series of public administration simulations developed by staff at the Center for Managerial Learning and Business Simulation. Based on years of experience with a supervisory in-basket simulation, the center's staff constructed a simulation called RAMPLAND for the Atlanta Regional Rehabilitation Office. The staff went on to develop and implement a simulation for the Southeastern National Park Service titled SCAMP (Southeastern Coastal and Mountain Park Service Simulation). RAMPLAND and SCAMP, both customized microworlds, require participant teams to move from one management level to another throughout a simulation week, assuming vertically interfacing roles. RAMPLAND participants begin as regional management, develop a strategic plan and budget, shift to middle management, and finally to supervisory management roles. In the latter capacity, they implement plans and budgets previously crafted, while in higher management roles.

In SCAMP, the role shifting is reversed. Park service management teams consisting of a chief park ranger, maintenance officer, and administrative officer conclude the week by presenting a strategic plan to their real regional director and staff.

Learning that transects vertical levels occurs as participants in the two simulations move from role to role, and as they (like their corporate counterparts in the Siemens simulation) "step outside the simulation" and reflect on their actions and interdependencies. Presentations to real top management produce considerable transfer of organizational learning. In the Siemens simulation and in RAMPLAND and SCAMP, interaction among organizational levels provides the perspective necessary to reduce vertical learning fragmentation in the real world organizations.

Aligning Leadership Development with Strategic Planning

In recent years, companies have recognized the need to incorporate leadership training in the context of corporate strategy development and implementation. Microworlds offer unique learning environments in which such integration can occur. Participants in complex behavioral simulations, such as Foodcorp and Globalcorp, begin with the ambiguous task of running the organization as they see fit. Their task typically concludes at a specified time, several hours later, at which point key executives address the other employees.

This is followed by a debriefing. Using participant observations and questionnaire data, the players explore issues of management style, decision-making techniques, and interpersonal dynamics. In one firm, for example, the decision-making power in the simulation, as in real life, became centralized; policies became dependent on top management, while subordinates became isolated and alienated. These sessions revealed the importance of influence and interpersonal skills to both subordinates and observers, although these issues remained obscure to upper-level management until the debriefing session. As the debrief revealed the dynamic interdependencies that led to decisions, participants were encouraged to improve individual and collective performances for future endeavors.

Connecting Short-Term and Long-Term Views

Policies, decisions, and strategies in complex organizations are often based on short-term thinking. Consequently, they may initially produce positive outcomes but prove costly in the long run. The Hanover Insurance Company microworld has taught this lesson well. Hanover Insurance is a highly successful, medium-sized property and liability insurance company that has been caught in a spiral of escalating settlement costs and premiums. The Hanover team, assisted by a systems group from MIT, built a microworld by identifying both hard and soft variables vital to the claims-adjusting process. Ultimately, they concluded that well-established practices throughout the insurance industry have led to massive underinvestment in the number of adjusters as well as in their salaries and experience levels. Managers failed to perceive the problem because adjusters kept hitting "production" targets with the number of claims settled. Rising settlement costs prompted more attention to controlling expenses, which led to further underinvestment in adjusters and further quality deterioration, thus creating a spiral. By following commonly practiced policies, managers unwittingly created their own problems.

The lesson learned from Hanover is a simple but vital one for organizational learning—management must view short-term activities and problems as interrelated, but inconclusive, pieces in the long-run development of the company.

The Beer Distribution Game, a board game refined by John Sterman of MIT, also illustrates how these programs attack systemic problems. A simple shift in the demand schedule at the retail level consistently results in massive disequilibriums throughout other aspects of the simulated beer industry. The impact of a single change on an entire system is dramatically repeated by human miscalculations, not actual shifts in demand.

PROMOTING FOCUS ON COMPETITION AND COLLABORATION

The simuworlds and microworlds discussed above were crafted from real industries and companies and mirror well the behavior and activity of corporate life. Participation requires subtle qualitative analysis of competitors, customers, suppliers, and other driving forces in an industry. As suggested by superior performance in real-world operations, the focus is on implementation of appropriate strategic plans within their environment, rather than a preoccupation with competitors. Several authors of complex behavioral simulations, intent on stimulating learning from collaborative behavior, have eliminated computer models and competing groups entirely. Other microworlds allow teams to play against a computer model but not against each other. Managers must perceive that the learning process is about them, their ways of thinking, their strategies, and the dynamics of the system, rather than the competitive computer model that underlies the simulation.

ENCOURAGING EXPERIMENTATION AND TRANSFER OF LEARNING

Field research suggests that assignments from which managers learn the most tend to be "tough duty": start-up projects, functional job shifts, fix-it situations, company turnaround jobs, and jobs that require a leap in scope. Microworlds and simuworlds provide practice in these types of experiences in a risk-free environment. Without the "do-or-die" consequences encountered in real life, participants are likely to learn through experimentation.

At the same time, however, research suggests that managers learn poorly from experience if there is no feedback or coaching. Microworld debriefings must be extensive and performed by experts in the simulation, in the subject matter, and in group processes.

The new practice fields, like their corporate counterparts, are so qualitatively complex that participants must specialize and learn different aspects of the problem at the same time, then share and integrate information. This is ensured, as in real life, by hierarchical and role-based organizations in which various participants receive different organizational information, or by the functional and environmental richness provided by case material and international briefings. Participants face the choice of engaging in team interactions that foster or hinder organizational learning, such as withholding or filtering information and "turf-building," or sharing openly and generously.

The reality of the simulated context is so great that participants often recreate an organizational and interpersonal system similar to the corporate world in which they are employed. Observations about parallels between their simulated and real worlds prepare participants to transfer learning to practice. To promote this transfer of learning, simulations couple reflection, experimentation, and action in the simulated world with data gathering and reflection in the real world.

INITIATING ORGANIZATIONAL LEARNING WITH SIMUWORLDS AND MICROWORLDS

Simuworlds and microworlds provide practice fields for many concepts vital to the development of leaders today. As simulations parallel organizational realities, increased dialogue helps to clarify patterns in the organization or expose weaknesses and strengths in strategic thinking. Interaction in the simulation can change the views and behaviors of the participants. The likelihood of this happening grows exponentially as organizations incorporate four elements in their learning transformation: (1) a healthy combination of systems theory and simulation that allows managers to see patterns and interactions in their organization; (2) incorporation of a wide array of participants from all levels and backgrounds in the organization; (3) top management participation in and support for uninhibited, prolific learning; and (4) sustained development that allows the simulation to become seamlessly integrated with the real organization. Next, we take a look at each element in action in different simulated environments.

Discovering Contradictions in Strategy Through Systems Theory

Participants sometimes compare their microworld experience to "confronting a gyroscope" for the first time. They often discover difficulties in team strategy that can be explained by systems theory. They react to "pushes and pulls" in the dynamic system being simulated. They learn how to align systems to arrive at success over time, and they learn to better understand the interconnectedness of events.

Consider, for example, the ability of a simuworld to replicate the actual growth pattern of the microcomputer industry. The adaptation of products in this industry has been so rapid over certain periods that firms have encountered great difficulty in maintaining sufficient production capacity to meet demand. In a microcomputer industry simuworld, teams will often oversell and underproduce, resulting in the inability to meet orders and producing slim profits. IBM has encountered this difficulty during several growth periods, each time allowing newcomers like Compaq Computer Corporation or Packard Bell to make a solid entry. But, unlike the real world, the pace of simuworld decisions can be varied, and what would be irreversible actions in the real world can be reviewed and retried. By simplifying circumstances, the simulation enhances participants' ability to focus on key issues.

Learning from Dynamic Interdependencies of Participants

With contemporary emphasis on teamwork, integration of functions, and global management, opportunities to practice team development are very valuable. Simuworlds and microworlds are effective practice fields for intercultural training because participants are "caught up" in the role-based activity, allowing their feelings and attitudes to emerge.

Simuworlds and microworlds include extensive behavioral debriefings and use data gathered from observations of the participants in action. A new customized microworld developed for Hoechst Celanese includes formal computerized feedback from simulation, teammates, and trained observers. This feedback addresses "competencies" for participants developed from 360-degree observations obtained from "real world" colleagues.

A few of the personal insights stimulated by similar feedback and open discussion of leadership and teamwork within Foodcorp include:

- "Those who say little may have the best ideas."
- "Creating a compelling image of the future is part of my job."
- "Blaming others is useless and destructive."
- "Life repeats itself until I learn; habits are hard to break."
- "I don't have to do it all myself."

Many of the world-class executive training programs today bring together diverse teams from global operations and usually initiate training with team-building exercises. The research available, although limited, suggests that participation in a simuworld or microworld can create team cohesiveness that is stronger than many traditional team-building exercises and arguably more cost efficient, since the simulations provide the additional advantage of including highly transferable managerial and organizational learning.

The team interactions that occur within simuworlds and microworlds are many and varied. Culturally diverse teams in a simuworld may experience bias resulting from a dominant language, a dominant gender, or a dominant functional background. Some participants have exhibited an "Ugly Westerner" overtone because of a linguistic advantage in English. Participants from male-dominated cultures often show frustration as they engage in their first male-female team interaction.

Through iterations of play and coaching, participants in the Multinational Management Game have learned to work through their differences without the threat of corporate upheaval. Teams dominated by English speakers have learned to occasionally speak Japanese so that Japanese division chiefs can more readily express their feelings. Female managers, excluded from decision making, have learned to remain silent for a time and emerge as leaders when

Asian men request their help in writing reports in English. One Western-dominated team chose not to "Americanize" some of the Japanese-English—choosing instead to allow final reports that were grammatically idiosyncratic. Another nationally diverse team chose to confirm a decision consensus, with deference to Japanese teammates, by applauding.

Top Management Involvement in Futuristic Learning

An excellent example of the potential of top management involvement and support of organizational learning comes from a futuristic simulation called the Merlin Exercise. Although it is important to understand the focus of the present, an understanding of the future may be even more important. As Wayne Gretsky, perhaps the world's best hockey player, explained, "When everyone else on the ice is trying to get to where the puck is, I try to get to where the puck is going to be."

The forecasted future is a paradigm that managers already understand. They can examine organizational strengths and weaknesses, explore core competencies and capabilities, analyze current trends, and chart the future projection of those trends. But our experience suggests that managers have difficulty releasing current assumptions and envisioning possible ideal futures—often viewing these as pipe dreams. Simulations built around the present dynamics of an industry may fail to anticipate quantum leaps in the competitive environment or stimulate "out of the box" thinking.

The Merlin Exercise was created to move leaders away from the prevalent model of "present knowledge thinking" and to encourage them to leap to a challenging "invented future" with significant competitive advantage. T. H. White (1959), in *The Once and Future King*, describes Merlin, the magician and advisor to King Arthur, as having an uncanny ability to know the future. When questioned, Merlin explained, "Nearly everything in the world goes forward. . . . This makes it quite easy for ordinary people to live . . . but unfortunately I was born at the wrong end of time, and have to live backwards from in front, while surrounded by a lot of people living forward from behind" (p. 34).

White's whimsy provides an apt metaphor for the "future first" perspective. Armed with traditional sources of competitive and environmental data, participants are asked to "create a future" that is unencumbered by the limitations of current knowledge. The Merlin process starts with the senior management of the enterprise, who engage in a highly participative conversation, recorded on charts or via computer "groupware." Next they are encouraged to shift all attention from present concerns to envisioning what the organization could become. Finally, with "out of the box" thinking comes a renewed sense of challenge and excitement that can be shared with the organization. This fosters creativity and exciting planning.

The Merlin Exercise has been used successfully as part of a three-year executive education initiative for the top 700 executives in a large U.S. based health care products corporation. "Merlin" presentations about their "invented future" to a vice chairman or CEO conclude the five-day program.

Learning from Seamless Integration of the Simulated and Real Organizations

Effective strategic planning generates dialogue in organizations and encourages planners to examine their mental models of strategy and operations. But mental models are largely tacit, expressing themselves as intuitions and "gut instincts." Moreover, they are difficult to communicate. Organizational learning must blend the mental models of individual managers with the models that are shared among learners—the team. Well-designed simulation models capture shared mental models and create holistic dialogue. Thus, they support the communication and understanding of strategy.

Chris Argyris (1994) argues that effective managerial learning must be based on real-life problems, followed promptly by action involving innovative application to the participants' organization. Consultants, vaguely anticipating such needs, modified a predecessor of MMG to become the shadow of a large chemical company. The discrete products were changed to chemical tanks, human resource management relationships were added, and the company began developing a customized simulation.

Some learning was as planned; some proved serendipitous. Initially, the middle managers, hoping to become general managers, listened to lectures on finance, marketing, and operations, and learned to complete planning exercises designed for the game. Complaining that their teams needed to learn how to plan in all functional areas simultaneously, the managers requested that a learning lab of audiotaped workbooks be designed. Afterward, during the first decision round, one team member would attend the lab and study operations while another focused on marketing or finance. On the second round, team members switched functions for study. Soon all members were cross-trained in the various functions.

Over the years, players have provided information about discrepancies to the company's industrial engineers who program the game. Many of the suggestions for redesign gave rise to cross-functional questions never addressed by the real company. During simulation rounds, engineers and operations managers, traditionally concerned about chemical tank purchases, now project how depreciation and write-offs affect cash flow. Marketing personnel, for the first time, may see the connection between production capacity utilization, unit costs, and pricing strategies. By means of the simulation, managers are freed to share learning naturally.

The organization has also developed a new motivation and commitment to learning. Experimentation or "big picture thinking" has become a way of life. What began as a management game has become a customized microworld, mimicking the real organization with great verisimilitude. Solutions in the simulation often lead to action in the real organization, resulting in genuine organizational learning. The practice field has become seamless with the real organization.

CONCLUSION

Simuworlds and microworlds, second-generation business games, and in-basket simulations, provide excellent practice fields for a learning organization. They provide a risk-free environment in which to experiment with ideas and strategies. When combined with systems theory, they prompt managers to discern previously overlooked patterns and interactions in their organization. Incorporating a wide array of participants from all organizational levels and backgrounds can enrich learning and promote even greater organizational learning. If fueled with top management involvement and support, learning payoffs can become prolific and uninhibited. When practice fields are cultivated in an organization for a sustained period of time, learning in simuworlds and microworlds becomes seamlessly integrated with the real organizations they shadow.

SELECTED BIBLIOGRAPHY

To view the work that spurred worldwide discussion and development of learning in organizations, see Peter Senge's *The Fifth Discipline: The Art and Practice of the Learning Organization* (New York: Doubleday, 1990). *Organizational Dynamics* published a collection of distinguished articles on this subject, including pieces by Kofman and Senge, Chris Argyris, William Isaacs, Edgar Schein, Dave Ulrich, Todd Jick and Mary Ann Von Glinow, John Slocum, David Lei, and Michael McGill. See *The Learning Organization in Action: A Special Report From Organizational Dynamics* (New York: American Management Association, 1994). See especially Fred Kofman and Peter M. Senge, "Communities of Commitment: The Heart of Learning Organizations," *Organizational Dynamics,* 22(2), pp. 5-23, first published in 1993. For a splendid rationale for learning as competitive advantage, see John W. Slocum Jr., Michael McGill, and David T. Lei, "The New Learning Strategy: Anytime, Anything, Anywhere," *Organizational Dynamics,* 23 (2), 1994, pp. 33-47.

For more on the need for learning in organizations, see R. W. Revans, "What is Action Learning?" in *The Journal of Management Development,* 15 (3), 1982, pp. 64-75; M. Pedler, J. Burgoyne, and T. Boydell, *The Learning Company* (New York: McGraw-Hill, 1991); and R. Hawlins, "Organizational Learning: Taking Stock and Facing the Challenge," *Management Learning,* 1 (25), 1994, pp. 71-82. For the field of research on learning from experience, see W. M. McCall Jr., M. M. Lombardo, and A. M. Morrison, *The Lessons of Experience: How Successful Executives Develop on the Job* (Lexington, MA: Lexington Books, 1988).

An extensive survey of business game usage is contained in A. J. Faria, "Business Gaming: Current Usage Levels," *The Journal of Management Development,* 8 (2), 1987, pp. 58-65; an exhaustive review of learning validity studies is contained in J. B. Keys and J. Wolfe, "The Role of Management Games in Education and Research," *The Journal of Management,* 16 (2), 1990, pp. 307-336. Interestingly, both games that we have called simuworlds (INTOPIA and MMG) are based on the microcomputer industry. See J. Bernard Keys and Robert A. Wells, *The Multinational Management Game,* 4th ed. (Little Rock, AR: Micro Business Publications, 1992), and Hans B. Thorelli, Robert L. Graves, and Juan-Claudio Lopez, *International Operations Simulation* (Englewood Cliffs, NJ: Prentice-Hall, 1992). More extensive review of research and applications with *The Multinational Management Game* can be found in "The Multinational Management Game: A Simuworld," by J. Bernard Keys, Robert A. Wells, and Alfred G. Edge, *The Journal of Management Development,* 13 (8), 1994, pp. 26-37; and "Cross-cultural Learning in a Multinational Business Environment," by Al Edge and Bernard Keys, *The Journal of Management Development,* 9 (2), 1990, pp. 43-49.

Other management games that can be classed as simuworlds, noted in Exhibit 1, include Ronald L. Jensen, *The Business Management Laboratory* (Homewood, IL: Irwin, 1992), and *Airline, A Strategic Management Simulation* (Englewood Cliffs, NJ: Prentice-Hall, 1994).

Many of the computerized management games and simuworlds available are reviewed by J. B. Keys and W. D. Biggs, "A Review of Business Games," in James W. Gentry (ed.), *The Guide to Business Games and Experiential Learning* (London: Nichols/GP Publishing, 1994). To review the development work done on The Looking Glass, see M. W. McCall Jr., and M. M. Lombardo, *Looking Glass, Inc.: The First Three Years* (Tech. Rep. No. 13. Greensboro, NC: Center for Creative Leadership, 1979), and Wilfred H. Drath and Robert E. Kaplan, *The Looking Glass Experience: A Story of Learning Through Action and Reflection* (Greensboro, NC: Center for Creative Leadership, 1984). Many of the other complex behavioral simulations listed in Exhibit 1 are reviewed in Roger L. M. Dunbar, Stephen A. Stumpf, Thomas P. Mullen, and Maria Arnone, "Management Development: Choosing the Right Leadership Simulation for the Task," *Journal of Management Education*, 16 (2), 1992, pp. 220-230. Others such as *People's Express, Hanover Claims Adjustment Simulation*, and *The Beer Distribution Game* are available through Innovation Associates, a consultancy directed by Peter Senge of MIT.

For a more extensive discussion of microworlds, refer to *The Fifth Discipline* by Senge noted above, or to Peter M. Senge and Robert M. Fulmer, "Simulations, Systems Thinking, and Anticipatory Learning," in *Anticipatory Learning for the Twenty-First Century*, Special issue of *The Journal of Management Development*, 12 (6), pp. 21-33.

Complex behavioral simulations or non-computerized microworlds and other simulations included in this article are described more fully, along with survey and case type research, in *The Journal of Management Development*, 13 (8), 1994; see especially the article by Stephen A. Stumpf, Mary Anne Watson, and Hermant Rustogi, "Leadership in the Global Village: Creating Practice Fields to Develop Learning Organizations," pp. 16-25, and the article by Robert M. Fulmer and Stephen G. Franklin Sr., "The Merlin Exercise: Creating Your Future through Strategic Anticipatory Learning," pp. 38-43 and T. H. White, *The Once and Future King* (New York: Putnam, 1959). The customized microworld development at Siemens is reviewed in J. S. Goodwin and R. M. Fulmer, "Management Development at Siemens Electronics: Hitting a Moving Target," *Journal of Management Development*, 11 (6), 1992, pp. 40-45. For more information on in-basket simulations and customized microworlds developed for public administration projects, see M. McDonald, F. Catroppa, and J. B. Keys, "Making Management Development Relevant with Simulations," *Journal of Management Development*, 19 (3), 1991.

Several sessions of MMG have been conducted with intercultural groups. See Al Edge and Bernard Keys, "Cross-cultural Learning in a Multinational Business Environment," in J. Bernard Keys, ed., *Management Games and Simulations,*

Special issue of *The Journal of Management Development*, 9 (2), 1990, pp. 43-49; A. G. Edge and M. French, "Management Development at the Japan-America Institute of Management Science," *The Journal of Management Development*, 5 (4), 1986, pp. 51-68; and Robert W. Hornaday, "Using a Computer Simulation in Multicultural Management Development: An Indonesian Example," *Journal of Management Development*, 12 (3), 1993, pp. 12-19.

Chapter 12

The Multinational Management Game: A Simuworld

J. Bernard Keys
Robert A. Wells
Alfred G. Edge

The experiential knowledge and understanding of a complex industry and its competing companies can be greatly enhanced by participating in a simuworld. Simuworlds differ from the well-known management games in several ways. Rather than being built on generic business concepts, they are designed around accurate published data about one industry, and they usually model more closely a single company within the industry. This chapter describes such a simuworld, The Multinational Management Game (MMG), which models the microcomputer industry and Compaq Computer Corporation (Keys, Edge, and Wells, 1994).

Participants begin MMG operations by analyzing a short case history and developing a five-year plan. Providing a real corporate history, in this case that of Compaq Computer Corporation, is an improvement over the generic case introductions of past games. This provides a connecting link of institutional memory, interrupted for a time by corporate (simulated) activity created by teams, but connected once again in the final five year plan. After eight or more years of MMG work is completed, participants are required to pres-

Reprinted with permission of authors and publisher from J. Bernard Keys, Robert A. Wells, and Alfred G. Edge, "The Multinational Management Game: A Simuworld." First published in *Journal of Management Development* (MCB University Press), 13(18), 1994, pp. 26-37.

ent a five-year strategic plan for the future. In order to allow participants to break away from lock-step planning and engage in product
line development and other strategies that are much more complex
than within the simulation, the game rules are relaxed and all strategic moves and creative opportunities are allowed for this presentation. At this point the participants are provided the most up-to-date
version of the Compaq Computer Case and industry notes available
(similar to material in Block 1—but expanded to thirty pages).

Please see the diagram of MMG Simuworld Play (Figure 12.1).

Industry notes include extensive data about products for the
future from technology reviews in *Business Week, Fortune,* and
other business journals. Instead of building new plans on the latest
products manufactured within the game play, participants are free to
envision a totally new product that addresses the new communications highway, computer entertainment games, edutainment, interactive video, the telecommunications highway, and so on. Although
the competitive computer game inhibits alliances and mergers, participants are allowed to develop (and support) ideas for vertical
alliances with suppliers or customers and horizontally integrated
alliances with competing firms or suppliers, such as Motorola,
Microsoft, Intel, and others in their strategic plan for the future.

PLAYING THE MMG SIMUWORLD

MMG participants are organized into teams of six to seven members and placed in charge of a $200 million company, producing
and selling microcomputers and related equipment, and competing
with other similar companies in the industry. Team members are
provided job descriptions, share personal backgrounds, and self-
select roles for their teams.

FIGURE 12.1. The Multinational Management Game

Sequence of Simuworld Play

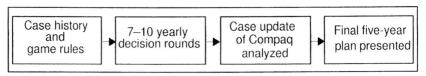

The simulated companies all look very much like Compaq Computer Corporation in its start-up years. Over a period of about eight simulated years the teams will try to make reasonable tactical decisions, converting heavy remaining inventories into cash, reducing employee turnover and increasing productivity by bringing low wage packages into line, and developing reasonable R&D, advertising, sales, and distribution policies. Effective teams will expand into international markets and will increase yearly sales to around $1 billion.

The start-up years are usually spent developing a viable organization and information processing system and clarifying team roles. Approximately five to seven hours of initial preparation per team member is required for game start-up. Major alternative strategic choices are outlined for participants, but other combinations may develop. Early years are often frustrating to teams, most of whom are functional specialists, as they attempt to balance sales with production schedules and to provide appropriate financing. As the tactical side of the business is mastered, teams use their corporate history, some industry notes, and research briefings about European and Asian markets to develop a five-year strategic plan. An MMG Simuworld seminar requires about four and one-half days for an executive program and about ten class periods for an MBA or Executive MBA program.

At year three, if a valid plan can be supported, teams are allowed to enter international markets of their choice, as exporters, producers, or both. After mastering the mechanics of the simulation and stabilizing domestic operations in Houston, Texas, participants are given several options. Teams usually follow a natural progression of exporting, followed by manufacturing overseas, then financing in other countries, and finally an integrated mix of operations throughout the world. In the present runs of the Simuworld, the most effective strategy usually proves to be the establishment of a producing site in Kuala Lumpur from which products are shipped back to the United States and forward to Europe. However, lower productivity in Malaysia and high tariff rates in Europe prevent this strategy from being a certain winner.

Global companies face more rapid and varied change than domestic companies, if for no other reason than the fact that something is likely to be changing on one or more of the international markets at any given time. MMG includes wage rates, productivity, and turnover rates that vary by producing country. The international/global dimension is portrayed by prime interest rates, inflation rates, tariff/VAT rates, and depreciation rates that are country specific. Also, varying economic growth factors and exchange rates for each country make MMG a very credible global simulation of real-world economic conditions.

After mastering case data and game mechanics (most correspond to real-world functions and terms), and developing a strategic plan, teams make yearly budgeting and scheduling decisions. The MMG Simu-world is designed so that participants view and feel the operations from a general management level and make decisions only about yearly budgets and schedules for that level. In this manner decision making becomes truly strategic in nature and an initial five-year plan and a revised plan for going international can be played out within a reasonable time frame. The actual inputs to decisions require very little computer time (and can be done by the administrator from written forms). Financial, operating, and industry results are returned for each team, simulating the results of a year of operation.

The emphasis of game play is on combinations of strategies, such as product innovation, price-cost combinations, or marketing development/distribution strategies, similar to those utilized by Compaq, IBM, Apple, and other PC companies.

To simulate the unruly and chaotic element of global operations MMG case incidents are frequently provided to force participants to respond to high-impact events throughout the world—a small war in one of their shipping harbor areas, a longshoremen's strike, or the loss of a key supplier because of a fire in a microchip plant. Computerized feedback responds by simulating these occurrences. Strategic Business Units overseas deal in the currencies of the producing sites, Malaysia dollars and deutsche marks, providing a realistic, but not overly complex, experience with exchange rate management and the risk of fluctuating rates.

THE CASE STUDY FOR THE MMG SIMUWORLD: COMPAQ COMPUTER CORPORATION

Compaq Computer, under the direction of Eckhard Pfieffer, has just completed one of the most successful turnaround strategies in the history of the industry. Compaq's phenomenal growth came to an end in 1990 because of the increasing technological expertise of other clone makers and a new reliance on cost-savings distribution channels. It was clear that Compaq could not duplicate their initial success without reformulating strategy. Joseph R. "Rod" Canion, the only president and CEO in the company's nine-year history, was ousted and replaced by Eckhard Pfieffer, German-born, European business chief, who had recently transferred to corporate headquarters as COO.

It takes years to acquire, as Compaq's Pfieffer has, a mature knowledge and feel for a major corporate enterprise. Few executives ever master the ability to think and conceptualize across the functional areas of the business at once. And rare indeed is the executive who can relate the many internal factors futuristically to environmental changes and trends, where competitive advantage will be sourced. Yet, in high-tech industries today, such as the microcomputer industry, these interrelated variables and more must be considered by the top management team in order to develop yearly and long-run plans. The Simuworld includes not only a business game but also a case experience, including many of these complexities, similar to the abridged case study shown. The case experience is provided as a concluding project at the close of game play.

The microcomputer industry is arguably the most important industry in the world, since it drives most high-tech manufacturing, aerospace industries, transportation, telecommunications, and research. It is certainly the most rapidly developing basic industry in the world, technologically. Because of its many interfaces, its exploding technology, its cutting-edge entrées, and its prolific familiarity, the PC industry is an excellent industry of choice for MMG.

Interestingly, the PC industry is changing so rapidly that even managers and executives within it are likely to be unfamiliar with much published information about their own and other firms. The MMG Simuworld with the Compaq case is an exceptional tool for updating them in a rapid and dynamic fashion.

The MMG computer game and case study are continually integrated in every way possible. For example, a few years ago, Compaq's stock price was just crushed on the stock market in spite of increasing profits and market share. Experts attribute the sizeable drop to increasing inventories in the $2 billion range and the sensi-

BLOCK 1. The New Compaq Computer Company (Abridged)
by John Gutknecht and Bernard Keys

In rebuilding the Compaq Computer Corporation, Eckhard Pfeiffer opted for a low-price high-volume strategy. He stopped testing every subassembly and leaned on suppliers to cut prices. Manufacturing costs were reduced by building an entire system on a single assembly line and cutting material costs by $200 million, without any apparent adverse effect on product quality.

In 1993, while sales increased 75 percent, employment was held to a 10 percent increase. Compaq's human resource development innovations greatly empowered cross-functional teams to speed product development. Productivity, measured in sales dollars generated per employee, approached $800,000 per year per employee in 1993, the highest in the PC industry.

Under Pfeiffer, Compaq increased market share by rapidly expanding distribution channels, becoming a leader in pricing, rapid product development, and excellent service and support. Additional worldwide entry included Hungary, Poland, Portugal, and China. Compaq's market share gain, measured by total revenue gains, was the largest share increase for any computer company. In 1994, Compaq was spending about one-third of its $170 million R&D budget on servers. In August of 1993, Compaq introduced a very popular desktop, the Presario, with many new product features and very competitive pricing, but sold out of the product in the fourth quarter. Compaq cemented its position as number one in PC-based servers worldwide with the ProLiant. Although Compaq's servers contribute only 5 percent of shipments to the company, they contribute 15 percent of revenue and 30 percent of profits.

Once the victim of price wars, Compaq was to become the aggressor. In 1992 Compaq announced price cuts of as much as 32 percent. The result was a continued downward spiral of industry prices. Compaq argues that this is a concerted strategy, representing a balancing act between competitiveness, growth, and profitability. They expect to make up the loss in margins by lowering below-the-line expenses and by stimulating sales growth in the higher-margin products.

From the moment Pfeiffer took over he began an advertising campaign proclaiming a new Compaq. Total ad spending was increased to $114 million in 1993, from the $82 million spent in 1992, and also up from approximately $55 million in 1991. Income before taxes as a percentage of sales increased from 7.2 percent in 1992 to 8.6 percent in 1993.

Because of increasing sales and channels of distribution the company's inventory doubled to $2.2 billion in 1994. This caused some wary investors to sell sizeable holdings and prompted a significant drop in the price of stock. The real challenge for Compaq and Pfeiffer is whether they can continue to be aggressive on pricing—by continuing the assault on costs—without sacrificing the top quality and innovation that was responsible for their early success.

tivity of stockholders to similar experiences with IBM's PS-1, which led to heavy losses. Our next modification of the stock price determinants of MMG will include inventory buildups, not just profits, debt-to-equity, and other commonly considered stock price determinants. Compaq's inventory buildup was planned to meet the heavy unit sales growth being experienced, but stock market sensitivity was not included in factors that should limit inventory size. This occurrence is a particularly good illustration of the system's concept of the *limits to rates of growth* and is similar to the kind of lesson learned by participants in the People's Express microworld (Senge, 1990).

LEARNING FROM MMG

Managerial learning is promoted throughout the MMG game play by numerous techniques. Frequent reflection periods are required in which teams must link game experiences to real-world experiences at work. Learning diaries with headings—*what I learned during decision making, what I learned about teamwork,* and *what I learned about strategy* this round of play—are frequently utilized. Much of the strategic learning comes at the points where strategic plans are updated. The major debrief at the end of team presentations following game play and the Compaq case analysis offers considerable learning opportunities. This debrief can be enriched by having top executive groups present to observe participant presentations.

When the MMG Simuworld is played over several weeks, an afternoon at a time, much more reflection and prompting of real company learning linkage can be promoted, as was the case with earlier versions that we used for Eastman Chemical, Xerox, Wilson, Inc., Teledyne-Stillman, and Maclanburg Duncan. From time to time we have tried to interest functional executives in their own corporate financial statements by occasionally shifting quickly from simulated statements to real corporate statements in the middle of a game debriefing, and making comparative analysis. In one such shift, none of the functional management heads, except the controller who was responsible for preparing them, recognized their own financial statements. Recently a branch bank head developed strategic plans for a presentation by a team at the same time she developed a real plan for her bank's board of directors. She was able to glean many new ideas supporting her real-life position while studying simulated activities.

Organizational learning, learning that seems to occur mutually across teams and that changes the way teams think, occurs within MMG in several ways. First, the major lesson learned from Simu-worlds is the systems dynamics lesson that *all corporate functions are interrelated* and that some systems incorporate *reinforcing feedback*, while some promote *balancing feedback*. Participants usually perceive these processes at work in their functional areas such as sales and marketing or in operations, but they seldom detect them as clearly across other functional areas. For example, we usually start teams with an initial buildup of inventories, but within a considerable growth cycle for the PC market. Few teams realize that increasing unit sales will create sizeable amounts of cash flow, and fewer still realize that a buildup of assets such as cash will lower many of the standard ratios that denote business success. Most teams have even more difficulty balancing the heavy growth of sales with production of PCs, a factor that requires several years of production strategy implementation. Consider the following learning diary entry.

> Round 3: This year we learned that cash budgeting is only effective if you correctly forecast what you will sell. The possibility that we might not sell all units was not included in the value of sales estimates. We are still behind on production capacity. If we could restart the game we would have increased our workstations in the first year.

In order to ensure that teams can master the complex detail of MMG in the time allotted, each member is required to develop individual strategic plans with an emphasis on the knowledge and experience gained in the assigned functional area, which is recorded on a PC disk. This process corresponds in a small way to what Peter Senge refers to as the discipline of *personal mastery* (Senge, 1990). Next, after having developed expertise in a functional area (and usually having developed some special biases within that area) teams must integrate individual planning disks into a complete strategic plan, what Senge calls *building shared vision* and *team learning* (Senge, 1990).

A second major lesson learned by MMG teams is that the *balancing of functional areas* is accomplished by the way in which one organizes and by the influence attributed to each team member. Teams often make critical errors in judgment early in the game by allowing a persuasive member to sway them unduly before fully learning about team strengths and mastering balancing processes. For example, in a recent game play a young plant manager persuaded his MMG team that the microcomputer industry was going to flatten in sales and that production capacity must be reduced. The error in judgment required about three simulated years to correct and led to a reorganization of the team. Somewhere near mid-game the more effective teams usually recognize that bureaucratic structures are inferior and they tend to reorganize, most often as cross-national and cross-functional teams. It is this reorganization that allows teams to cope with what Senge (1990) calls *emotional tension*, tension that develops between the ideal vision of team members and the reality of trying to balance functional areas. Observe the following learning diary entries that relate to such learning.

> Round 6: We have developed major conflict in terms of operational decisions. Our inventory and production is out of hand and there some conflict in resolving this problem. It is not a matter of not knowing how to solve it, but more of deciding which process to use. Market share projections are too aggressive by sales and marketing. Production and operations tend to be more conservative and more realistic.

> Round 8: Our organization has shifted to one of cross-functional teams and will remain this way. Our organizational structure is divided by region (North American, Asian and European). We will also organize by products as we change manufacturing over to new products.

A third major learning opportunity in the MMG Simuworld is another form of *team learning*. The tasks assigned are so complex and the time period is so compressed that teams quickly realize they must learn different things at the same time and that they must learn to conserve learning energy. In one Fortune 500 chemical company consulting project we developed a learning lab for participants to accomplish this task. Tape-notebooks were supplied to which members of each team rotated from round to round. For example, on round one a team sent one member to learn sales forecasting, another to learn production scheduling, and another to learn cash flow projection, bringing the team up to speed quickly on the yearly planning process. Members then rotated visits to notebooks for the next year of play. In the meantime the member trained assisted the other team members, using the newfound expertise. This process has continued for years in the organization, with many managers proceeding through MMG participation, rotating through the horizontal planning process notebooks, and upgrading the level of corporate-wide understanding and vocabulary used in day-to-day conversations. Organizational learning has also been stimulated by the customized simuworld, which continues to grow and develop within the company, forcing industrial engineers to engage in *dialogue* with accountants, marketing managers, and other key players about corporate-wide tasks that never interested them previously (Schein, 1994).

Effective teams in MMG soon discover that they must learn how to develop a *resonance or synergy through dialogue*. According to Schein, dialogue allows a team "to reach a higher level of consciousness and creativity through the gradual creation of a shared set of meanings and a *common* thinking process" (Schein, 1994). Some of this development can be seen in the following learning diary entries by J., a young woman, on one MMG team:

> Round 2: Each member is beginning to find his/her own responsibilities. Our operation tends to be fairly well organized with small subteams working on different projects or spreadsheets. For example, two work on decisions to build or hire while two or three look at debt and stock issues. Then we mold the decisions and test on an income statement spreadsheet—if inadequate we reassess the decisions and develop another avenue.

> Round 3: Team development is continuing to improve with sub-teams development and sub-team project assignments. Team leadership is also improving with our discussions and decision-making routine becoming more organized and to the

point. However, decisions are becoming more complex and more time-consuming.

William Isaacs, director of the *dialogue project* at MIT's Organizational Learning Center, suggests that dialogue represents *triple-loop learning,* the ability to "set up environments or *fields* in which learning can take place" (Isaacs, 1994, p. 54). The following diary entry probably depicts two learning concepts: first, the important concept that *today's decisions become tomorrow's plans,* and perhaps an example of the creation of *fields in which learning can take place.*

> Round 4: This round the transfer pricing issues took most of our time. We tried to allocate appropriate profits to the respective countries, and we tried to ensure that our decisions would lead us in the path of our strategic plans. The greatest problem was deciding whether or not we should change our organizational structure after we each composed our own individual strategic plans. If we do change, many of the team members will have to rework most of their planning; this will be very aggravating for those that do have to rethink, newly prepare, and reevaluate their proposed strategies. We have divided into sub-teams with half working on the international strategy. The other half of the group is compiling the composite strategy plan from all of the individual plans.

A fourth type of learning that occurs in MMG teams is *learning to work with intercultural groups.* This learning depends, of course, on assembling teams with a cultural mix, which is often the case in a multinational game. MMG has been used frequently for this purpose at the Pacific Asian Management Institute, University of Hawaii, utilizing an intercultural Asian and Western team mix. The Simuworld serves well by allowing participants to resolve cultural differences within a realistic task-oriented project. MMG has also been used as a central laboratory at the Japan-American Institute of Management Science operated by Hitachi. In the American Management Program, students from Japan and other Asian countries learn American styles of strategy and management. Students in the Japan Management Program from Western countries learn Japanese management styles. Learning is greatly accelerated by using live "boards of directors" from local organizations in the Honolulu area. A team member at the Japan-American Institute of Management Science in Honolulu reported:

> Our team consisted of management trainees from the USA, Japan, Thailand and Indonesia. Each of us had a different cultural style for dealing with problems. At first we also tended to develop very different strategies for the next year. However we learned how to respect other's opinions, and how to reach a decision that would satisfy everybody in the group. After we made decisions we began clapping our hands, as the Japanese teammates did, and as Japanese companies do. This is done to show the hope that a goal can be reached.

MMG provides a vicarious learning experience that is very valuable in today's global business world: that of conducting a country briefing and preparing for international business entry. One unit of the game manual provides considerable information on the more industrialized Southeast Asian countries (including Japan) with Malaysia as a producing site, and most European countries, with Berlin as a producing site. The data provided are rich enough to provide considerable challenge to team members. Each team member is assigned one major market and producing site to analyze and in which to become an expert. Priortizing these for entry then becomes a major strategic issue of the team.

MMG has been used in many industrialized countries of the world and in several developing countries. Free enterprise concepts and country-specific concepts often seem easier to demonstrate experientially than to explain in lecture. This was the purpose of MMG participation focusing on the North American market at Janus Pannonius University, PEC, Hungary. The Sangyong Group, Seoul, South Korea enrolled managers in MMG to teach them how to do business in the United States. International programs such as those at the University of Louisville, the College of William and Mary in Williamsburg, VA, and Georgetown University in Washington, DC, have used the game as an undergraduate international laboratory.

Finally, our research with management games and with the MMG Simuworld suggests that many unanticipated things are

BLOCK 2. Dynamic Strategies That Can Be Learned from MMG

- How to deal with the unruly and chaotic world of varying economic conditions. (Global companies always have crises occurring somewhere.)
- How to price products while meeting the threat of inflation, changing interest rates, varying exchange rates, and differing requirements for transfer prices worldwide.
- How to manage assets and expenditures without incurring high-cost special loans.
- How to develop competitive advantage through cost advantages, pricing differentials, offshore production, balanced marketing expenditures, and well-chosen regional distribution throughout the world when dealing with high-tech global products.
- How to manage complexity with teamwork by building on functional specialties, without allowing functional myopia.
- How to enter international markets in order to establish a competitive base without creating undue losses overseas or at home.
- How to utilize systems dynamics to develop long-run success and avoid short-term thinking.
- How to allocate scarce corporate resources between competing alternatives.
- How to examine technological and consumer trends of the industry to determine where future product innovations will come from.
- How to take advantage of knowledge of international markets, while achieving economies of scale of a global product.

---

learned from such property-rich laboratories. So many learning stimuli are available that it is very difficult to anticipate exactly what learning concept a team or team member will focus on in each simulated year of play. Perhaps this is why Arthur D. Little consultants have chosen to utilize MMG as an experiential final exam for MBA classes.

SUMMARY

Block 2 presents a summary of dynamic strategies that experience with teams participating in the MMG Simuworld has suggested can be learned.

The MMG Simuworld can be designed to lead to an action learning project, to precede a strategic planning period (as occurred fortuitously with the bank unit manager mentioned earlier), or to precede a global market planning and entry (which in turn could be organized as an action learning project). MMG participants can greatly profit from the administration of the Beer Game (see Chapter 11, this volume) in order to prompt functionally-oriented participants to take a systems view within the game. Action learning assignments can be made before the MMG game seminar and carried forward over the weeks or months following, as has been done with other business games (Jubilerer, 1991). The MMG and the Compaq Case can be utilized first, followed by a "live case" about current problems. MMG could be followed by the Merlin Exercise described in Chapter 11.

The MMG Simuworld is a multinational management game and case combination simulating the manufacturing, marketing, and financing of microcomputer products within a continually developing case study of the most rapidly developing industry in the world. Since the PC industry is poised to lead and be highly integrated with the exploding advances in telecommunications, interactive learning, entertainment, virtual reality simulations, and digital and voice-driven conversions, the game is oriented well to develop and stretch the minds of participants from many industries. It is a useful laboratory for updating managers within the microprocessing and related industries. Also, MMG design makes it highly suitable as a laboratory in which other tools of organizational and anticipatory learning can be utilized.

REFERENCES

Isaacs, W. N. (1994). Taking flight: Dialogue, collective thinking, and organizational learning. In *The Learning Organization in Action*. New York: American Management Association, 40-55.

Jubilerer, J. (1991). Action learning for competitive advantage. *Financier,* 15 (9): 16-19.

Keys, J. B., A. Edge, and R. A. Wells (1994). *The Multinational Management Game*. Little Rock, AR: Business Publications.

Schein, E. H. (1994). On dialogue, culture, and organizational learning. In *The Learning Organization in Action*. New York: The American Management Association. 56-67.

Senge, P. (1990). *The Fifth Discipline*. New York: Doubleday Currency.

Chapter 13

Leadership in a Global Village: Creating Practice Fields to Develop Learning Organizations

Stephen A. Stumpf
Mary Anne Watson
Hermant Rustogi

Global leaders must learn to lead multicultural microworlds through creating shared visions and common mental models. They must manage diversity less by appreciating and utilizing national and cultural differences, and more by establishing an organizational culture that *transcends* these differences. Programs for developing global leaders must go beyond teaching people to appreciate or accommodate cultural diversity to the task of developing people capable of creating an organizational culture that can *cohere* diverse groups (McBride, 1992). Peter Senge (1990) has proposed one such approach—a learning laboratory. We have used this approach in the context of the global village ideas proposed by Marshall McLuhan (1964; McLuhan and Fiore, 1968) to create a microworld practice field that facilitates systems thinking and organizational learning.

For a microworld practice field to be of greatest value it needs to be constructed so as to combine meaningful cultural and national issues with realistic interpersonal dynamics. This chapter examines

Reprinted with permission of authors and publisher. From Stephen A. Stumpf, Mary Anne Watson, and Hermant Rustogi, "Leadership in a Global Village: Creating Practice Fields to Develop Learning Organizations." First published in *Journal of Management Development* (MCB University Press), 13(8), 1994, pp. 16-25.

how two microworld practice fields—Foodcorp, International and Globalcorp—accomplish the task of creating a global village. Both are management development tools that are best thought of as behavioral simulations (not computer simulations) that create a realistic context for people to interact on business and global issues.

Three objectives are typically shared when these practice fields are used to facilitate systems thinking and organizational learning. These objectives are: (1) to surface cultural assumptions in the simulated context where they can be observed, tracked, and discussed relative to various effectiveness criteria; (2) to provide a practice opportunity for creating a global team capable of performing with a shared vision and common mental models; and (3) to develop leaders who can create as well as accommodate cultural norms worldwide. This chapter describes two practice fields and their common approach to facilitating systems thinking and organizational learning. We provide two examples of how microworld practice fields are used and share the results of the research underway.

GLOBAL VILLAGE PRACTICE FIELDS

Behavioral simulations stand apart from computer simulations in that they attempt to reproduce individual and collective behaviors that would normally be observed in a managerial work environment, including some degree of political, cultural, and conflict activity (McCall and Lombardo, 1982; Stumpf, 1988). The behavioral simulations that we discuss here are ones that attempt to mirror the top management roles and responsibilities of a global company.

The reality of the organizational setting in a behavioral simulation is obtained through the use of extensive background information and in-baskets for each simulated role—roles that are interconnected to reflect organizational realities. The content of in-baskets as well as the design for the organization is based on actual data and events collected from ongoing organizations. It is through the realism of the materials provided that the practice field stimulates representative behaviors from its participants (Dutton and Stumpf, 1991).

A realistic microworld practice field creates the possibility for dynamic interactions among participants. These interactions tend to be representative of the participants' on-the-job performances over the six-to-ten hour duration of the simulation. By analogy, we would expect a soccer team to be more inclined to exhibit gamelike behavior on a true soccer field than in a gymnasium. The greater the similarity of the practice setting to the performance setting, the more likely the practice behaviors will be representative of the performance-setting behaviors.

In the Foodcorp and Globalcorp simulations, participants are given a choice of several roles that vary in terms of hierarchical position, product or functional responsibility, issues to be addressed, and status. These roles create the organizational structure. For example, Foodcorp International, a food manufacturing organization, simulates thirteen senior management roles, three levels of hierarchy, two product groups, and two subsidiaries (Sonny's Restaurants and Farm Fresh Yogurt). Foodcorp's products (dry goods and frozen foods) are sold to distributors and retail supermarkets throughout the United States and in sixty other countries through thirty manufacturing plants, fifteen marketing affiliates, seven licenses, and six regional export sales organizations. Foodcorp is a fairly large firm within its industry, with 25,000 employees and $2.7 billion in sales.

Foodcorp uses a matrix organizational structure and has several committees to augment this structure. New product development activity, internal corporate venturing, joint ventures, international licensing agreements, and diversification/consolidation activities are integral to Foodcorp and the food processing industry. Consumer marketing (including brand development and advertising) and production quality are key issues domestically and internationally.

In comparison, Globalcorp (a public version of the proprietary Financorp simulation) is a diversified international financial services conglomerate with $27 billion in assets. Each of its thirteen senior management roles has corporate strategy development and business portfolio management responsibilities. The consumer banking sector is composed of a branch banking group, a credit card group, and a consumer credit group. The commercial banking sector includes an investment banking group, an institutional banking group, and a transaction services group. The financial product and services sector is composed of an information/investment services group, an insurance products group, and a research and development group. Each of the nine groups has two or three lines of business that offer a full array of products or services with profit-center responsibility.

Unlike the more homogeneous line-of-business situation and cross-functional activity common to Foodcorp, Globalcorp involves active coordination and competition across lines of business. The three levels of Globalcorp hierarchy are augmented by a committee structure that encourages cross-sector and cross-business discussion of customers (e.g., who owns the customer?), new business ventures, acquisitions, mergers, divestitures, and line-of-business direction.

CREATING A GLOBAL VILLAGE EXPERIENCE FOR ORGANIZATIONAL LEARNING

Some of the attributes of Foodcorp and Globalcorp that make them more lifelike than other methods for teaching systems thinking and organizational learning are the presence of a formal hierarchy among participants, division of labor, and realistic information contained in a hefty in-basket. Several other characteristics enhance the real-life quality of the simulation, such as the existence of various standing committees; prescheduled committee meetings that can be attended, rescheduled, or ignored by participants; and the incoming and outgoing mail throughout the simulation that is created by participants as they attend to or ignore various issues.

The large number of issues contained (e.g., more than eighteen major issues and more than thirty minor ones, with each role confronting about a third of these issues) make it a rich environment and context. This rich, interconnected, interactive context tends to minimize the dominance of any single participant's style and approach. The result is the creation of a group approach and culture. The temporal and artificial nature of the training experience actually assists participants in creating a microworld—a smaller, more immediate world that takes on a life of its own during the simulation and debriefings that follow.

The materials in Foodcorp and Globalcorp mirror real organizational experiences. Prior to the simulation participants self-select a role and thereby assume an organizational title, an associated status and position in the hierarchy, and role responsibilities. They are given a corporate annual report, an organizational chart, information describing the functions performed by other role holders including their managers, and direct reports. Participants devote from five to ten hours each to reading, analyzing, and internalizing this material along with dozens of pages of memos, correspondence, phone messages, and reports that are unique to the position they have assumed. While some of this effort is performed individually, small group meetings and presentations are conducted to thoroughly familiarize each participant with his or her position, its key issues, and significant company attributes.

Upon arriving at the simulation location participants are provided with individual office space, desks, a conference room, in-baskets, and writing materials. As an initial structure for their work day, they receive schedules of meetings, agendas of issues, budget reports, and memos containing information about current and unsolved problems as well as various opportunities. In addition, mail pickups and deliveries are scheduled throughout the day. All of these organizational trappings are designed to support a belief that the simulation is a real and valid experience.

Foodcorp and Globalcorp begin with a complex and ambiguous task: Participants are asked to run the organization as they see fit. The simulation typically concludes at a specified time six or more hours later with an address by the president and other key executives to the other employees. What issues are explored or ignored, who gets involved in decision making, how formal and personal power are used, what climate is created and how it affects the participants, and the actions to be taken or not taken emerge from the participants within the context of the simulation. These attributes of their microworld are captured by questionnaire, tallied, and used as part of the feedback process during the debriefing sessions.

While an organizational structure exists and some meetings are preplanned at the start of the simulation, participants are free to manage the organization as they choose. The fact that each role is initially constrained by the content of the information in it (e.g., data in memos, annual reports, and job descriptions) does not constrain how individuals interact to get additional information or how information is interpreted, shared, or used. They may (or may not) keep one another informed on possible actions on key issues, collect relevant information, summarize its implications, and formulate, become advocates for, and convince relevant others to accept new policy proposals.

As participants become involved in strategy-making activities during Foodcorp and Globalcorp, they are confronted with the time pressures, uncertainties, and dependencies associated with bounded rationality constraints (March and Simon, 1968). As they experience and become more aware of their limited capacities to comprehend, they may feel threatened. This, in turn, may reduce their adaptive capacities. Participants may restrict their information processing, narrow their fields of attention, overlook details, and reduce contact with other organization members in order to cope with the demands of a senior management position. To the extent that these behaviors occur, they are noted by a trained facilitator who is observing the process.

While each microworld that is created is unique, there are patterns that can be noted across groups, particularly if the groups are all employees of the same firm. For example, in one firm in which we have worked, the decision-making power within the simulation (and in real life) often becomes centralized. Policies become dependent on the overall vision and comprehension of those occupying roles at the top of the simulated organization's hierarchy. Subordinates get isolated and may even become alienated.

The importance of influence and interpersonal skills that enable the relevant participants to be included in decision making becomes evident to these subordinates as well as observers. But it often escapes those occupying the most senior roles until it is raised for discussion in a debriefing session. An irony in this process is that in order for senior management to maintain an understanding of activities within the firm that have strategy implications, they must depend on the inputs of participants occupying roles lower in the hierarchy. These participants are often feeling isolated and left out. They focus their attention on local matters, ignore opportunities to influence their senior management counterparts, and further cut themselves off from a more strategic and global perspective.

In the eight to ten hours of feedback and analysis that take place after the simulation experience, participants become more aware of these dynamic interdependencies, how their interdependencies evolved over time, and the behavioral roles they and others enacted in this policy-making process. They become aware of the systems dynamics within the microworld that *they* created and the extent to which it was a viable global village. This legitimizes their exploring the cultural assumptions they held that influenced their business decisions. By reviewing these decisions and the thoughts and behaviors that led to the decisions, participants are able to explore how their collective cultural diversity led to a microworld of shared perceptions. It is through this debriefing process that participants become eager to learn how to improve individual and collective performances in future endeavors.

Participant response to the Foodcorp and Globalcorp behavioral simulations has been uniformly positive. No one has dismissed the experience as unrealistic or unrepresentative. In fact, facilitators of the feedback process encourage participants to discount those aspects of the experience that are unrealistic or unrepresentative to them. Post-feedback session evaluations of the program have highlighted a tremendous amount of relevant learning that participants think and feel they obtained. Follow-up research has confirmed these evaluations—participants remember the experience and the lessons they learned several years later. Eighty-six percent of the more than 2,000 participants surveyed have expressed a desire to attend another behavioral simulation to further their insights and development (Stumpf and Mullen, 1992).

TWO PRACTICE FIELD APPLICATIONS

The growing awareness by organizational leaders of a need to develop global managers to perform effectively in a global market-place has led to rapid growth in global training programs. Several of these programs have chosen to focus on the development of man-agement talent suited to leading a diverse workforce and satisfying customers from different cultures. The organizations sponsoring these programs know that their managers must learn to frame expe-rience in a way that allows for common interpretation and unified action (Peters and Waterman, 1982; Pondy, 1976). These managers must learn how to effectively guide the behaviors of a culturally diverse workforce through the creation of a shared vision and a com-mon understanding of the organization's actions. One way of doing this is through the creation of a microworld with a culture so strong that it coheres the actions of diverse groups around the goals, beliefs, and practices of the firm. Developing managers who can build a unifying microculture requires providing them with experiences to practice creating and shaping a microworld (McBride, 1992).

Two organizational programs—one conducted by Northern Telecom and the other by Citicorp—exemplify the use of Foodcorp and Globalcorp as practice fields for managers to exhibit and develop leadership skills in creating a global village. By reflecting on how they created a global village—through the vision, values, behaviors, and actions of participants—these managers begin a process of systems thinking and organizational learning.

While the similarities of the programs offered by these two firms far outweigh the differences, the differences are particularly noteworthy. Northern Telecom, a midsize telecommunications equipment manufacturer headquartered in Canada, wanted a practice field experience that placed their managers in a matrix organizational structure facing a highly competitive, global marketplace with a line of products that had potential for rapid growth in select markets. While some competition across product lines was desired, the practice field needed to reflect a focused organization that was trying to grow in Europe, the Pacific Rim, and South America. Foodcorp fit their needs.

In contrast, Citicorp, a large, international, financial services firm headquartered in the United States, wanted a practice field that reflected a decentralized, multi-product-line firm that was diverse in its product offerings. As there is little in common among many of Citicorp's banking and financial service businesses, it wanted a practice field to have a large number of profit centers within it to parallel the Citicorp organization. Globalcorp reflects both the financial services nature of Citicorp and its line-of-business profit center approach.

Both the Northern Telecom and Citicorp programs were conducted over a week with participants in residence, focused on developing leadership skills with respect to global issues and a diverse workforce, and included lecture/discussion components to set the stage for the practice field session. Both programs included a multirater "feedback from home" assessment instrument as part of the program so that participants would have manager, peer, and direct report views of their skills based on previous job performances.

Participation in these programs was voluntary, prestigious, and limited to people who managed other managers (middle and upper-middle managers) and/or people who had significant responsibility for a line of business or function. The enrollment in each program was handled through the human resources function. Each program had, by design, a culturally diverse group of attendees. This added to the challenges of managing a diverse workforce and attending to a variety of cultural differences in the ways in which issues are approached and people interact.

Northern Telecom's objectives in using Foodcorp were for participants to:

- experience new forms of leadership behavior and the micro-culture they create as Northern Telecom managers;
- understand the interdependencies and tradeoffs inherent in modern organizational structures (e.g., matrix relationships);
- create and communicate a vision for that portion of the business for which each is responsible; and
- develop greater personal awareness of strengths and developmental needs in light of Northern Telecom's mission, vision, and values.

In addition, the week-long program was designed to:

- endorse an environment that supports people development and continuous learning, and outline their commitment to continuous improvement in people, processes, and systems;
- identify the impact of global marketplace/workforce issues in executing their roles as leaders in achieving the corporate vision and living its core values;
- describe the factors that contribute to effective, positive change, and determine ways to resolve organizational barriers to facilitate change; and
- demonstrate the ability to apply team skills in building organizational networks and alliances.

The Citicorp program was designed to help managers cope with the problems of leading effectively within the complex, fast-paced Citicorp culture. Issues such as dealing with ambiguity, balancing action with control, choosing priorities, and operating within constraints are addressed within the program. Specific objectives were to:

- define the challenges of managing effectively within the Citicorp culture;
- practice strategic leadership and differentiate it from strategic planning and tactical management;
- build upon and learn from Citicorp experiences and processes across businesses and time;
- experience the process of creating a culture in an organization similar in size and scope to Citicorp;
- identify, from a strategic perspective, the profitability and service dynamics of each business;
- understand the interplay between products offered, distribution systems used, and customer segments served in different global markets;
- identify the interdependencies among business lines and the tension between internal structure and external demands and perceptions; and
- develop a plan for applying the program learnings to the workplace.

LEADERSHIP IN A GLOBAL VILLAGE: THE RESULTS

Were the objectives in these two programs accomplished, and how did the behavioral simulation used help to accomplish them? Based on participant feedback following each offering of these programs and subsequent follow-up interviews, the program objectives were substantially met. Program evaluations of "the extent to which the program objectives were met" averaged for each of the fourteen program offerings (forty-eight behavioral simulations involving 357 people) from 4.2 to 4.7 on a 5-point scale ("5" being the most favorable response).

In each program, and for each application of Foodcorp and Globalcorp, the participants created their own global village; they became a separate entity with a distinctive culture, approach to issues, vision, and values for the duration of the simulation activity. These microworlds were the practice fields for the concepts espoused earlier in the program.

Based on participant and observer postsimulation assessments, extensive practice efforts were made by all but a few participants. These efforts were the behaviors that became the raw data for many hours of feedback discussion immediately following the simulation. Their practice efforts and the microworld they created were explored by them—first individually, then as a global village. Through discussion, participants were able to identify opportunities to transfer both the successful and "still needs development" efforts of each person and his or her microworld to their respective work settings.

As a closing activity for each microworld that was created, participants were asked to summarize two generalizable personal insights and key learning points for their organization. These were documented on flip charts and fed back to other participants in other simulations as well as the parent organization. For the forty-eight microworlds discussed here, the following insights and organizational learnings were shared by five or more microworld groups:

Insights Mentioned	*Frequency*
Those who say little may have the best ideas.	32
Creating a compelling image of the future is part of my job.	29
Blaming others is useless and destructive.	23
There are probably many right answers.	19
My personal style will dominate my skills if I let it.	15
Walking the talk is tough work.	12
Intentions and actions are not the same.	11
Life repeats itself until I learn; habits are hard to break.	9
I don't have to do it all myself.	8

Organizational Learning Mentioned	*Frequency*
There is no one to blame, only problems to be solved.	34
Visions are of little value unless they are shared and compelling.	30

The enemy is us.	28
Simple solutions obstruct creative thinking.	21
Yesterday's solutions are often today's problems.	17
Structure must follow strategy.	12
Messy processes are not necessarily inferior to organized ones.	10
The past is not a reliable indicator of the future.	8

SUMMARY

Unlike other "practice sessions" where one or two program ideas are tried in a controlled, simplified setting, the Foodcorp and Global-corp simulations brought out each participant's typical approach to issues and people—including views of cultural diversity. Postsimulation discussions indicated that participants were trying hard to apply what they learned, but were often overwhelmed by the complexity and realness of the simulation activities and their interactions with each other as the leaders of the simulated company. Under stress, they did what came most naturally to them. Many tried to create microworlds that paralleled their real worlds. Outdated understandings and mental models of how things worked were hard to let go of—even when doing so was part of the program.

Without intending to do so, participants often recreated in their microworld an inferior organizational system similar to the one that they had been living in, independent of the program concepts or their expressed desire to change. It was not until participants were asked to reflect on their actions and behaviors through a facilitated debriefing process that the above-noted personal and organizational insights emerged. It is these insights and organizational learnings that are now being tracked in follow-up interviews. The interviews conducted to date confirm the nature of the personal insights and have begun to identify how the organizational learnings are being applied to specific business situations.

REFERENCES

Dutton, J. and Stumpf, S. A. (1991). Using behavioral simulation to study strategic processes. *Simulation and Gaming,* 2 (2), 149-173.

March, J. G. and H. A. Simon (1968). *Organizations*. New York: Wiley.

McBride, M. (1992). Management development in the global village: Beyond culture—a microworld approach. *Journal of Management Development,* 11 (7), 48-57.

McCall, M. W., Jr. and M. M. Lombardo (1982). Using simulation for leadership and management research. *Management Science*, 28, 533-549.

McLuhan, M. (1964). *Understanding media*, New York: McGraw-Hill.

McLuhan, M. and Q. Fiore (1968). *War and peace in the global village*. New York: Simon and Schuster.

Peters, T. J. and R. H. Waterman (1982). *In search of excellence: Lessons from America's best run companies*. New York: Harper and Row.

Pondy, L. R. (1976). Leadership is a language game. In McCall, M. and M. Lombardo (Eds.), *Leadership: Where else can we go?* Durham, NC: Duke University Press

Senge, P. M. (1990). *The fifth discipline: The art and practice of the learning organization*. New York: Doubleday Currency.

Stumpf, S. A. (1988). Business simulation for skill diagnosis and development. In London, M. and E. Mone (Eds.), *Career growth and human resource strategies*. New York: Quorum Books, 195-206.

Stumpf, S. A. and T. Mullen. (1992). *Taking charge: Strategic leadership in the middle game*. Englewood Cliffs, NJ: Prentice-Hall.

Summary:
What We Learned
About the Seven Imperatives

In the introduction to this text we reviewed seven imperatives for executive education and organizational learning in the global world:

- Think and act globally
- Become an equidistant global learning organization
- Focus on the global system, not its parts
- Develop global leadership skills
- Empower teams to create a global future
- Make anticipatory learning a core competence in your organization
- Use practice fields to revinvent yourself and the global organization

Let us review what we have learned about these seven imperatives from the chapters included in this book.

THINK AND ACT GLOBALLY

To think and act globally, Kanter and Corn remind us (Chapter 2), may actually mean overlooking global differences—searching for other causes of problems first. They stress first and foremost that the global actor and thinker does not stereotype cultures. These same authors dramatize this need with the example of the American who served in Japan during World War II and returned to marry one of the docile women he saw there. He was dismayed to learn after the marriage that she came from the one part of Japan that did not fit his sterotype—one that encouraged assertive, dominant women.

Adler and Bartholomew (Chapter 3) continued the learning journey well. It is an economy's human resources, not its natural resources, that will determine success in the global world. Japan is a prime example. With fewer natural resources and less land mass than most industrialized countries of the world, they have created a legendary success story. Their strategies were, of necessity, global from the period following World War II, and they borrowed from every culture in the world.

BECOME A GLOBAL LEARNING ORGANIZATION

Expatriates only make up one small part of the system, say Adler and Bartholemew (Chapter 3). All managers must adapt and all must help create a synergistic organizational culture that transcends any one culture. In the global firm, or what Adler and Bartholomew call the transnational firm, power is no longer centered in a single headquarters and the organization is no longer dominated by any one culture. These authors offer insight that permeates the imperatives of this book:

> . . . the integration required in transnational firms is based on cultural synergy—on combining the many cultures into a unique organizational culture—rather than on simply integrating foreigners into the dominant culture of the headquarters nationality. . . . Transnational managers require additional new skills to be effective in their less hierarchical, networked firms: first, the ability to work with people of other cultures as equals; second, the ability to learn in order to continually enhance organizational capability. Transnational managers must learn how to collaborate with partners worldwide, gaining as much knowledge as possible from each interaction and transmitting that knowledge quickly and effectively throughout the worldwide network of operations.

Global firms must have transnational human resource management systems to be successful.

EMPOWER TEAMS TO CREATE A GLOBAL FUTURE

Mixed nationalities on teams can bring richer and more appropriate solutions to global problems. The critical factor is that of choosing the right mix. Davison describes one such team in operation.

The . . . CEO managing a Finnish/UK merger stresses team spirit, common language, consensus through debate. He encourages managers to participate in the debates outside their areas of responsibility and to tell when he is wrong . . . Although the headquarters are based in Finland, only the CEO and the financial controller are based there. The other three top vice presidents were free to choose any European headquarters as their operating base. It works because there is a high level of trust and a very disciplined communication pattern. Every month they have a board meeting at one of the regional headquarters or company offices somewhere in the world. Between meetings they have a telephone conference every Monday to share information and conduct a very organized set of telephone conferences. . . . The benefit of being geographically dispersed is that the top team is always out in the company, encouraging networking and cross-fertilization and bringing a firsthand knowledge of events to the board meetings.

Often part-time teams that function in planning and networking serve best, rather than those engaged in regular work, says Sue Canney Davison (Chapter 4).

To ensure that all possible learning is gleaned from projects, organizations may wish to engage teams in action learning processes. Each member of a team shares a problem or project, usually in case form, and commits to meet regularly, assist each other with ideas for solutions, and continues till all problems are solved or all projects are complete (Louise Keys, Chapter 8). Team members can be from the same or different organizations. When Davison's admonition to use teams that are from mixed nationalities or diverse cultures is needed, even richer learning is likely to occur.

FOCUS ON THE GLOBAL SYSTEM, NOT ITS PARTS

Systems dynamics, according to Senge and Fulmer in Chapter 10, suggests that role players in organizations form mental models of "how things are." These models are largely tacit and difficult to communicate. Further, certain models are shared by learners in organizations. To learn, all the various decision makers must learn together. Systems thinking as articulated by the MIT Organizational Learning group helps individuals see patterns and helps organizational members focus on the big picture. There is a trend today of increasing management involvement in modeling the organization, aided by new computer software that allows them to participate more directly in building organizational models and in participating in management simulations and games.

One of the important tools of the systems strategist is scenario development. Scenarios are stories that give meaning to events. Like novelists, the scenario team weaves together plots driving forces and trends. Gutman (Chapter 6) reviews the way scenario planning developed at Shell during the 1970s to assist in studying social, political, and economic trends that were likely to affect the oil markets. These tools of planning draw out the slow-moving trends that will affect the industry in the future. Gutman cites the "Johnson & Johnson 2002" case, which required more than 100 interviews in six countries to assess key issues in Johnson & Johnson's business and to reflect global challenges for the future.

Whenever a new strategic issue confronts policymakers, it initiates a process of debate and dialogue. Microworlds and simuworlds, discussed next, can enhance this debate and dialogue. Simuworlds and microworlds bridge planning and training/learning by including learning in both the development and the utilization side of a simulation.

Gutman outlines the way senarios, cases, and systems thinking can be combined with anticipatory learning:

1. The corporate planning staff formulates broad scenarios of the marketplace ten to fifteen years hence, and groups of line managers use those scenarios for direction.
2. Future-oriented cases are developed to encourage common "mental models" of the business enviroment at different levels of the business.
3. A broad group of managers is exposed to systems dynamics concepts through computerized "microworlds" that elicit skills and orientations for the future.

DEVELOP GLOBAL LEADERSHIP SKILLS

A model of the effective global leader suggested by the articles in this book would include several key characteristics.

The global manager understands the worldwide business environment from a global perspective. The traditional manager, on the other hand, focuses on a single foreign country and on managing relationships between headquarters and that country (Adler and Bartholomew, Chapter 3). There is the high-performance international team composed of mixed nationalities (Chapter 4) and the "contingency model of international management development methodology selection" (Chapter 5). The global leader does not stereotype culture but views the world from a global perspective. The global leader is aware of certain themes that permeate life in various cultures and probably knows several cultures intimately. Such a person speaks more than one language. The globally competent leader has been trained in cognitive, behavioral, and performance programs for international leadership, including cases or simulations, assimilators or microculture experiences. The global leader's model of organizational learning is likely to include not merely improvements in performance (Chapter 1) but anticipatory—participative and futuristic—learning as well.

The leader is likely to have several field experiences. He or she may have participated in an action learning program geared to culturally diverse teams. The globally competent manager may have been called upon to work as an internal or external consultant in international training, and has probably provided briefings about a country upon return from the field. The globally competent manager may have participated in a microworld or simuworld that deals with global trade and strategies.

The contingency model for international management development presented in Chapter 5 calls for international training by lecture and cases in the cognitive competency area, behavioral training such as in the cultural assimilator, and performance competency training from simulations or field experiences. Brislin's 100 cross-cultural incidents and eighteen themes central to understanding cross-cultural interactions are useful for general intercultural training. They are also useful as an aid to expatriate trainers to help elicit memory about specific events in another culture upon returning to the trainers' home country.

The case study of training Russian managers presented by Gancel and Perlo integrates many of the concepts presented in this book. It targets a specific branch of industry and involves European textile and clothing industries with Russian participants on an operational level. Thus some initial rapport was provided by combining trainers and participants of similar industry and technical background (see Kanter and Corn, Chapter 2). Its content, pedagogy, and methodology were developed only after the in-depth examination of the daily challenges Russian industrialists face (see Chapters 3, 5, and 6). It goes beyond management training per se and aims at developing business relations between Russian and Western European industrialists in order to support the Russians and allow subsequent skills to be immediately applied. This approach follows the admonitions of Chris Argyris, reviewed in Chapter 11 under the heading "Learning from Seamless Integration of the Simulated and Real Organizations," that effective learning must be based on real-life problems followed promptly by action.

MAKE ANTICIPATORY LEARNING A CORE COMPETENCY IN YOUR ORGANIZATION

Slocum, McGill, and Lei, writing in Organizational Dynamics, propose that learning must include "strategic intent to learn, commitment to experimentation, and an emphasis on learning from past successes and failures" (Chapter 11). Fulmer and Teegen, in Chapter 1, suggest that "all learning is not equal." Some is maintenance oriented, merely trying to discover ways to do better what we already know how to do. Some is shock learning, precipitated by crisis and forced on us. Some learning, however, is both participitative and futuristic. This is learning that anticipates future environments, opportunities, and threats, and changes today in anticipation of occurrences in the future. Decentralized learning that engages diverse cultures and that includes mixed nationalities is likely to produce very rich knowledge and idea based. When learning is anticipatory and based on opportunities for a wide range of participants to provide inputs across the global organization, it "creates a global synergism for the future."

Organizational learning is well illustrated by action learning programs such as those at the University of Michigan's Global Leadership Program, which train managers in all areas of competency, cognitive, behavioral, and performance (Chapter 5). Fast-track managers from sponsored companies participate on culturally diverse teams, with the scheduled project of developing strategies for entering various international markets. Teams develop cohesiveness in Outward-Bound programs on Maine's Hurricane Island. They may lay a foundation for worldwide performance by building a global world model and critiquing their own firms on a global scale. As a capstone experience the teams visit three different countries and establish networking for their companies. Before departure teams are given country briefings. This program not only illustrates the action learning model, but also demonstrates ways to develop cultural synergy and exemplifies leadership development and strategic management integration.

USE PRACTICE FIELDS TO REGULARLY REINVENT YOURSELF

Learning in organizations is often fragmented by several learning barriers. Individuals in each functional specialty and in each country of a global company see only one aspect of a larger problem. This fragments learning horizontally across the global organization. Top management planners fail to perceive the interaction required with lower management and lower management fails to conceptualize plans beyond their own functional areas. This fragments learning vertically in the organization. Strategic planning and leadership training is often segmented, and according to Adler and Bartholomew, the latter often lags behind globalization of the former. Managers often fail to grasp the connections between short-term actions and long-term results. This obscures an understanding of cause and effect. In addition, planners in organizations tend to experiment or take risks only when forced to do so by crisis.

Microworlds and simuworlds, such as those described in Chapters 10 and 11, the rehearsal rooms of the manager, are excellent in helping organizations overcome the five learning barriers. Microworlds such as Globalcorp and Foodcorp, described in Chapters 11 and 12, built on in-basket architecture, involve participants in the simulation and free natural behavior. Since these exercises include multiple hierarchies they are particularly effective at assisting in integrating thinking vertically in the organization. Persons who fail to bring subordinates into the planning initiatives find out about their mistakes in the debriefing session. The integration of leadership training and strategic planning is built into complex behavioral microworlds and computerized simuworlds. For example, the teams participating in the Siemens Electronics Simulation, to prepare for a merger, developed a better view vertically within their organization. Representatives from real operating divisions assigned to manage the simulated headquarters group developed a new appreciation for some of the complexities associated with the role of managers at the headquarters. Many of the problems that the newly merged organization was to face in its transition were replicated within the confines of the one-week simulation.

The simuworld, based on computerized management game architecture such as The Multinational Management Game and others described in Chapters 11 and 13, includes as a major strength the ability to view organizations as a big picture. The ability to learn across functions, countries, and cultures is enhanced. Participants must plan across marketing, operations, and finance, and engage in strategies across world markets and diverse cultures. Since time and space are compressed in a simulation, it is easier to see cause and effect between functions and between short-term decisions and long-term plans.

Similarly, simulation programs noted in the performance sector of the contingency model for selecting international training methods (Chapter 5), such as the American Management Program and the Japan Management Program at the Japan-American Institute of Management Science in Honolulu, reinforce our thinking about contingency models and culturally diverse practice fields. Students from Japan study American management, and students from the Western world study Japanese management for five months. In both programs students from Eastern and Western cultures are brought together in teams for a number of experiential laboratories using simulations such as The Multinational Management Game (Chapter 12).

These experiences enable participants to explore organizational and strategic change alternatives within culturally diverse teams, to make mistakes, and to learn from the other cultures, but to avoid damaging the organizations by which they are employed. The contingency model of Chapter 5, with its listing of training methods, and the accompanying literature, provides a handy reference to training methodology likely to provide strength for the competency desired.

No simulation prompts experimentation of thinking and creativity better than the free-form Merlin Exercise. Executives who engage in this exercise suspend "present-knowledge-thinking" and forget the forecasted future. Instead they move forward in their thinking as did Merlin the Magician in King Arthur's court, to live backward from the future. They make a leap in thinking, armed with traditional sources of competitive and environmental data, but unencumbered by the limitations of current knowledge, to create an "invented future" with significant competitive advantage. By engaging senior management via charts or group-ware in highly participative dialogue, attention is shifted from present concerns to "out-of-box" thinking. To be sure, hindrances and limitations will be reviewed again at some point, but often these are less restraining than was envisioned before the ideal future was invented.

Global organizations engage in microworlds, simuworlds, customized simulations, and the Merlin Exercise to continually reinvent themselves.

Resources and Materials
for the Global Learning Organization

ORGANIZATIONAL LEARNING CENTERS

The Center for Executive Development
124 Mt. Auburn, Suite 520
Cambridge, MA 02128
(617) 557-6771

The Center for Managerial Learning
and Business Simulation (CML)
College of Business Administration
Georgia Southern University
P.O. Box 8127
Statesboro, Georgia 30460-8127
(912) 681-5457

Monitor Corporation
Cambridge, MA 02163
(617) 252-2276
(617) 252-2255

Innovation Associates, Inc.
4613 Wellborne Drive
P.O. Box 309
Sherrills Ford, NC 28673-0309

JMW Consultants
1 Station Place
Stamford, CT 06902
(203) 352-5047

Society for Organizational Learning (SoL)
222 Third Street, Suite 2323
Cambridge, MA 02141
(617) 491-0262

ELEA S.p.A
Consultancy of Olivetta
via Dei Bruni, 27
Firenze, Italy
Tel. 39-55 475603/475500
Fax. 39-55 483793

MANAGEMENT SIMULATION AND GAMING CENTERS

Burgundy Group, Inc.
100 E. Saint Vrain Street
Colorado Springs, CO 80903-1143
(719) 634-8956

Center for Creative Leadership
5000 Laurinda Drive
P.O. Box 26300
Greensboro, NC 27438-6300
(919) 288-7210

Center for Managerial Learning and
Business Simulation (CML)
College of Business Administration
Georgia Southern University
P.O.Box 8127
Statesboro, GA 30460-8127
(912) 681-5457
FAX (912) 681-0292

EduTRek
Tower Place #2000
3340 Peachtree Road, NE
Atlanta, GA 30326
(404) 812-8250

Interpretive Software
1932 Arlington Blvd.
Charlottesville, VA 22903-1560
(804) 979-0245

The Learning Partnership
Affiliate of the MSP Institute
301 Caspian Street
Tampa, FL 33606
(813) 254-9668
FAX 813-251-0079

Strategic Management Group, Inc.
3624 Market Street
Philadelphia, PA 19110
(215) 387-4000

Management Games
Wilson Baptista Junior
Rua Pium-i 312 / 303A
30310-080 Belo Horizonte, MG
Brazil
Tel. +5531 282-3976
e-mail: wilson@bis.com.br

Index

Page numbers followed by the letter "e" indicate exhibits; those followed by the letter "f" indicate figures; and those followed by the letter "t" indicate tables.

Acquisition process (foreign), 43-44
Acting globally, 243-244
Action Learning, 3,6-7,88,108-109, 151-152
 adaptations, 155-159
 approaches to, 153-155
 definition of, 152-153
Adaptable, 13
Adaptive family, 96
Adler, N.J.
 leadership training, 249
 and learning, 11,17,243-244
 synergistic, 12
 and management, 247
 transnational, 2
 and managing globally competent people, 5,13,49-69
 and selective perception, 97
After-experience recommendation, 147
Albert, R., 102,129,132
Allied-Signal postmerger simulations, 185-186
Alpha Company, 118
Ambiguity, 140
American Management Association, 6,194
American Management Program (AMP), 110,250
AMP. *See* American Management Program
Andrews, E.S., 101
Anglo cluster, 93

Anticipatory learning, 11,15-22
 as core competency, 248-249
 future-oriented, 184
 scenarios and cases for, 117-125
 and systems dynamics, 181-190
Anxiety, 140
 and foreign takeover, 40
Apple Computer, 9
Appraising and Coaching Staff, 166
Argyris, C., 16,42,101,182,248
 and seamless integration, learning from, 209
Art of the Long View, The, 120
"As you like it," business learning approach, 18
Assignment (overseas), 91
 accomplishing, 96
Assimilators, cultural, 102-103
Attitude, and cross-cultural interaction, 42
Attraction, similarity leading to, 130
Attribution, 142
Avoiding stereotypes, 138

Baba, V.V., 98
Backstage culture, 97
BaFa BaFa Simulation, 103
Bailey, E., 5,122
Baker, J.C., 91,104
Balancing of functional areas, 223
Barker, J.R., 106
Barney, J., 16

Barriers, to learning, 249
  overcoming, 199-204
Bartholomew, S.
  leadership training, 249
  and learning, 11,17,243-244
    synergistic, 12
  and management, 247
    transnational, 2
  and managing globally competent
    people, 5,13,49-69
Bartlett, C., 2,56
Bartwick, J.M., 17
Battelle Research Institute, 122
"Because I say so," business
    learning approach, 18
Beck, J.E., 100,108,158
Beer Distribution Game, 204,228
Behavior, 97
Behavioral competency, 98
  developing with experiential
    methods, 101-105
Behavioral simulation, 107
Behavioral training, 93
Belonging, 140
Berger, M.A., 101
"Best Proven Practices," 57
Beta Gmbh, 118
Bhawuk, D.P.S., 131,139
"Big global picture," focusing
    on, 4,183
"Big picture"
  learning, 195. *See also* Learning
  thinking, 210
Black, J.S., 91,92,96,101
Bleicken, 5,87,91-112
Bogorya, Y., 100,101,102,109
Bolt, J.F., 93
Borderless World, The, 1,12
Botkin, J., 7,16,17
"Boundaryless" organization, 4
Bower, G.H., 97
Braddick, B., 108
Brislin, R., 5-6,103,109,129-148
Broaddus, D., 146
Bryne, D., 130

Burgundy Group, 201
Burke, M.J., 100
Burnett, K., 109
Business
  compatibility, 36-37
  globalization of, 52-56
  success, 39-40
"Bust the bureaucracy," 74

Caie, B., 156
Canney Davison, S., 7
Carnevale, A.P., 108
Cascio, W., 5
Case incidents and intercultural
    training, 101
Case studies, 122-124
  international management
    development, 161-177
  Russia, 167-177,248
Categorization, 141
Central country value, tendencies
    of, 26
Challenge, 121
Change, 26
  and global competition, 8
  and growth, 142
  and leaders, 5
Change management seminar, 173
Change Masters, 12,18,19. *See also*
    Kanter, R.M.
Citicorp, 236
Citizens of country, interaction
    of, 130
Claims Laboratory, 187
Clark, K.B., 15
Clarkson, 3
Client participation, significant, 183
Clientele (multicultural),
    professionals who work
    with, 144-145
Clover, W.H., 155
Club of Rome, 11,16,17
Cognitive, side of scenario planning,
    120

Cognitive competency, 98
Collaboration, focus on, 204
College students, 145-146
Colorful incident, overreacting
    to, 138
Common thinking process, 224
Communication
    in an international context,
    131,165
    open and mutual respect, 38-39
Company-wide network, 74
Compaq Computer Corporation, 206,
    215,217,220
    as MMG simuworld, 218-219,221
Competence
    with experiential methods,
    101-105
    political, 170
    social, 170-171
    technical, 170
    three stages of, 98
    and training required, 96-97
Competition, focus on, 204
Competitive advantage, 7
Competitive demands, 65
Competitiveness (national), creating,
    49
Computer-simulation model, 184
Conflict, 2
    danger of with foreign takeover
    anxiety, 40
    intercultural, and creativity, 83-84
Confrontation, 140
"Confronting a gyroscope," 206
Constraints, removing, 74-75
Consulting, multicultural
    environment, 164
Contingency model, 251
    following cross-cultural training,
    111
    and international management,
    247
Contextual factors, and cross-cultural
    relationship success, 34-41

Contrast America, role-play exercise,
    103
Cooper, J., 131
Coordinating International Projects,
    166
Core competency, anticipatory
    learning as, 248-249
Corn, R. I., 2,13,23,46,243,248
Corporate Culture and Performance,
    5
Corporate pool, 57
Correctness of choice, 132
Cost, assessment of and geographical
    distance, 75
"Create tomorrow," 8
"Creating a corporate culture," 156
Creating an international team,
    74-78,80f
"Creating our future," business
    learning approach, 19-20
Creativity, and intercultural conflict,
    83-84
Credibility, 175
Critical incidents (100), 134-139
    themes around development
    of, 139-142
Critical uncertainties, 121
Cross-border merger, 43,45
Cross-border relationships, 24
Cross-cultural encounter, 5,130,131
Cross-cultural experiences, 88,131,
    137,139
Cross-cultural incidents (100),
    134-139,247
    themes around development
    of, 139-142
Cross-cultural interaction, 131
    between expatriate managers
    and local staff, 53
    and cross-cultural incidents (100),
    247
    and general assimilator, 144
Cross-cultural interaction
    (continued)

and globalization, 52
negative sides of, 41-42
social context of, 133
and trainees, 138-139
Cross-cultural orientation, 131,140
Cross-cultural relationship success,
    23-46
and contextual factors as key
    determinants of, 34-41
Cross-cultural teams, 13
Cross-cultural tension, levels of, 40
Cross-cultural training, 101,102
contingency model following
    development of, 111
programs, 68,89,131,133
Crump, L., 102,103
Cultural assimilators, 102-103
format, 132-134
Cultural awareness, 163-164
Cultural cluster, eight, 93
Cultural differences
analyzing, 13
approach for managers, 24-26
in decision-making styles, 30
employee sensitivity to possibility
    of, 39
and interpersonal difficulties
    with foreign colleagues, 32
level of, 92
national, 29-30
in search of, 24-26
vs. technical differences, 38
and tension, 42
Cultural empathy, 96
Cultural fatigue, 97
Cultural feedback, 81
Cultural heterogeneity, 43
Cultural mode, getting beyond, 176
Cultural synergy, 55,57-58
Cultural tendencies
of country, 26
of group, 26
Cultural value issues, 25-26
Culture vs. context, 30-33
Culture sensitizer, 132

Culture shock, 97
Culture-general assimilator, 88
uses for, 142-147
Culture-specific training, 143
Cushner, K., 129,132,134,146
Customized microworlds, 197
Cusumano, M.A., 6
Cyert, R.M., 124

David, K., 92,97,104
Davison, S.C., 13,73-86,244-245
Day, R.R., 100
de Gues, A., 7,119,120
Dealbuster, 25
Decentralized learning, 12,248.
    See also Learning
Dechant, K., 101,108,109
Decision-making process, 84
Decision-making styles, cultural
    differences in, 30
Deep-end approach, 109
Degree of similarity, 92
Delphi forecasting, 20
Delta et Cie. S.A., 118
Dempsey, P., 102
Developing International Networks,
    166-167
Development (transnational),
    60-62,63e
Development of international
    management, 6
DeVries, D., 107
Dialogue, 224
Difference
and cultural value issues, 25-26
in national cultures, 29-30
Differentiation, 142
Disconfirmed expectancies, 140
Diversity, 7
Domestic firm, 53
Domestic game research, 106
Domestic training, contingency
    model, 98
Dominant culture learning, 11-12

"Do-or-die" consequences, 204
Double-loop learning, 16,182
Drigin forces, identifying, 121
Dunbar, E., 92,104,107
Duncan, N., 122
Dutton, J.E., 107,230

Early, P.C., 100,103
Eccles, J., 138
Edge, A.G., 102,103,105,106,110
    Multinational Management Game,
        The, 215-228
Eight cultural clusters, 93
El-Namaki, M., 93
Emotional tension, 223
Employee
    attributing foreign colleagues
        negative behavior
        to nationality, 44
    reaction to cross-cultural
        interaction, 41-42
    reaction to foreign ownership,
        45,46
    sensitivity to cultural differences,
        39
Equal, all learning is not, 16-18
Equidistant manager, 12
Ericsson, 61
Evolution, 121
Executive (global), developing,
        87-89
Expatriate (ion), 53,54-55,67,91
    preparation, 165
    selection of managers, 96
    success, 96
    training, competency achieved
        by, 98
Experienced-based learning, 97-98,
        109
Experiential learning, 101-105
Experimentation, 204-205
Experimentation *(continued)*
    "big picture" thinking, 210

Explanatory factor, culture
    vs. context as, 30-33

Fabritek, 34,42
Faira, A.J., 105
Family, adaptive and supportive, 96
Fast-track managers, 249
Fatigue, cultural, 97
Feedback, establishing, 81
Feedback structure, 16
Feudal village (social sphere), 169
Fiedler, F.E., 102,129,132,147
Field experience, 109
Fifth Discipline, The, 4
Financial management seminar, 173
Finney, M., 97,104
Fiore, Q., 229
Flagship program, 156
Fleck, R., 106
Follow-up research, 235
Foodcorp (microworld), 196-197,
        230-240,250
Forecasted future to invented future,
        20-21
Forecasting vs. creating the future,
        20
Foreign acquisitions study, 26-27
    pilot project for, 27-30
Foreign assignment, 62
Foreign language, proficiency,
        104-105
Forrester, J.W., 181,183
Fortune 1,000, 91
Framework scenario, 122
Franklin, S. Sr., 21
Free-form simulation process, 197
French, M., 102,106,110
Fulmer, R.M.
    and anticipatory learning,
        15-22,118
    and systems dynamics, 181-190,
        245

Fulmer, R.M. *(continued)*
    integration of systems thinking
        and learning, 4
    and learning, 11,12,248
    and Merlin Exercise, 8,9
    microworlds/simuworlds, 193-211
Fundamental attribution error,
        44,136
Future
    forecasted to invented, 20-21
    manager model for moving
        toward, 21-22
Future-oriented, anticipatory learning
        as, 17,18
Future-oriented cases, 123-124
Future research, 111-112
Futures Group, 122
Futuristic learning, 208-209
Futuristic thinking, 8

Galligan, P., 157,158
Games, international, 105-106
Gamma NKK, 118
Gancel, 87,88,161-177
General Electric (GE),
        7,108,151,157,159
Generative learning, 182-183.
        See also Learning
Geographical distance
    assessing cost of, 75
    managing, 78-80
Ghoshal, 56
Ghoshal, S., 2
Gilbert, D., 136
Global anticipatory learning.
        See Anticipatory learning
Global Business Network, 122
Global Change Master Learning, 12
Global competition, and change, 8
Global executive, developing, 87-89
Global future, and teams, 6-7,
        244-245
Global leadership skills, developing,
        5-6,247-248

Global learning matrix, 12t
Global learning organization
    become a, 244
    becoming equidistant, 3
Global manager, 247. *See also*
        Manager
    need to develop, 235
Global organizational learning, 3,7-8
Global strategic integration, 58-59
Global system, focusing on,
        3-4,245-246
Global Teenager, 121
Global village
    experience for organizational
        learning, 232-235
    practice fields, 230-232
    results of leadership in, 238-240
Globalcorp (microworld), 196-197,
        230-240,250
Globalization, and learning, 11-13
Globalization of business, 52-56
Globally, thinking and acting,
        243-244
Globally competent people,
        managing, 13,49-69
Graham, J.K., 93
Graves, R.L., 106
Group coordination, 201
Group cultural tendencies, 26
Gruetzi, 28,34,35,37,38,44
    and business success, 39,40
Gudykunst, W.B., 97,100,102,103
Gullahorn, J., 131
"Gut instincts," 181
Guth, G., 106
Gutman, J., 6,117-125,246

Haley, U.C., 107
Hall, E.T., 131
Hambirck, D., 85
Hamel, G., 8
Hammer, M., 4,97,100,102,103
Hands-on learning, 101. *See also*
        Learning
Harvard Business Review, 6,119

Harvard Business School, 159
Harvey, M., 91
Hays, R.H., 15,96
Hennessy, E., 185
Heskitt, J.L., 18-19
Hewlitt, T., 147
Hierarchical structure, 53,141
Hilgard, E.R., 97
Hinton, R.W., 106
Hofstede, G., 18,30,93,96
Horizontal fragmentation,
    overcoming, 200
Hornaday, R.W., 106
House, R.J., 104
"How things are" mental model, 245
Human resource system
    (transnational), 56-58,244
    executives, 69,118
    integration, 59-65
Hunt, T.G., 106
Hydrotech, 28,30,34,35,36
    anxiety and foreign takeover,
        40,41
    and business success, 39,40
    and in-group favoritism, 43
    and investment, 37-38

ICM. *See* Inter Cultural Management
    Associates
Illusions (transnational), 65-69
Ilola, L.M., 146
Implementation
    of international team, basics of, 80
    of task, taking into account, 77
Importance of group, 141
In time apart, 79
In time together, 79
Inappropriate training, 91
In-basket architecture/simulation,
    194,196,210,230,250
Incentive, and recruitment, 60
Incidents, 100 cross-cultural, 247
    themes around development
        of, 139-142

Individual learning, 60
Individualism-Collectivism, 18
Industrial development, history
    of in emerging economies, 4
Influence, 53
    of nationality, appreciating, 75-76
Information-processing skills, 131
In-group favoritism, 43
In-group vs. out-goup
    experience, 142
    members, 43
Innovative learning, 11
Inpatriate, 54-55
    assignments, 54
INSEAD, 6
Instrumental learning, 182. *See also*
    Learning
Insufficient training, 91
Inter Cultural Management
    Associates (ICM), 2,161.
    See also Russia, case study of
Interaction of citizens of country,
    130
Intercultural analysis, 147
Intercultural communication, 131
Intercultural management training
    programs, 89
Intercultural training, case incidents
    for, 101. *See also* Training
Interdependencies of participants,
    learning from, 206-208
Interference, investment without,
    37-38
International assignment,
    management training
    for, 91-93,94t-95t,96-97
Internship, 174-175
International communication, 165
International conflict to creativity,
    83-84
International firm, 53-54
International management,
    53,165-166
    centers, 155-156
    development, 6,87-88

International management,
    development *(continued)*
    case studies of, 161-177
    contingency plan for, 92,247
    games and simulations, 105-106
International manager(s)
    method for choosing, 5
    proficiency in host language, 104
International negotiation, 164
International Operations Simulation
    (INTOPIA), 195
International raw materials market
    seminar, 174
International team
    creating/managing an, 74-78,80f
    establishing
        context of, 73-74
        feedback, cultural and personal,
            81
    and geographical distance,
        managing, 78-80
    implementing basics, 80
    intercultural conflict
        and creativity, 83-84
    lessons
        for leaders of, 84-95
        for managers setting up, 77-78
        for participants, 84-85
    members, not leaving anyone out,
        84
    mixing nationalities in, 73-74
    participation, balancing, 82-83
    working languages, choosing,
        81-82
    working within, 80-86
International trade fairs seminar, 173
International training
    and cultural awareness, 163-164
    design/development, 162-163
    needs analysis for, 162
    research, 100
    for trainers, 163
Internationalization, 161
Internationalizing vs.
        implementation strategy, 49

Interpersonal style, differences in, 31
    problems with foreign colleagues,
        32
Invented future, 20-21,251
Investment
    and operational autonomy, 37
    without interference, 37-38

JAIMES. *See* Japan-American
        Institute of Management
        Science
James, H., 7
Japan Management Program (JMP),
        110,225,250
Japan-American Institute of
        Management Science
        (JAIMES), Honolulu, 103,
        105,110,225,250
JMP. *See* Japan Management
        Program
Job ability, factors of, 96
Johnson & Johnson, 19,124,246
Joint venture, 35
Jones, M.L., 153,154
*Journal of Managerial Learning,
        The,* 15
Jubilerer, J., 159
Jussim, L., 138

Kahn, H., 120
Kanter, R.M., 2,6,12,13,18,
        23-46,243,248
Kaplan, R.E., 107
Keys, J.B., 91-112
    microworlds/simuworlds, 193-211
    Multinational Management Game,
        The, 215-228
Keys, L., 5,6,87,88,151-159
Knowledge, 3,8. *See also* Learning
Kofman, F., 193,199
Kolb, D.A., 97,102
Kotter, J.P., 5,18-19

Landis, D., 139,140
Language, 140-141
  choosing working, 81-82
  as excuse for lack of team
    participation, 81-82
  problems, 30
  proficiency, foreign, 104-105
Lanier, A., 91,96
Lannor, C., 184,186
Larreche, J.C., 105
Larsen, R., 19
Latham, G.P., 102
Lawrie, J., 153
Leader(s)
  and change, 5
  choosing for international team,
    76-77
Leadership, and strategic planning,
    202-203
Leadership in a global village,
    results, 238-240
Leadership skills (global),
    developing, 5-6,247-248
Leadership training, 249
Leading Change, 5
Learning, 3,7-8. *See also*
    Organizational learning
  about a structure, 16
  action, 3,6-7,88,108-109
  barriers, 249
    overcoming, 199-204
  and culture-assimilator format,
    132
  decentralized, 12,248
  double-loop, 16,182
  equality of, 16-18
  experience-based, 97-98
  experiential methods, 101-105
  generative, 182-183
  and globalization, 11-13
  individual, 60
  instrumental, 182
  maintenance-oriented, 11,12,
    17,248

Learning, maintenance-oriented
    (continued)
  "Because I say so" approach,
    18
  from MMG, 221-227
  organizational. *See also*
    Organizational Learning
    creating a global village
      experience for, 232-235
    global leader's model of, 247
    reducing high risk of, 197,199
  performance oriented, 105
  shock, 11,17248
  single-country focused, 53-54
  single-loop, 16,182
  transfer of and experimentation,
    204-205
  triple loop, 225
  work experience as a source of, 97
Learning, business approaches
    to, 19f
  "As you like it," 18
  "Because I say so," 18
  "Change master," 19
  "Creating our future," 19
  "Learning to Create a Synergistic
    Future Globally," 12
Learning cycle model, 97
Learning laboratory, 105
Learning organization, 7,107
  developing, 179-180
  microworlds/simuworlds for, 198e
Learning Organization, The, 15
Learning the ropes, 135-139
Learning vs. beating the computer,
    189
Learning vs. microworlds, 189-190
Learning vs. teaching, 188
Learning vs. winning, 188-189
Least-cost outcomes, 54
Least-cost products/services,
    producing, 54
Lei, D.T., 3,7,248
Lessons of Experience, The, 109

Lessons and international teams
   for leaders of, 84-95
   for managers setting up, 77-78
   for participants, 84-85
Lewin, K., 97
Lewis, A., 153,154
LGI. *See* Looking Glass, Inc.
Lindsay, C., 102
Little black book executives, 170
Living Company, The, 7
Local nationals, dealing with, 96
Local responsiveness, 60
Lombardo, M., 107,108,230
Long-term views, 203-204
Looking Glass, Inc. (LGI), 196

Madon, S., 138
Maintenance learning, 11,12,17,248
   "Because I say so" approach, 18
Malone, P., 136
Malpass, R.S., 132
Management
   development methods, 99-100
   problems, and national cultural
      differences, 24
   training, model for, 91-93,
      94t-95t,96-97
Manager(s). *See also* Managing
      globally competent people
   cultural differences approach
      for, 24-26
   expatriate, selection of, 96
   fast-track, 249
   future training of, 111
   global, 247
      need to develop, 235
   international. *See* International
      manager(s)
   lessons for setting up international
      teams, 77. *See also*
      International team
   model for moving toward the
      future, 21-22
   results-oriented, 31

Manager(s) *(continued)*
   senior, 32,118
   supervising a multicultural
      workforce, 96
   traditional 247
   transnational scope
      in development, 60-62
      in recruiting, 59-60
      in retaining, 62-64
      in utilizing/utilization, 64-65
   transnationally competent,
      50,51t,52
   use of microworlds, 184
Managing director, role of, 169-171
Managing globally competent
      people, 13,46-69
Managing an international team,
      74-78
Managing Internationally, 165-166
March, J.G., 124,153,154,234
Margerison, C.J., 156
Market segmentation, 168
Markstrat competition, 105
Marquardt, M., 3
Marshall, 6
Marsick, V., 108,156,157
Masculinity-Femininity, 18
Mason, D.H., 122
Materials development, 129-131
McBride, M., 107,229,236
McCall, W.M. Jr., 107,108,109,230
McGill, M., 3,7,248
McIntyre, D.J., 104
McLuhan, M., 229
Mendenhall, M., 92,93,96,101,104
Mental models, 181-182
Merlin Exercise, 8,9
   a free-form simulation process,
      197,251
   and futuristic thinking, 12-13,21
   and invented future, 21,208,209
Merlin Process. *See* Merlin Exercise
Mestenhauser, J., 146

Metalfab, 28
anxiety and foreign takeover,
40,41
and business compatibility, 36
and cross-cultural interaction
negative side of, 42
and organizational problems,
43,44
and decision-making styles,
cultural differences in, 30
and investment, 37-38
and relationship desirability, 34,35
Metaplan, 85
Method for choosing international
managers, 5
Microcultural experiences, 109
Microsoft, 6
Microworld, 107,246,249-250
evolution of as practice field,
194-195
examples of, 184-187
leadership/strategy in, 196-197
for learning organization, 198e
and organizational learning,
205-210
using, 187-190
Mihal, W.L., 93
MiL. *See* Swedish Management
Institute
Millett, S.M., 118,122
Mistakes, overseas assignments are,
91
Mistrust, 41
MIT Organizational Learning group,
203,246
Mitchell, T., 102,129,132
Mixed nationalities, 247
MMG. *See* Multinational
Management Game, The
MMG Simuworld. *See* Multinational
Management Game, The
Modeling process, 92
Morecroft, J.D.W., 184
Morrison, A.M., 108
Mullen, T.P., 107,235

Multicultural clientele, professionals
who work with, 144-145
Multicultural environment,
consulting in, 164
Multicultural workforce, supervising,
96
Multinational, 67
firm, 54-55
Multinational Management Game,
The (MMG)
and "big picture" learning, 195
learning from, 221-227
participants of, 207
simuworld, 215-228,250,251
Compaq Computer Corporation,
218-219,221
playing, 216-218,216f
Mumford, A., 108
Murakami, M., 158
Murray, A.H., 97
Murray, F.T., 97

National competitiveness, 49
National cultural differences, 29-30
and decision-making styles, 30
and interpersonal styles, 31
management problems caused
by, 24
and organizational problems,
42-45
National orientation, 25
National stereotypes, 33
Nationality
appreciating influence of, 75-76
mixed, 247
in a team, 73-74
negative behavior attributed to, 44
Nationals, dealing with local, 96
Needs analysis, and international
training, 162
Negative behavior attributed to
nationality, 44
Negative side of cross-cultural
interaction, 41-42

New Rules, 5
No Limits to Learning, 7,17
Noel, J.U.L., 101
Noonan, P., 188
North, D., 124,125
Northeast Consulting Sources, 122
Northern Telecom, 236,237

Oberg, K., 131
O'Brien, G., 147
Oddou, G., 92,93,96,104
Ohmae, K., 1,2,3,12,66
Olivetti, 61
Once and Future King, The,
    20-21,208
On-the-job learning, 107-109
Operational autonomy, and
    investment, 37
Operational consequences, 33
Organization, 3
Organizational Dynamics, 194
Organizational learning, 7,60,
    222,249. *See also* Learning
  creating a global village
      experience for, 232-235
  global leader's model of, 247
  imperative, 15-16
  matrix, 18-20
  and mental models, 181-182
  and microworlds/simuworlds,
      205-210
  reducing high risk of, 197,199
Organizational problems, and
    national culture, 42-45
Organizational similarity, 36
Organizational strategy, 93
O'Reilly, B., 110,157,158
Osigweh, C.A.B., 101
Out-group vs. in-group members, 43
"Out-of-box" thinking, 208,251
Outward-Bound program (Hurricane
    Island, Maine), 110,158,249
Overseas assignments, 91
  accomplishing, 96

Packard Bell, 206
Paige, R.M., 146
Pang, J., 105
Participant, interdependencies
    of, 206-208
Participant selection, 174
Participation, balancing, 82-83
Participative, anticipatory learning
    as, 17,18
Partnerships (potential), 175-176
Passage of time, 40-41
Passport hierarchy, 55
People, 3
  mix of in an international team, 74
People's Express, 9,186-187
Performance competency, 98
  developing, 105-109
Performance incentive, 63
Performance-oriented learning, 105
Perlo, 2,87,88,161-177
Personal feedback, 81
Personal mastery, 222
Peters, T.J., 235
Phatak, A.V., 3
Pilot project for foreign acquisitions
    study, 27-30
Pinder, C.C., 96
Policy-making process, 235
Political competency, 170
Pondy, L.R., 235
Porter, M., 151,159
Positive orientation, 34
Postsimulation assessments, 239
Power, 53
Power Distance, 18
Practice fields. *See also* Microworld;
    Simuworld
  evolution of, 194-195
  global village, 230-232
  use of, 249-251
Prahalad, C.K., 8
Predeparture training, 91
Predetermined elements, 121
Prejudice, and cross-cultural
    interaction, 41-42

Present-knowledge thinking, 251
Privatizations, 168-169
Process (transnational),
  57-58,61-62,63-64
  in recruiting, 60
Product development cycle seminar,
  173
Program objectives (ICM), 172
Programmed knowledge (P), 152
Providing Leadership, 166
Prudential Assurance Company, 154
Ptak, C., 131

Questioning insight (Q), 152-153

RAMPLAND (simulation), 202
Randles, F., 122
Rationale, sharing with international
  team, 75
Ratiu, I., 97,108
Recommendations (transnational)
  65-69
Recruiting, 59-60
  transnational, 61e
Reengineering, 4
Reinvention, 8-9
Relationship desirability, 34-36
Representation (transnational), 57,63
  in recruiting, 60
  in utilization, 64-65
Reputation, 35
Respect (mutual), 45
  and open communication, 38-39
Response, 121
Responsiveness (local), 60
Results-oriented manager, 31
Retaining managers, transnational
  approach to, 62-64
Revans, R.
  and action learning, 3,151,152,
    153,154,155,193
  and reinvention, 8
Richmond, B., 184

Rituals, 141
Role-play, 100,103-104
  exercise, Contrast America, 103
  in intercultural settings, 103
Roles, 141
Ronen, S., 93
Ross, L., 136
Russia, case study of, 167-177248
Rustogi, H., 229-240

Salancik, G.R., 132
Sashkin, M., 6
Seamless integration, learning
  from, 209-210
SCAMP (simulation), 202
Scenarios, 246
  planning, 119-122
Schein, E.H., 224
Schoemaker, P.J.H., 120,121
Schon, D., 16,189
Schroeder, K.G., 96
Schwartz, P., 120,121,122
Schwind, H., 91
Scope (transnational), 55-56
Second-language English speakers,
  81-82
Selby, R.W., 6
Selective perception, 97
Seminar design, ICM, 172-174
Senge, P.M., 15,193
  and anticipatory learning, 21
  and systems dynamics, 181-190,
    245
  building shared vision, 222
  informal network, 18
  and learning, 16
  laboratory, 229
  overcoming barriers to, 199
  and systems thinking, 4
Senior manager, 32,118. *See also*
  Manager
Sensitivity Training, 100,103-104
Shell, 62,64,117,246
  and scenario planning, 119,120
Shenkar, O., 7,93

Shock learning, 11,17,248. *See also*
    Learning
Short-term views, 203-204
Siemens Electronics Simulation,
    185-186,200,250
Significant client participation, 183
Similarity
    degree of, 92
    leading to attraction, 130
Simon, H.A., 234
Simulation, international, 105-106
Simuworld, 246,249-250
    evolution of as practice field,
        194-195
    for learning organization, 198e
    MMG
        Compaq Computer Corporation,
            218-219,221
        playing, 216-218,216f
        and organizational learning,
            205-210
Singapore Institute of Management,
    105
Single-country focused learning,
    53-54
Single-loop learning, 16,182
SLIDA. *See* Sri Lanka Institute of
    Development Administration
Sloan, H.M., 106
Slocum, J. Jr., 3,7,194,248
Snell, S., 85-86
Snow, C., 85
Social competency, 170-171
Social learning theory, 101
Social relationships and technology,
    97
Social sphere, 169
Space, 140
    and cultural differences in the use
        of, 131
SRI International. *See* Stanford
    Research Institute
Sri Lanka Institute of Development
    Administration (SLIDA),
    154-155

Stanford Research Institute (SRI
    International), 120,122
Stappenbeck, G.J., 106
Stata, R., 15,16,182
"Step outside the moment," 201
Sterman, J., 204
Stewart, T., 4
Stock, D.A., 104
Strategic assignment, 92
Strategic planning, 249
    and leadership, 202-203
Strategy, internationalizing
    vs. implementation, 49
Stress, 96-97
Structure
    change in, 16,182
    learning about a, 16
Structure vs. process, 4
Students (college), 145-146
Study abroad
    coordinator, 143
    participants, returning, 146-147
Stumpf, 107,229-240
    microworlds/simuworlds, 193-211
Success, expatriate, 96. *See also*
    Expatriate
Supervising a multicultural
    workforce, 96
Supportive family, 96
Survival-level language training, 104
Sustained improvement by
    performance, 15
Swedish Management Institute
    (MiL), 156-157
Synergy through dialogue, 224
Systems dynamics, and anticipatory
    learning, 181-190
Systems Dynamics Group (MIT), 4
Systems-flow process, 193-194
Systems theory, and contradictions
    in strategy, 206
Systems thinking, 4,246

Target population (ICM), 172
Task, implementation of, 77
Team learning, 223
Team-based business planning, 201
Teams. *See also* International team
   and a global future, 6-7,244-245
   lessons for managers setting up,
     77-78
Technical competency, 170
Technical orientation
   common, 36-37
   vs. national orientation, 25
Technical vs. cultural differences, 38
Technology, 3
   and managing international teams,
     79
   and social relationships, 97
Teegen, H., 8,9,11,12,15-22,248
Temple, C.S., 106
Temporal, P., 109
Tenaglia, M., 118
Tension, 25
   and cultural differences, 42
Terpstra, V., 92,97,104
Thinking globally, 243-244
Thompson, A.A., 106
Thorelli, H.B., 106
Threat, and cross-cultural interaction,
     41-42
Tichy, N., 88,157
Time, 140
   cultural differences in the use
     of, 131
   passage of, 40-41
   pressures, and managing
     resources, 201
Top Management Decision
     Simulation, 194
Turf building, 205
Traditional manager, 247
Train-the-trainers program, 163
Trainee, 92
Training
   challenge of, 167-168
   and competency, 96-97

Training *(continued)*
   cross-cultural, 101,102
     programs, 68,89
   insufficient/inappropriate, 91
   intercultural, case incidents
     for, 101
   international, research, 100
   management, for international
     assignments, 91-93,94t-95t,
     96-97
   predeparture, 91
Training method
   assessment of effectiveness
     of, 111-112
   theoretical base for, 97-99
Training model, summary and
     application of, 110-111
Training program, cross-cultural,
     68,131
Training rigor, 92
Trait-situation distinction, 138
Transnational, 17. *See also*
     Transnational scope
   development, 60-62,63e
   firm, 55-56,62
   human resource system, 56-58
     executives, 69
     integration, 59-65
   illusions, 65-69
   managers, 55-56
   process, 57-58,61-62,63-64
     in recruiting, 60
   recruiting, 59-60,61e
   representation, 57,63
     in recruiting, 60
     in utilization, 64-65
   retaining managers, 62-64
   and today's firms, 58-65
   utilizing/utilization, 64-65
Transnational human resource
     management system,
     56-58,244
   executives, 69
   integration, 59-65

Transnational management, learning
    approach. *See* Action
    Learning
Transnational scope, 56-57,59. *See
    also* Transnational
    managerial development, 60-62
    and recruiting, 59-60
    retaining managers, 62-64
    in utilizing/utilization, 64-65
Transpatriate, 62
Triad Power, 1
Triandis, H.C., 102,129,132
Triple-loop learning, 225
TRW, 155
Tung, R.L., 91-92,102
21st Century Report, 50
Two-way communication, 102

"Ugly Westerner" overtone, 207
Uncertainty Avoidance, 18
Unilever, 57
United Parcel Service (UPS), 17
University of Michigan's Global
    Leadership Program,
    110,157-158249
Us vs. them mentality, 188
Useem, J., 130
Useem, R., 130
U-shaped adjustment curve, 131
Utilizing/utilization (transnational
    scope), 64-65

Validation sample, 133
Values, 141
Vertical fragmentation, overcoming,
    200-202

Views, short-term and long-term,
    203-204
Virtual world, 189
Von Glinow, M.A., 97,104

Wack, P., 119,120,122
Waterman, R.H., 235
Watson, M.A., 229-240
Wayagaya, 83
Webster, J., 107
Welch, J., 4
Wells, R.A., 106
    Multinational Management Game,
    The, 215-228
Wheatley, W.I., 106
Wheelwright, C.C., 15
When Giants Learn to Dance, 6
White, T.H., 20,208
Whorf, B.L., 104
Wilson, I., 122
Win-lose mentality, 188
Winners and Losers, 121
Wiseman, R.L., 97,100,102,103
Wolfe, J., 105,106
Wolniansky, N., 100
Worchel, S., 102
Work, 140
Work experience, as source of
    learning, 97. *See also*
    Learning
Working language, choosing, 81-82
World-wide integration, 60
W-shaped adjustment curve, 131

Yip, G.S., 2
Yoshida, T., 139

Order Your Own Copy of
This Important Book for Your Personal Library!

EXECUTIVE DEVELOPMENT AND ORGANIZATIONAL LEARNING FOR GLOBAL BUSINESS

_____ in hardbound at $49.95 (ISBN: 1-56024-983-8)

_____ in softbound at $29.95 (ISBN:0-7890-0479-8)

COST OF BOOKS_____

OUTSIDE USA/CANADA/
MEXICO: ADD 20%_____

POSTAGE & HANDLING_____
*(US: $3.00 for first book & $1.25
for each additional book)
Outside US: $4.75 for first book
& $1.75 for each additional book)*

SUBTOTAL_____

IN CANADA: ADD 7% GST _____

STATE TAX_____
*(NY, OH & MN residents, please
add appropriate local sales tax)*

FINAL TOTAL_____
*(If paying in Canadian funds,
convert using the current
exchange rate. UNESCO
coupons welcome.)*

☐ **BILL ME LATER:** ($5 service charge will be added)
(Bill-me option is good on US/Canada/Mexico orders only;
not good to jobbers, wholesalers, or subscription agencies.)

☐ Check here if billing address is different from
shipping address and attach purchase order and
billing address information.

Signature_____

☐ **PAYMENT ENCLOSED: $_____**

☐ **PLEASE CHARGE TO MY CREDIT CARD.**

☐ Visa ☐ MasterCard ☐ AmEx ☐ Discover
☐ Diners Club
Account # _____

Exp. Date _____

Signature _____

Prices in US dollars and subject to change without notice.

NAME _____

INSTITUTION _____

ADDRESS _____

CITY _____

STATE/ZIP _____

COUNTRY _____ COUNTY (NY residents only) _____

TEL _____ FAX _____

E-MAIL_____
May we use your e-mail address for confirmations and other types of information? ☐ Yes ☐ No

Order From Your Local Bookstore or Directly From
The Haworth Press, Inc.
10 Alice Street, Binghamton, New York 13904-1580 • USA
TELEPHONE: 1-800-HAWORTH (1-800-429-6784) / Outside US/Canada: (607) 722-5857
FAX: 1-800-895-0582 / Outside US/Canada: (607) 772-6362
E-mail: getinfo@haworth.com
PLEASE PHOTOCOPY THIS FORM FOR YOUR PERSONAL USE.

BOF96